CONFRONTATIONS

Other Books by Louis Rapoport

The Lost Jews: Last of the Ethiopian Falashas
Redemption Song: The Story of Operation Moses
Anatoly and Avital Sharansky: The Journey Home
(Co-author, editor)

LOUIS RAPOPORT

CONFRONTATIONS

Quinlan Press
Boston

Published by Quinlan Press
131 Beverly Street, Boston, MA 02114

Printed in the United States of America, 1988

Library of Congress Cataloging-in-Publication Data

Rapoport, Louis.
  Confrontation : Israeli life in the year of the uprising.

  1. Israel. I. Title.
DS102.5.R37   1988   956.94   87-43311
ISBN 1-55770-032-X

To Sylvia, Ehud, Adi, Avigal and Gavriela

Parts of this book have appeared in different form in *Commentary,* the *Village Voice, Present Tense, Moment,* the *Los Angeles Times,* the *Boston Globe,* the *Washington Post, Washington Jewish Week,* the *San Francisco Chronicle* and the *Jerusalem Post.*

CONTENTS

"And your children shall wander in the Wilderness forty years."
—Numbers 14:33

"No, I am not a millenarian, and a passionate belief in life's regenerative powers makes me believe that the catastrophe I foretell will only be one more of many this planet has already seen."
—Friedrich Percyval Reck-Malleczewen
Diary of a Man in Despair

"Israel is merely reproducing today a very old drama in modern costume—while, in the scorching light of the Judean hills, eternity looks on through the window of time..."
—Arthur Koestler
Promise and Fulfilment

"I want to be buried as a Jew, not as a bohemian."
—Philip Roth
Zuckerman Unbound

I

IN THE YEAR 2008, when Israel celebrates its sixtieth birthday, those of us who are still alive will have witnessed a terrible struggle, the near schism of the Jewish people, the emergence of a Palestinian state in Jordan and half of the West Bank, and a happy ending to it all: love, pity, pride, compassion, sacrifice and redemption.

It's either that or destruction and ruin, without any hope for a Hollywood ending.

Now, Israel is forty. It is said that we don't understand life any better at that watershed age than we did at twenty; but the difference is that we know it, and can finally admit it.

When Israel was nineteen and appeared to be on the verge of destruction, the whole world watched what was termed a "miraculous" six-day victory. It recalled a 1948 joke: During the siege of Jerusalem, two old Jews were overheard talking. "We can only be saved either by a miracle or by a natural event," said one. "What natural event?" asked the second man. "Why, the coming of the Messiah, of course."

The result of the 1967 event was that Israel greatly expanded—to an imperial empire less than a quarter the size of Montana. This victory, according to the left-liberal conventional wisdom of recent years, cost Israel its soul and may bring about its destruction. The Palestinian uprising that began in December 1987 reinforced the belief that Israel cannot continue to lord it over a hostile population, one that had now become aflame with revolution; and most of the world was saying the same thing. But not everyone. The Israeli nationalist-messianic right felt that the results of the 1967 war presented clear evidence that the Lord had kept his promise, returning to its rightful owners the Entire Land of Israel, plus Sinai (the desert peninsula, which was later traded to Egypt for peace, represented 23,000 of the 26,000 square miles conquered by Israel; of the remaining territories, the Gaza Strip is 120 square miles in its entirety, much smaller than greater Los Angeles).

The rightist camp also believes that Israel could be destroyed—if the leftist camp gets its way and the conquered territories are given back to the enemy. For both camps, the Palestinian revolt served to throw everything into focus, to boil things down to the basic questions that must be answered in the near future if disaster is to be averted.

WHEN ABBA EBAN addressed an emergency conference meeting in Jerusalem in January 1988, six weeks after the Palestinian uprising began, he noted glumly that Israel's fortieth birthday did not give much cause for celebration. Even though the state of Israel is a success story, he said, the entire Zionist enterprise was endangered by the continued rule over 1.5 million Palestinians. Other Israelis were saying that we are in a no-win situation, that the Arabs will always interpret Israeli peace overtures as weakness, that they are bent on destroying us, that the whole world has turned against us—as was prophesied thousands of years ago.

In the many millions of words that were written about the Palestinian winter uprising, a bit of space was devoted to the not unimportant question of what set off the revolt, and its psychological background. Most reporters and commentators said that it was a rumor that four Gazans had been intentionally killed by Israelis in an auto accident. Only one Israeli leader, Prime Minister Yitzhak Shamir, saw it differently, and his view went virtually unnoticed by the media. However, one of the country's most balanced commentators, political scientist Allan E. Shapiro, did notice: ''Bad luck and bad judgement have plagued Israel's efforts to deal with the disturbances in the territories,'' he wrote. ''The bad luck began with the [November 25, 1987] glider attack on the army base in the north. Prime Minister Shamir was probably correct when he said that this event cancelled out the deterrent effect of Israel's overwhelming military superiority on the readiness of the Palestinians to take physical risks in their opposition to the occupation.''

In other quarters, Shamir's notion—that the mission by the Palestinian guerrilla during ''the night of the gliders'' was what opened the floodgates to the uprising—was ridiculed roundly. Gideon Rafael, a former Foreign Ministry functionary who had once been Israel's UN ambassador, wrote that ''the prime minister, in support of his hard-pressed colleague [Defense Minister Yitzhak Rabin], volunteered the rather surprising explanation for the innovative policy of club and clobber. In his view the successful one-man glider suicide mission against a negligently guarded army camp had considerably reduced the Palestinians' fear of the power of the army.''

If Mr. Rafael had visited Gaza during the first weeks of the uprising, he would have heard the chant of the rock-throwers. ''Six to one, six to one,'' they repeated continuously, referring to the fact that the Palestinian fighter had entered an Israeli army base and killed six soldiers before he himself was cut down. It was a source of great pride to the Palestinians, whose heroes in the past have always attacked civilians, killing children on kibbutzim or women on buses.

Mr. Shamir was right. He was in a position to understand, for forty years earlier he had been the leader of the Stern group of Jewish guerrillas who fought for independence. The mentality was not foreign to him. Another leader of the prestate Jewish underground fighters, the late Justice Minister Shmuel Tamir, once remarked to an old comrade, after visiting PLO-affiliated Palestinians, that ''there is something in common between us.'' Although he knew that the PLO men went after civilian targets, and therefore were a world apart from the prestate Jewish terrorist groups, he meant that something of the same spirit was there.

Shamir has been there too. But at least half of Israel viewed the prime minister as an obstacle to peace, a tree trunk of a man incapable of making with the Palestinians. As the revolt in the territories rumbled into the summer of 1988, it remained to be seen whether it would be possible for Shamir or his successor to overcome the very deep and significant divisions among Israelis, and to move toward a solution.
Israelis, and to move toward a solution.

But the Palestinian side has always presented a much bigger problem. The Palestinians' chosen leaders are murderous and incompetent, and the average Palestinian is not interested in coexistence with Israel—he wants all of it. The stone-throwing kids and their parents who encourage them all say it quite frankly for everyone to hear. After three Palestinians were killed during rioting in Nablus, a local fireman told Israeli reporters: ''Even if God comes down from heaven, there will be no peace between you and us.'' Pointing to his son, he said: ''After you plant the seed of hate in a boy like this, not even a million years will be enough time to heal the wounds.'' This is their belief, and it can only lead to a disaster, unless there is a fundamental change—among Palestinians and Israelis.

But despite all the hatred and intransigence, all the doom and gloom, the events that occurred as Israel began to mark its fortieth birthday may enhance the possibility of a final settlement to the Arab-Israel conflict. For a great awakening has occurred among many Israelis who did not understand that continued domination over a large and growing population of hostile Arabs spells disaster for all the people of the State of Israel. Among the casualties of the revolt was the status quo, and the country was shaken to its very roots.

THOSE WHO REPORT ON ISRAEL or analyze its policies are naturally subjective—there is no such thing as an "objective observer." But as Arthur Koestler wrote forty years ago (in *Promise and Fulfilment*, his epic book about the birth of Israel), "the good judge, like the playwright and historian, absorbs the subjective truth contained in each of the conflicting pleas, and his verdict is a synthesis of their part-truths, not their denial."

Every Jew who makes Israel his home is a judge, though few are equipped with the proper tools: the necessary knowledge or the understanding heart. But qualifications don't really matter. We are forced by circumstance to judge all the time. Every parent who worries about bombs on buses or a child in the army is a judge. Everyone who watches our soldiers confront the stone-throwers, every single person who lives in this increasingly polarized society, is called upon to make judgements.

The verdict reached by this writer, an American-born Israeli citizen, is that Israel, despite its staggering problems and the evil shadings it shares with all nations, will wrestle its way through the labyrinth, and that one day in the not-too-distant future, millions of Jews and many non-Jews will flock to a Jerusalem that is both earthly and heavenly. Undoubtedly it will be tough going. The threat of a civil war may be real—though I'm not one who believes it. One result of the Palestinian uprising is the brutalization of an already difficult, abrasive society. Economic calamity apparently awaits us all—there seems to be little debate about that. No one knows what will happen in the wake of the Gulf War, whether the Moslem Fundamentalist revolution and the Palestinian nationalist revolution and the Syrian Ba'ath revolution will merge and try once again to push the Jews into the sea. No one knows when the Messiah will make his first appearance: tomorrow, or in 2008, or in fifty years, or in a thousand, although current betting seems to favor the more immediate future.

I myself am a secular Jew, who immigrated to Israel in January 1973 at the age of thirty, and who worked as a journalist while raising a family. But though Judaism remains for me remote from the wrangling everyday world, I believe unabashedly that God lives innocently in Jerusalem, that his hand is becoming increasingly visible, and that the sages of Israel are right in their belief that we have entered the era of Redemption. The Palestinian march toward statehood is just a part of the saga that will truly be part of the greatest story ever told.

In Israel, the poet Yehuda Amichai once wrote, people live inside prophecies that have come true. But day-to-day life in Israel is a story that doesn't get written by outsiders. Foreign correspondents, and most of the local press corps, are kept frantically busy covering the Arab-Israeli conflict, what appears to be an unending series of controversies, rifts, scandals and affairs, all redolent of politics or ethics, all here today and gone tomorrow. The world media sends in eight hundred reporters to cover the Palestinian uprising, but much of what the world sees is the dross on the surface—*Newsweek* will feature a Defiant Palestinian wrapped in a kaffiyeh fashioned from a Palestinian flag, but it doesn't tell the reader much about the reasons why Israel doesn't hand a state to its conquered subjects; ABC will make invidious comparisons between South Africa and Israel, without presenting any historical context, any true understanding of Jewish history. In one telecast, that network's anchorman intoned mellifluously that Israel had barred the media from sections of the territories, thus making Israel exactly like "South Africa or Iran and Iraq in the Gulf War." Why didn't he mention the American ban on the media in the Grenada intervention, or England's bar on the media in the Falklands war?

It's not only the double standard: texture is also missing. *Time* magazine or NBC News cannot convey more than a superficial, often inaccurate picture of Israel. They often do not check out a story, or they are stymied by the slow-working Army Spokesman's Office. For example, wide coverage was given to the story that Israeli troops were pushing Palestinians out of helicopters—shades of Vietnam! Only it was a total fabrication. Another glaring incident was the long report in a local Tel Aviv newspaper, *Ha'Ir,* by Arab journalist Makram Khoury Mahul, about horrible atrocities in Gaza. Subsequent investigation by the Army and Ze'ev Schiff, the highly respected military correspondent of *Ha'aretz*, showed that the story was a fabrication. Of course, there were deplorable incidents, like the now infamous televised beating of two of the captured rock-throwers by four Israeli troops. But Vietnam, or India, or World War II, it's not. Lost in much of the reporting is a clear understanding of the Israeli psyche, of the mundane realities and conditions of ordinary life that remain just below the surface. The existence of racism and exploitation cannot be denied, but the Israeli attitude towards its Arab citizens and the Arabs of the territories should be looked at in the broader context: the problem of national and religious identity, the often vicious divisions among the children of Israel, a siege mentality, the bureaucratic nightmares, the tussle and pull and hustle of the fruit and vegetable market, the heartaches of schoolchildren and their harried parents, the comic-tragic absurdities of fifty-year-old reservists charging up a stony hill.

The hatred for the local media, as well as for the foreign, reached fever pitch in Israel in its fortieth year; and there was much justification for the disgust and consternation. The Palestinians' propaganda department would set up a demonstration, calling all the print and broadcast journalists and telling them where and when. I joined one of these hapless convoys in Ramallah and witnessed how a demonstration is staged for the benefit of the cameramen. But despite strong reservations about the motivations and reporting skills of many of the overweaningly proud journalists, I am not one of those who believes the media are the culprit, or that they should be barred from the territories. On the contrary, despite all of the negatives, despite the often sickeningly leftist persuasion of most of the press people, the media were getting across a story that could no longer be suppressed. The picture in the mirror was definitely distorted; but breaking the mirror is not the remedy. "Behold, I will send my messenger." Don't kill him.

In judging Israel, the questions seem endless. Are the Jews really the Chosen People, and does that mean they have to behave differently from other peoples; or that they are just like everyone else, only more so? Does Israel belong to the Israelis—including Israeli Arabs—or to the Jewish People? Will the Kulturkampf between religious and secular Jews end in disaster? Is there really any hope for coexistence between Arabs and Jews? Can we negotiate with the PLO? Why are growing numbers of Israelis leaving the country? Why would Soviet Jews want to live here? What motivates the Jews who seek to oust the Moslems from the Temple Mount? How do Israelis cope with an economy that always seems to be on the skids? What does the mass return to religious observance portend? Will we always be in a state of war? Will the confrontations never end?

A tiny minority of Israelis remain unpolarized and see both good and bad in the two main camps into which the country is divided. The majority, across the spectrum, believes that despite all of its superpower-sized problems, Israel will prevail, whether it becomes a "Light Unto the Nations" or just a normal country—the goal of secular Zionism.

I do not believe that Israel's creation forty years ago was a freak phenomenon of history, as Arthur Koestler wrote. On the contrary, history itself can be read through the eyes of the Jewish experience. The forty years in the desert are over. And perhaps the culmination of history will coincide with the fate of the renascent nation of Israel—the Judean drama the whole global village is watching.

II

EVERY YEAR, the issue of the Temple Mount gets hotter, though it has yet to ignite the imagination of most Israelis, who remain strangely indifferent to the fate of God's little acre.

In October 1987, as Israel began the build-up to the year-long celebrations of its fortieth birthday, thousands of Moslems massed on the Temple Mount to protest against a group of nationalistic Jews who, at least twice every year, try to pray there. Only a few head-bashings occurred on this occasion, and no one was seriously injured when the crowd was dispersed with tear gas. Likewise, a few weeks later, in the midst of what would become known as the Palestinian uprising, another confrontation occurred. Tear gas wafted into the Moslem shrines, and an Israeli policeman was badly beaten inside the Dome of the Rock.

The history of the Temple Mount has been marked by violence. In 1969 a born-again Australian Christian set fire to the silver-domed al-Aksa mosque, one of the two Moslem shrines on the mount. In April 1982 a crazed follower of Meir Kahane shot and killed an unarmed Moslem guard. But the biggest threat to continued Moslem sovereignty over this holiest of Jewish sites and third-holiest Moslem site occurred in 1984, when the Jewish underground—composed of some of the best young men from the best national-religious homes—planned to blow up the golden Dome of the Rock.

The Temple Mount lies in the heart of Old Jerusalem. According to Jewish lore it is the navel of the universe, the site of both the First and Second Temples. The Dome of the Rock is built around a huge, flat, pitted piece of granite, the legendary site of Abraham's near-sacrifice of his son, Isaac. The Moslems, a couple of millennia later, conquered Jerusalem and spun the legend that Mohammed and his horse ascended to heaven from this rock. Christians, too, regard the site as holy, since their Lord Jesus was said to have preached at the Second Temple. Not surprisingly, this small plot of land, which figures so prominently in the histories of the three monotheistic religions, has become the most fiercely contested plot of land in the world.

Israel captured the Mount in the 1967 war and put it into the hands of the Moslem *wakf*, or trust, because Moshe Dayan feared that the entire Moslem world would conduct a holy war if Israel did otherwise. Under the *wakf*'s administration, neither Jews nor Christians are allowed to pray there.

Members of the mid-1980s Jewish underground—some of whom are still in prison for murdering three Arab university students or for maiming two West Bank mayors or for conspiracy—thought they could hasten the advent of the Messiah and Redemption by blowing up the Dome of the Rock. They thought of themselves as construction workers who must first dynamite the condemned building before they can begin laying the foundations for the new edifice—in this case, the Third Temple. This belief is still held by many members of Gush Emunim (Bloc of the Faithful), the Jewish settler movement. Even though the members of the underground are deeply religious, they apparently ignored the Judaic tradition, which says that no human hands will build the Third Temple: it will either descend from the heavens as a whole, or appear in an instant when the Messiah instructs Elijah to blow the trumpet four times.

The Jewish terrorists, all of them prominent members of Gush Emunim, thought God was with them as they assembled the explosives to destroy the massive Dome, a treasure of classical Moslem art. That feeling has always caused trouble. The Messianic terrorists share a spirit with the religious extremists of all nations, an intoxication that is sweeping the world, including America with its tens of millions of fundamentalist Christians.

In this climate, a group of minor actors has been moving about the stage attempting to forge strong links between some Christian evangelicals and the zealots of Jewish religious nationalism, a sort of marriage between Evangeline and Gabriel, an attempt to raise the collective consciousness, to educate the people so that they understand why their sons should be slaughtered in the coming holy war. There is a definite comic-opera flavor to the whole story, despite its seriousness.

Enter Stanley Goldfoot, a lanky South African-born Israeli who was once an intelligence man in the Stern group underground and one of those jailed by the young State of Israel in connection with the murder of UN envoy Count Bernadotte in 1948. He hardly spoke any Hebrew, but he could easily pass for a British officer, and his obvious histrionic abilities made him an asset to the outlawed group headed by Yitzhak Shamir, the future prime minister.

In the early 1970s, the well-heeled Goldfoot (the pun is inevitable) was the publisher of a right-wing journal called *The Times of Israel* and one of the founders of the Faithful of the Temple Mount, a rather lame little group that makes periodic and peaceful attempts to pray on the disputed Mount—it was their attempt in October 1987 that set off the Moslem riot. But Goldfoot left the Faithful in the 1980s and soon after set up the Jerusalem Temple Foundation, with a board consisting of himself and five American evangelicals. He sloughed off charges by some members that he had sold his soul and become an instrument for fundamentalist Christians attempting to convert Jews. Researching a piece about the Temple Mount I asked him about a $50,000 gift from one of his board members—Oklahoma oil and land wheeler-dealer Terry Risenhoover. He remained closemouthed. I had interviewed him several months earlier, and he had denied that there ever was a $50,000 donation. But in my second interview he shared a guffaw with his wife and said: "That $50,000 was given expressly to establish the headquarters of the Jerusalem Temple Foundation...Private people came up with the money—for a library, reading room, offices—but I decided it's not the right time. Too much of a headache." The atmosphere was wrong. Chipping in, his wife said that the Jewish antimissionary activists might blow up the headquarters.

Just before my article was supposed to come out, I was scooped by a long piece in The *New Republic* by Barbara and Michael Ledeen—the latter a former aide to Alexander Haig, a regular contributor to *Commentary* and a future figure in the Irangate scandal. The article portrayed Goldfoot, in a not unfriendly manner, as the main conduit for funds from American fundamentalists to Jewish fundamentalists in Israel, including money for the defense of a tiny sect of messianic Jews, the Lifta group, who had tried to blow up the Dome of the Rock a few months before the Gush Emunim terrorists' plan.

The Ledeens' article made the Goldfoot operation seem big-time, indeed. But it wasn't. It was no surprise, however, that a popular Israeli tabloid newspaper, *Hadashot*, splashed the story on its front page and claimed—totally inaccurately—that "millions of dollars" were being funneled from the evangelicals to Israeli Temple Mount fanatics. Goldfoot told me that Ledeen was "a good friend" of his. He added, in a stage whisper, that "all you journalists are liars." But I sensed that he was not displeased by the publicity.

The Ledeens' article and the exaggerated *Hadashot* report based on it drew immediate fire and brimstone from Texas evangelical minister Dr. Hilton Sutton, of Mission to America, also a board member of Goldfoot's Jerusalem Foundation. Sutton threatened to sue both publications for saying that Mission to America had contributed large sums to the Jewish terrorist underground. In fact, the terrorists needed very little money to finance their operations, and it was highly unlikely that they would have sought any outside funds whatsoever. Sutton, ignoring Michael Ledeen's staunchly conservative background, said it was all part of a "left-wing plot" against avid supporters of Israel. But something was happening, and Mr. Sutton didn't know what it was.

To some minds, the links forged between a group of American evangelical leaders and right-wing Israelis like Stanley Goldfoot were significant and worrisome. Some of the personalities on his board were important. Lambert Dolphin, for example, was the head of a key section of the world's most massive research conglomerate, the Stanford Research Institute, a $200-million-a-year concern whose main client is the U.S. government. Board member Terry Risenhoover, a regular at the Reagan White House, had chaired the annual "National Prayer Breakfast in Honor of Israel."

But there was something overblown about the whole story, a sense of agitprop accepted as reality. Goldfoot's organization apparently had no general membership at all. When pressed, he told me he had "thirty-forty million" supporters.

A FAMILY CREST hangs above the entrance to Goldfoot's spacious Jerusalem penthouse located on one of the city's priciest streets. When asked what it represented, Goldfoot, who describes himself as an "entrepreneur," answered resonantly, "I made it up." But then, maybe the whole thing is a fairy tale?

Before the arrest of the Temple Mount plotters—both the Lifta group and the Gush Emunim terrorists—Goldfoot and Dolphin planned to hover one day just before dawn in a helicopter a thousand feet above the Temple Mount and the Holy of Holies (where the sacred Ark of the Covenant was kept) and to X-ray and probe the innards of the mount with Dolphin's sophisticated equipment—an induced polarization set, a Cesium Beam Magnetometer, a downhole Borescope television and a high-power Dipole-Dipole Resistivity Set—to find out just what in tarnation was down there.

Dolphin, a frequent visitor to Israel, had used this gear at ancient Herodian and Hebron. His real interest, however, and that of his fellow evangelical and fundamentalist preachers and laymen, was the Temple Mount, for they believe that Jesus cannot "come again" until the Temple Mount is restored to the Jews and the Temple is rebuilt—and then destroyed a third time. "It was in the Second Temple that Jesus worshipped, taught and threw out the money-changers on two occasions. It was in the Temple Court that the Christian Church was born," reads an official Stanford Research Institute International brochure put out by Dolphin.

Goldfoot has frequently addressed groups of evangelicals touring Israel about the importance of the Mount, and he apparently made a bit of a splash touring America on the evangelical circuit. When he spoke before Reverend Chuck Smith's Calvary Chapel in Costa Mesa, California, the church's lavish 3,000-seat auditorium was filled to overflowing. The reverend had sent a Cadillac equipped with a bar and telephone to pick Goldfoot up at the airport, and it was champagne-flight treatment all the way.

Goldfoot told me that he listened regularly to the tape of his speech before going to bed, "just to hear the applause." They loved him there in Costa Mesa, as he recited Jewish prayers that implore the Almighty to "build Thy Temple speedily." To the wild applause of the believers, he said, "Jerusalem is not truly liberated yet—its heart is still under alien control. There is no freedom of worship on the Temple Mount, not for the Jews and not for the Christians...the *wakf* employs thugs who will prevent you from praying there." He did not add that if the Jewish Orthodox establishment ever came to administer the Mount, his Christian friends might still be barred from praying there.

But, then, Goldfoot plays a loose game with history. In describing Christian holy sites on the Mount in an interview, he mentions the spot where Jesus's brother, St. James, was martyred—"stabbed or stoned to death." Who killed St. James and laid him out on a long white table? "Why, Moslems, of course," answers Goldfoot. He catches his error— we have to wait another six hundred years or so for Mohammed and his followers to appear—and says, "Well, not Moslems, of course. The people at the time"—he lowers his mellifluous voice—"between you and me and the lamppost, it was the Jews that killed him.''

Perhaps I am striking the wrong tone here, but a certain amount of flippancy is unavoidable. Tycoon Terry Risenhoover, who chaired the White House prayer breakfast in which most of the major American-Jewish organizations took part, may not even be Terry Risenhoover. He went up to the Temple Mount with the silver-haired Goldfoot one day and said, ''I am Nehemiah''—a statement that raised even Goldfoot's eyebrows. (Nehemiah, or Zerubbabel, was the restorer of the Temple in ancient times, and according to Jewish legend is to be the Messiah's herald one great day.) In an unguarded moment, Goldfoot told me that Risenhoover was under investigation by the FBI in a land-fraud case.

I could not ascertain just how much money Risenhoover gave Goldfoot. One reliable Christian source told me that the sum far exceeded $50,000, and that only poison fruit had grown from its seeding. When an American-Jewish colleague of mine asked Risenhoover about the money, he was told, ''Repent, and make aliyah''—which he was planning to do if he could raise something like $50,000 as a down payment on a small apartment.

I sent a brief letter to Risenhoover and received a seventeen-page typed response he had written with Douglas W. Krieger, executive director of the Jerusalem Temple Foundation. My query about money elicited this line: ''We have not given enough—that is how much we have given.'' Numerous biblical quotes followed.

Risenhoover, a fortyish ''classical Southern Baptist'' whose ventures have included drilling for oil in Israel, believes with his colleagues that God has stirred them up to prepare for their Messiah's Second Coming. They quote Revelation, chapter 11, saying that a final spiritual battle will take place over the Temple site and that Israel and the Church will together triumph. In their eyes, the evil King of the North has transformed himself into the USSR. A major war is coming, one that will also involve Egypt, and Damascus may be destroyed. On the millennial maps of the evangelicals Israel includes great chunks of Egypt, Lebanon and Syria.

Risenhoover and Krieger, like Dolphin, condemned attempts to blow up the Dome of the Rock, but they also assailed the ''violence'' being done to the sacred site ''when Jewish prayer books are seized by Temple Mount guards from devout Jewish women.'' The board members said they didn't believe that all Jews must convert to Christianity, but that a Christian isn't worth his salt unless he ''bears witness'' and at least tries to woo the Jews.

THE ISRAELIS involved in all of this are mostly fringe characters, but their stand on the Temple Mount issue is supported by the biggest party on the far right, Tehiya, whose strength is expected to double in the 1988

Knesset elections—they may control ten of the 120 seats in the parliament and serve in a coalition government. Yisrael Medad, Tehiya's parliamentary secretary, works with Goldfoot and also with El Har Hashem ("To the Mountain of God"), another minor group campaigning for Jewish rights on the Mount. Medad guided Risenhoover and Dolphin during one of their trips to Israel, and introduced them to the "Temple lobby" at the Knesset. Unlike Goldfoot, Medad, an affable West Bank settler and Gush Emunim activist, admits to wanting "political and monetary support from the Christian fundamentalists...We're looking to the Christians for help, not out of any theological identity of views, but because we haven't got any support from Jews." Medad said this to me several months before the existence of the Jewish underground was revealed. Medad added that the Temple issue had become a new and critical focus of leaders of the "believers' camp," since it combined religious and nationalist goals.

Religious politics does indeed make strange bedfellows: the links between the small group of individual evangelicals and Israeli Templars are indicative of a much broader alliance between the reborn Christians and American Jews on a variety of issues. The liberal churches are seen as increasingly pro-Palestinian, while the conservative evangelicals and fundamentalists are down-the-line pro-Israel. AIPAC, the Israel lobby in Washington, has taken on a full-time Christian liaison, whose main task is to deal with the born-agains. The Israeli government has been no less enthusiastic, although one of Prime Minister Yitzhak Shamir's top aides has been wary of some individual evangelical leaders. Referring to Terry Risenhoover, for instance, the official told me: "He's making his way rapidly, because he is loaded. But he is way out...as is Goldfoot."

Reverend Jim DeLoach, of Houston, Texas, another of the five Christians on the six-man board of the Jerusalem Temple Foundation, grew up in Alabama and used to be anti-Semitic—until he was "reborn" at twenty-two and began to see "that the Bible was a Jewish book." On his right hand he wears a diamond ring combining the Star of David with a Latin cross. On his lapel is pinned a double flag—America and Israel.

When I met DeLoach, he appeared to be unfazed by Orthodox Jewish critics or other opponents of the emerging alliance between the evangelicals and Israel—"They have legitimate gripes, like against missionizing"— but he would not come out squarely against missions to the Jews. Asked about the money given by evangelicals to Goldfoot, he said: "We know that there was Gentile involvement in the financing and building of both the First and Second Temples. So why not the Third?"

DeLoach and his fellow board members issued a prospectus in 1984 that outlined their future projects, including financial assistance to Yeshiva

Ateret Cohanim ("priestly crown") in the Moslem Quarter of Jerusalem's Old City, about a hundred yards from the Temple Mount. The Temple rites are being studied at this yeshiva, which is also active in "redeeming" Moslem Quarter buildings, many of which were once owned by Jews. The Goldfoot operation also pledged funding for the yeshiva in "preparation for the construction of the Third Temple in Jerusalem." The architect's plans were already completed in the early 1980s by the late Jacob Yehuda, a recluse who spent forty years on the project and was considered a genius by various Temple Mount sects. So the Third Temple is all set to go. Just a matter of time—and clearance.

The Dome of the Rock, of course, does not necessarily have to be blown up first. Aryeh Kotzer, principal of a school in Rishon Lezion and a former Stern underground fighter, published a booklet in which he maintained that the Dome of the Rock is simply to be incorporated as a part of the Third Temple. Other, quite reasonable people have proposed dismantling the huge edifice and moving it elsewhere.

I VISITED THE ATERET COHANIM yeshiva not as a Cohen but as an inquiring reporter, though naturally I would be willing to don the ephod and serve in the Temple when the call comes.

Ateret Cohanim traces its roots to Rabbi Abraham Yitzhak Hacohen Kook (known as "the Rav Kook"), the first chief rabbi of the Jewish community in Mandate Palestine, and his son, Zvi Yehuda Kook, who was the spiritual leader of Gush Emunim. The senior Kook once said that the Cohanim, descendants of Aaron and members of the priestly caste, must prepare themselves for the Redemption, since the Messiah might come and order the Temple to be rebuilt, and no one would be ready. The Rav Kook, considered the leading Judaic spirit of modern times, eventually dropped the idea, but Menachem Hacohen Dan picked it up over forty years later and founded the yeshiva in 1978.

The Ateret Cohanim people believe they are the vanguard of a movement that is about to take off. The yeshiva's rabbis forbid their students from going up to the Temple Mount—so near, yet so far away—until there is an official rabbinical ruling allowing Jews to pray there: observant Jews are barred from the Mount by the Rabbinate for fear that they might violate the underground chamber known as the Holy of Holies. So nationalist Jews who try to exercise the right to pray on the Mount are violating the precepts of the Judaic authorities. The yeshiva is contemptuous of such groups as the Faithful of the Temple Mount, which are "ineffective and unimportant," according to yeshiva spokesman Menachem Bar-Shalom.

The yeshiva conducts seminars, a field school and three-day conventions every Passover and Succot on the general subject of the Temple and on specifics about such subjects as animal sacrifice. The students study the works of Rav Kook and his contemporary, the Hafetz Haim, on priestly duties. Rav Kook wrote that God's message concerning the rebuilding of the Temple was at hand: "That great and glorious day is drawing nigh." He called for study of the rituals and the rites so that everyone would be ready for the Day of Glory. And the messianic fever is palpable among the people at the yeshiva. One of the leaders of the Jewish underground, Yehuda Livni, was among those who were "inspired" after attending lectures on the Temple at Ateret Cohanim.

"The Temple is the top of the pyramid of the Jewish people," says the yeshiva's chief rabbi, Shlomo Aviner. The former rabbi of Keshet, a religious settlement in the Golan Heights which spawned at least three of the Jewish underground leaders, Aviner believes that the time has not yet come to build the Temple. It is important to bring about Jewish revival first. His message is not to jump the gun. Methods of terror are completely off base. "It's being done by people who think you can jump, to bring Redemption in an hour." He said he was not concerned one way or the other about the involvement of the evangelicals. "It depends on us, not America."

PRIME MINISTER YITZHAK SHAMIR'S adviser on Diaspora affairs, Harry Hurwitz, was one of the officials who supported the emerging alliance between the evangelicals and the Jews. It is much better for AIPAC to "go up to [Capitol] Hill with these Christians to lobby for Israel—because they are the most powerful Christian element in America," he told me.

Why have these traditionally anti-Semitic elements in America turned into philo-Semites, pro-Israel fanatics? "Maybe they think something is happening here," Hurwitz answered. He recalled his delight at being guest of honor at the Alabama governor's mansion back in 1981, soon after the evangelical-Jewish romance began. Governor Fob James gave a big bash to celebrate Israel's thirty-third birthday, inspired by his wife, a born-again Christian. Hundreds of participants signed an "I Love Israel" proclamation. They served kosher food. A huge Magen David with thirty-three outsized candles floated in the executive swimming pool...Joy to the Jews.

THAT THE TEMPLE MOUNT was the prime concern of the Jewish underground came as a surprise even to seasoned reporters who have covered the Mount and the various fringe groups or individuals who have tried to alter the status quo by violent means. For the underground, broken in May 1984, was drawn from the heart of the settler movement. They were not fringe nuts like American *baal teshuva* (penitent) Allen Goodman, the Rabbi Kahane fan who went on a rampage on the Mount and murdered a Moslem guard. Goodman, whose legal costs were paid by the good rabbi, said he had intended to liberate the Mount and become "king of the Jews."

The Lifta sect (named after the place where they lived, an abandoned Arab neighborhood on the northern outskirts of Jerusalem) that tried to blow up both Moslem shrines on the Mount in early 1984 also appeared to be very much an aberrant group: whenever they left their squatter-homes during daylight they would walk backwards so as not to offend the Sun. Also on the fringe was one Yoel Lerner, a leader of Kahane's Kach party, who was convicted in October 1982 of planning to blow up the Dome of the Rock. And the born-again Christian arsonist Michael Rohan was clearly deranged.

It should come as no surprise that yet another group of religious nationalists was possessed by similar devils. Unbeknownst to the bearded, hippie-ish Lifta sect or the bearded yet squeaky clean Gush Emunim underground, a third group working at the same time also had plans for the Dome of the Rock. Rabbi Kahane's former number-two man, Rabbi Ariel, and twenty-eight followers from the yeshiva at Kiryat Arba (the Jewish settlement next to Hebron) were discovered in an underground passage near the Mount in 1984 and placed under arrest. But their aims were never very clear, and the judge released them for lack of evidence.

For some time, the addition of evangelical Christianity to the already poisonous witch's brew of various Temple Mount sects appeared likely to exacerbate the situation. But the Gush Emunim people are distrustful of any Christian involvement, and they do not take Goldfoot seriously. Meir Kahane, assuming his typical heroic posture, told me that he "repulsed Christian overtures connected to the Temple Mount." He asserted that Jan Willem van der Hoeven, chief spokesman of the fanatically pro-Israel "Christian Embassy" in Jerusalem, had contacted him, "but I repulsed him—he's a missionary..."

"The Christians would love me to bomb the mosque because they believe it would bring Jesus. I don't want Christians," Kahane said contemptuously.

Van der Hoeven, of course, never made any offers to Kahane, but he did express criticism of the Israeli government for its "don't rock the boat" over the question of the Temple Mount. The Moslems are usurpers, he said, which is, of course, true. He said that the Mount should be returned to the Jews, "even if it means Armageddon." Which it might. But the fundamentalist spokesman did not condone violence in any form. "I don't think God needs violence or illegality to accomplish his ways," he said, a sentiment Kahane would fulminate against.

NOT ONLY MARGINAL THEATRICAL CHARACTERS like Stanley Goldfoot support the goals of the Jewish terrorists or assert Jewish rights on the Temple Mount. On Yom Kippur of 1983, for example, police tried to prevent former chief rabbi Shlomo Goren from holding prayers in a room beneath the Mount. But they relented when the armed forces chief of staff, Moshe Levy, showed up to join Goren in prayer.

Goren, considered a great sage by many observant Jews, has long had a particular interest in the Temple Mount. In the early 1980s, after a clash between Moslems and Jews in a mysterious tunnel under the Mount, he told me that the recently rediscovered passageway might lead to the Holy of Holies, housing the lost Ark of the Covenant and other Temple treasures. According to Maimonides, King Solomon built the honeycomb of tunnels under the Temple because he foresaw its future destruction and sought a secret place for the Temple treasure.

The white-bearded Rabbi Goren said that he had seen "the light" in the tunnel, but could not reveal more because of "secret and mystical reasons and also archaeological, historic and religious reasons." What about political reasons? "Not political reasons!" he exclaimed.

Goren said that it was against Jewish belief to reveal the real story of where the Ark is hidden. "The secret will be revealed just prior to building the Third Temple."

Rabbi Adin Steinzalz, considered one of the greatest Talmudic scholars in Jewish history, told me that "the Holy of Holies was part of the Temple and no longer exists. There may be a tunnel that leads to the area. We know the Temple Mount was tunneled and cross-tunneled. Even in Second Temple times, in the first century of the Common Era, we have information that the Ark was buried in one of the tunnels." According to Jewish tradition, the place is to remain a secret until the Redemption, when a stream will break forth from the Temple Mount and reveal the Ark and other treasures. But Steinzalz added that he didn't believe there would be any push to find the ancient Jewish treasures because "the Arabs would be emphatically against it. They don't want the Temple Mount tied to Jewish things."

Indeed, the Moslem *wakf* guides on the Mount tend to forget what came before the Moslem shrines.

The Moslems are every bit as malevolent as the worst of the Jews and Christians—much more so. The site of the Temple does not belong to them. It belongs to the Jews. One day it will belong to all humanity. It is all a question of timing. The rabbi of the Western Wall, Meir Yehuda Getz, put it this way: "We don't want to make problems [with the Moslems]. There's no need. We'll know when the time comes. Then there won't *be* any problems."

The Imam of the silver-domed al-Aksa mosque on the Temple Mount—site of the assassination of King Hussein's grandfather Abdallah, slain because he dared to seek a dialogue with the Jews—is still calling for Jihad, a holy war that "sweeps away the state of the Jews and the infidelity it represents." The Imam, Sheikh As'ad al-Tamimi, in a statement made in the fall of 1987, blessed the fundamentalist Moslems of "Palestine" who seek, through terroristic means, to destroy Israel. It is to be hoped that one great day, Mr. Tamini, and his Jewish and Christian counterparts, will finally be enlightened about the God that they all claim to represent.

For years, the periodic violence on the Mount came and went with the wind, with nobody paying too much heed. My own feeling has been that the apathy most Israelis felt about all of this activity around the Temple Mount was providential, allowing events to take their own course. Sluggishness prevailed. At a meeting in Jerusalem of the Faithful of the Temple Mount, a threadbare man named Ze'ev reported on his latest efforts to excite a nationalist-religious Knesset member, Haim Druckman, about the Mount. "He fell asleep as I was talking," the outraged zealot said. "I'm ashamed of Druckman." But that drowsiness, and the respite it provided, may be over now, as Israel has been shaken awake by the big Palestinian bang that opened the Fortieth Year. The Temple Mount has become a focal point of the Palestinian uprising, and no one can predict what will happen to God's little acre.

Richard T. Nowitz

III

THE ISRAELI TELEPHONE SYSTEM, the bane of all intelligence, has long had a deservedly notorious reputation. It is the incarnation of inefficiency and small-mindedness. Even the friendliest visitors to the country can't help but categorize Israel as Third or Fourth World after a few exasperating attempts to make a simple phone call. But we are not entirely without hope. One of the great expectations in the nation's fortieth year is that the planned privatization of the telephone company, Bezek, will finally correct a nagging problem.

If Israel had left the whole matter in the hands of Ma Bell in 1948, surely it would not now have a debt as big as the annual Gross National Product—some $25 billion. The waste of time and money is mind-boggling; sometimes you have to dial a number five or more times before you get through, and you'll have spoken to several wrong numbers along the way, reaching people from all walks of life who are accustomed to mistakes and inured to distress.

The government-owned telephone company gets thousands of complaints every month from people who don't understand why they have to wait a year or three to get a phone, angry consumers who seek to clear up obvious errors made by the company (you are guilty until you can prove you are innocent, for the customer is always wrong), and the panicky souls whose incoming calls have been cut off for no reason at all. Whenever the rains come, Bezek hears from thousands of distressed customers who want to know when their phones will overcome the weather. A simple phone call will suffice to do business in the U.S., but in Israel you often cannot clear things up or get what you want over the phone. And to correct any fault you must usually travel to some office in the vast bureaucratic maze to handle things in person.

Just calling the phone company can be a maddening experience. In an unscientific survey, I dialed the phone company's number, 556333, four times and got only a dead response. The fifth time, a recorded message, backed by Muzak, said: "This is Bezek, shalom, we will get to you according to your turn in the queue." Five minutes later, the recording stopped, and nobody answered. Dead again. This happened twice. Finally, I reached an all-too-human voice on the other end, a Bezek operator chatting with a friend. "Just a minute," she said gruffly, and then hung up on me, probably in order to resume her conversation or to finish her glass of tea. I tried again, and the pattern repeated itself. After forty minutes of uninterrupted attempts, I finally got through to another rude clerk, who told me, "No one's here now. It's the day before a holiday."

Some of the operators are not at all rude. One very friendly lady, whom I spoke to on two occasions during a week-long attempt to get my phone line fixed, commiserated with me fully. "This isn't America, sweetie," she said, and then joked, "So why don't you pay your phone bills?" It was fun talking with her. I told her my whole history—about my severe financial problems, how it was all exacerbated by having to use pay phones, most of which are chronically ill, and she believed in my case, and tried to soothe me. My phone, however, stayed disconnected.

But this is nothing. A friend got a monthly bill not long ago for 10,000 shekels (about $7,000). My own bill that same month was $400, four times the usual. Down at the modernized, computerized Bezek offices, we both waited in line for two hours in order to be told that we were undoubtedly lying. In any case, the clerk told me as she helped me fill out a long form, it takes six weeks to check a bill. And you can't get an itemized bill listing all long-distance calls, she said. In the meantime, if you don't pay the bill your phone will be cut off; and it is no easy matter to have it reconnected—in fact, it's a nightmare, unless you have a relative or close friend who works for Bezek.

My telephone has had a long run of bad luck. When three students rented our Jerusalem apartment for a year, they were stunned by the incredibly high bills they were getting, some as high as 8,000 shekels ($5,000). It took eight frustrating visits over a period of five months to get the phone company even to deal with the problem. One of the students recounted Visit Number Four—halfway through the long struggle for justice—in a letter asking me to help them:

> Adina and Joseph went for a scheduled appointment and were initially refused entrance. They were told that it was impossible to see Mr. Pardess, that he wasn't in and that there was no place to wait for him: all of which was untrue. They managed to get through anyway, after waiting for one hour (during which time Adina missed an important exam at the university and Joseph was late for work). Mr. Pardess, after listening for two minutes to their explanation of the problems, sent them downstairs to Mr. Klein, who he said would take care of the matter immediately.

> Mr. Klein shares an office with Gadi, who a month earlier had brought Adina (who really is as gentle as her name) to tears. Now, Gadi immediately said that he refused to deal with them. Adina told the whole long story to Mr. Klein, who said, "We'll check it out" and told Gadi to go through the files. Gadi brought out the files *from his drawer* and only then began to look into the problem, which he had promised to investigate two months previously. Then, apparently working intentionally slowly, he leafed through the lists while chatting with secretaries and drinking coffee. Because Adina had to return to her classes and Joseph to work, one of them politely asked how long this would take. Mr. Klein and Gadi began yelling at them, saying that they should be thanking them for working on the problem at all. Mr. Klein then told them to leave his office. Adina and Joseph asked him what to do with the bills, and said they could not possibly afford such outrageously high sums which weren't even theirs. Mr. Klein refused to say how long it would take them to get a reply...

Such scenes are repeated thousands of times every day in hundreds of Israeli institutions and offices. The stupid and sometimes sadistic bureaucracy is usually cited as one of the four or five main reasons why so many Israelis leave their country, and why so many Western immigrants don't stay. But in the last few years, the computer revolution has helped immeasurably to bring Israel out of an Ottoman-Soviet-British colonial age and into the new era. The dusty files full of red-tape papers stored in inaccessible places will soon be a thing of the past. The necessity of breaking up the big bureaucratic institutions—the phone company, the Histadrut labor federation, the Jewish Agency, the health funds and dozens of other concerns—is finally being recognized.

In the United States people are complaining about the breakdown in services—the "Israelization of America"—while in Israel it is finally getting a bit better. Some perverse souls even celebrate the general inefficiency. "This really is Uganda," a colleague of mine once quipped as we waited for Godot in a stalled bus. "I think that's why I like it."

Richard T. Nowitz

IV

TWO OR THREE TIMES every year, the life of the average Israeli family is disrupted by the army. The nation's regular army is quite small—tiny in comparison to the standing armies of Israel's neighbors—so Israel must rely on reserve forces, for back-up as well as for front-line fighting, in case of a new outbreak of the forty-year war.

The average Israeli male enters the regular army at age eighteen and serves for three years. He then serves at least five weeks to two months of reserve duty (and much more during a war year—the forecast for reserve duty in 1988-89 is at least sixty-two days because of the Palestinian uprising) every year until he reaches the age of fifty. At that age he is put into Haga, the urban patrol force whose pot-bellied men are equipped with ancient "Czechi" rifles and whose main function is to check bags and purses at markets, cinemas, and other public places thirty days a year. Only at the age of fifty-five can he stop being a soldier/guard. His absence from home and work causes no small amount of havoc and distress in a pressure-cooker society, but Israelis generally are used to it, and somehow make do.

Of course, within the reserves, there are many units composed of top combat soldiers, including grizzled veterans of several wars. The majority of the reserves, however, is made up of middle-aged men who are far from their fighting prime. Some of the men complain of shinsplints and aching knees as they climb like goats under the light of a half-moon and a blanket of stars. They come from all walks of life and every kind of background—a corporal with a criminal past, a sergeant who is a nuclear physicist, an Ethiopian new immigrant, even an occasional "black hat" (most of the so-called ultra-Orthodox are anti-Zionist and refuse to serve in the army). In the vernacular, these reservists are known as *shlav bet-nikim*—literally, "level B," but more accurately, "seconds."

A large number of these men welcome the thirty-day call-ups for guard- or border-patrol duty—and even the tough week-long or two-week-long training spells—as a chance to get away from the job, the city, the family. And they are basically good soldiers. But a sizable number do not want to patrol the borders in the cold night or capture a steep cliff during training maneuvers. Many have legitimate reasons for trying to get discharged from one or two particular call-ups: health or family problems, financial troubles, travel connected to work. Others—malingerers, discontents or men who simply cannot take the army—will try every trick they know to get out. Most reservists especially dread the intensity of the first and last days of service, the always contentious issuing and returning of arms and equipment. But even the worst soldiers—I number myself among them—know that when the crunch comes, even the sloppiest, laziest *shlav bet-nik* will do his utmost for the tribe of Israel. But too many segments in the reserve army—and even in the regular army—have grown soft and ill-prepared. One of the reasons why the November 1987 glider attack by a Palestinian fighter so disturbed the nation was that the attacker entered a regular army base where no one was ready, even though there had been a thirty-minute warning. The single guard at the gate ran away, and the gunman was able to shoot down six young soldiers before he himself was killed. It was one of the few times a Palestinian gunman selected a military target, instead of killing civilians, the usual PLO tactic. It was seen by some Israelis as a warning, a sign of decay.

The somewhat seamy unit I serve with is composed of battle-weary veterans and untested immigrants—insiders and outsiders—many of whom are over forty years old. The unit usually supplements regular army forces in the Golan Heights, serving somewhere along the necklace of forts that dot the volcanic hills along the border. The desolate Golan, which was captured by Israel in the 1967 war and all but formally annexed in December 1981, is where everyone expects Syria to launch a massive attack today or tomorrow. Although the constant threat of war faded slightly with the signing of the peace accords with Egypt a decade ago, it rose again with Lebanon and Iraq-Iran, and now the Palestinian uprising also serves as a constant reminder that we are all dancing on top of a volcano.

It is not hard for the Israeli reservist to understand why he must serve when, for one example, he looks at the world from the heights between Israel and Syria.

PROPHETS OF DOOM say that the Golan region is a stage set for a major conflagration, one that could even involve the superpowers. In the surprise Arab attack of Yom Kippur 1973, the Syrians reconquered the Golan and came within a few miles of the Sea of Galilee, with its many Jewish settlements that lie at the mercy of the master of the Heights. For two days Israel was threatened with extinction by hundreds of fire-belching tanks aimed at the country's heartland. The memory of that war lingers on.

According to some reports, Israel has installed nuclear Jericho II missiles underground in the Golan. Of course, no Israeli official will even comment on such a report, but Moscow Radio, in its Hebrew-language broadcasts, repeatedly warned Israel during the summer of 1987 that it must disarm the Jericho IIs (whose range extends to southern Russia), or else. The warnings from Moscow were not ignored by at least one of Israel's two major political parties. Since 1986 reports have persisted that the Labor Party is willing to negotiate an Israeli withdrawal from the Golan (most of whose eight thousand Jewish settlers are Labor supporters) as part of a deal involving the restoration of Soviet-Israeli relations, Soviet backing for an international peace conference on the Middle East, and an easing of restrictions on Soviet-Jewish emigration. Conceivably, the Jericho II missiles would be included in the package. It all seems far more probable in Israel's fortieth year than it did in its thirty-ninth, when political leaders from across the spectrum were saying that the Golan is far too strategic to Israel's security, and that neither of the major political parties was ready to make anything but cosmetic border changes, at the most.

In any case, the political maneuvering in the upper echelons of various governments becomes quite relevant to all the reservists, including the sad sacks, who are periodically plugged into the forts along the Golan Heights.

FROM THE TOP OF TEL FARIS, an extinct volcano on the border between Israel and Syria, the Golan fans out in an eerie plain as flat as Poland's, open country that seems to invoke war: "Perfect tank country," exclaimed the young lieutenant in charge of my platoon, as he briefed us on the local topography and explained what we should be watching for. There was no doubt about it: the Great Rift land, dotted by a long line of volcanic hills thrust up from the earth, looks like it was fashioned for warfare by some demonic hand. "Tanks love to play here," the officer said.

Tel Faris, one of the highest forts in the central Golan, is perched three thousand feet above the plain on a volcano that ceased erupting in the Middle Pleistocene Age, some 500,000 years ago. The black basalt hill was at the center of the most fevered fighting of the Yom Kippur War, and the Syrians captured and held it for a while. The nearby Rafid crossroads was the spot where six hundred Syrian tanks broke through the border in a three-pronged attack in October 1973 and headed into the bone marrow of the Galilee.

The fortress itself rises up darkly like a stepped Mayan temple of baled basalt and limestone. A torn Israeli flag snaps in the wind above the black rocks and bristling antennae. When the Syrians captured Tel Faris and the other forts along the border they took no prisoners. Israeli soldiers who recaptured the forts found murdered middle-aged Israeli reservists mutilated, their testicles stuffed in their mouths. One noncommissioned officer at Tel Faris told me that "Israel has never really punished Syria for its crimes. One day, we will."

About a year before Israel's withdrawal from Lebanon in the summer of 1985, Henry Kissinger was warning that a confrontation between Syria and Israel was very likely because of their deep involvement in that benighted country. Ironically, that confrontation became much more likely after Israel pulled out of Lebanon. Syria has been able to withdraw two of its total of eight divisions from that country, redeploying them on the Golan front. As Israel entered its fortieth year, a massive build-up of forces on both sides took place. Two formidable armies were now nose-to-nose, concentrated in a tiny area.

A visitor to Tel Faris cannot really get a sense of this build-up by looking at either country through large, mounted 20 x 120 binoculars. The big fleets of tanks, artillery and missiles are all hidden beneath camouflage or flat, giant pillboxes that are called "pita," after the similarly shaped bread. But there remains a palpable sense of foreboding. Hafez Assad, the sphinx of Syria, appears to be obsessed with the Golan. He threatens to make trouble if the Golan Heights is not put at the top of the agenda in future peace negotiations.

There are several ways he can do that: installing longer-range missiles, engaging Israeli planes in more dogfights, giving free rein to his Palestinian terrorist proxies, or stirring up the discontent among Israel's Druse population, many of whom live in the Golan Heights.

THE ARABIC PEOPLE who practice the Druse religion and who are scattered throughout Lebanon, Syria and Israel have long been a target for Syrian manipulation. Although most Israeli Druse identify strongly with their country and with other Israelis, and although many Druse serve in top positions in the Israel Defense Forces, a great deal of disillusionment set in among them during the Lebanon war, when Israel sided with the Christians instead of the Druse of Lebanon. The Israeli Druse's gradual estrangement from other Israelis really began the year before the war, in December 1981, when the Knesset enacted the Golan Law, applying Israeli law to the Heights, a step just short of complete annexation. Most of the population of the Golan was Druse, some twelve thousand of them, and they did not want to be forced to become Israeli citizens, since thousands of their relatives lived just across the border on the Syrian side.

Israeli Druse were also affected by these events, according to one of my fellow reservists, Ahmed, a Druse schoolteacher who slept in a nearby bunk several stories beneath the crest of Tel Faris. Every so often, Ahmed said, a Labor Party politician would suggest that part of the Golan really was negotiable, or that the four Druse villages in the Golan might be returned to Syrian sovereignty for some *quid pro quo*, such as freedom for the five thousand Syrian Jews. "Such talk did great damage," Ahmed added. "People asked how Israel could expect the Golan Druse to take Israeli citizenship if there were even the remotest chance that their villages might become part of Syria again." It was no surprise that serious security problems developed among the Golan Druse, giving Assad an opportunity to damage Israel. Two months after the Palestinian uprising began in Gaza and the West Bank, the Golan Druse joined the rampage. As in the other territories, Israeli security forces responded with tear gas, rubber bullets and sporadic forays into the alleyways and back streets of Majdal Shams and the other Druse villages.

Ahmed, an affable, stocky man, told me that he was worried about Israel's inconsistent policy towards the minorities. He said that the mixed signals Israeli Druse were getting could lead to harmful alienation. "It's not a question of bad intentions," he said, "just the usual *bardak*—the mess—we know so well from the army and the bureaucracy."

Though Ahmed was well liked by most of the other reservists, a definite distance existed—because he was not a Jew. Some of the reservists who had emigrated from Russia or the United States or Argentina also were considered outsiders, albeit of a different kind. Sometimes the immigrants felt far removed from the "Israeli Israelis"; but at other times they felt that the old boy network was within their reach. Ferenczi (not his real name), a filmmaker who emigrated from Hungary in the late 1970s, was one of those who felt very remote from most of his fellow reservists.

FERENCZI SAT NEXT TO ME in the Tel Faris tower during an afternoon watch. We took turns looking down into Syria, while the other read or just daydreamed. On a clear day you could see Damascus, we were told, but there were few such days—the fog engulfed us almost every day, even in summer.

"I can't believe what I'm seeing," Ferenczi said suddenly, summoning me to take a look. There, a hundred yards across the border, at 56 degrees northeast, near a burnt-out tank at the Rafid crossroads and close to a UN observer post, a Syrian shepherd, undoubtedly aware that he was being observed by the Israeli enemy, thrust his penis into a white-nosed mule while a hundred sheep cropped the grass around the bestial love scene.

We learned later that this shepherd, whose face was partially concealed by a red-and-white-checkered kaffiyeh, had already acquired a measure of fame among the regular army people manning the fort. He brought to mind Saul Bellow's menacing, powerfully built black man exposing his privates and holding them like a club in order to threaten Mr. Sammler.

The Syrians cultivate a barbaric image; they don't have to be demonized by others, since they provide this service themselves. Most of Israel saw a film on the evening news showing graduating Syrian women soldiers eating live snakes (what the TV House people refused to telecast was the segment showing the men soldiers biting into live puppies and drinking their blood). In the film, President Assad and his chief of staff politely applauded this display, as if it had been a Maypole dance. Considered too rough for American audiences, the film was not telecast by U.S. networks.

After we were relieved by two other reservists, who apparently doubted the veracity of our story, Ferenczi and I headed down into the volcano. Two sharp-winged gray swallows brushed my face as they swept into the steel and concrete tunnel, looking for the omnipresent mice. Ferenczi said that the bestiality we had witnessed was the perfect metaphor for describing Israel's existential situation. "I only wish I had been able to film it."

Ferenczi suffered his way through almost every tour of army duty, and this was one of the worst for him. He was blind to the positive aspects of army duty, to the realization that despite its many warts, the Israeli reserve army was among the best in the world. He called his wife every day from the fort inside the bowels of the volcano, during the two-hour period when it was Tel Faris's turn to get an open line. He complained to her constantly. He was a bitter man, fighting a losing battle to sustain himself and his family in a merciless economy. His bible in Budapest was *Good Soldier Schweik*, which still rang true in Israel. He felt he was a target for the lowlife characters in our unit, who mocked his accent and teased him meanly whenever he retreated into his pile of Hungarian books. Every time he said "yo" (yes) to his wife on the phone, a thickset sergeant, Saguy, and his coarse, lazy sidekick, Abrasha, imitated Ferenczi, yelling, "Yo, Yoooooo, Yo!" and laughing over their rummy game.

Although Ferenczi was not an observant Jew, he had great respect for the religion, so he was deeply offended when Saguy and five other reservists brought the carcass of a wild hog to a nearby outpost and strung it up for slaughter. They had killed the huge boar fifty yards from the electronic fence our unit patrolled every night. Now they divided up the meat for distribution to three forts. "It's straight out of *Lord of the Flies*," commented Ferenczi, who refused to take part in eating the pork stew cooked in the kosher kitchen that night.

The boar was the biggest prize the reservists had snagged in two weeks of hunting porcupines, rabbits, quail and snakes along the fence they patrolled in eight-hour shifts. Their main concern was not the Syrians, but that some gung-ho Israeli officer or, God forbid, the company commander ("Nails"), would discover that the patrol was snoozing in their parked armored personnel carrier or hunting or riding instead of hoofing it along the electronic fence. Mohammed, a Bedouin army scout, had warned Ferenczi and me to keep our eyes on the Israeli side of the border, and Sergeant Saguy concurred. The Syrians were no threat, but the *colonel*, buzzing around in his little Jeep, could make your life miserable. Saguy, who was built like a bronzed circus strongman, made an obscene gesture and said *zayan betakchat*, a favorite barracks expression meaning "penis-in-the-ass." But these were just words. The Syrian shepherd acted.

Three weeks into our tour of duty, Ferenczi's wife told him that she had exceeded the $800 limit on their bank overdraft, on which they paid astronomical interest. Now the bank was returning her checks, including ones for their smallest child's nursery school, a dentist's bill and the electric bill. When he got off the phone, he was in despair. He didn't know who to turn to for financial help. "This is what worries me," he told me. "Not Syria."

ACCORDING TO MORDECHAI GUR, a Labor Party politician and a former armed forces chief of staff, the greatest threat against Israel has always come from the north, "even in Biblical times." He told me in an interview that the Golan is too small and too strategic for anything but the most minimal withdrawal.

Apparently, leaders of the Likud party would not be prepared to make even cosmetic changes. Yitzhak Shamir and Ariel Sharon have said that the Golan is an integral part of Israel, not subject to negotiations. But while the Likud position on the Golan is unequivocal, Labor politicians have purposefully been vague—the words "Golan Heights" were deliberately kept out of the 1983 Labor Party election platform. The U.S. position is that UN Resolution 242 applies, that Israel will withdraw (the question of the extent of that withdrawal is not stated) from the territories, including the Golan Heights, in exchange for peace.

Labor has never spelled out how much Israel would pull back in exchange for a peace treaty with Syria, because there is simply no room to pull back—nothing more than the length of a couple of football fields. "Contrary to the situation in Judea and Samaria, where we can suggest the Allon Plan or other territorial compromises, we can't say anthing about the Golan because of the smallness and the topography of the area—for all practical purposes, it's part of Israel, and there's no room for negotiation," according to Gur.

Gur, like many other military experts, said he was extremely worried about the build-up of forces by both sides along the Golan front. Despite all the talk about the effectiveness of sophisticated U.S.-supplied F-16 fighters and other weapons, nothing in warfare has really changed in recent years: "The strength of the ground forces decides the battle. Tanks and foot soldiers. One army has to move to another's territory."

The man who led the paratroopers who unified Jerusalem in 1967 said he believed in the inevitability of war with Israel's worst enemy, the Syrians. "It's not just in the Bible that they speak of the northern front as the worst. It has always been a problem. It's a matter of people, tradition, and it has *always* been a phenomenon—the Syrians are not made for compromise.

"Syria and Israel can now pour in more forces than the Germans and Russians did around Stalingrad [in the biggest battle of World War II], and in a much smaller area. War would be very costly for both sides."

Syria appears to be prepared to go to war even if Egypt honors its peace treaty with Israel and the war becomes a one-front battle. In March 1988, Assad mocked the U. S. peace proposals formulated in the early weeks of the Palestinian uprising, saying that Secretary of State George Shultz came to Damascus "carrying dead and spoiled projects." He told a chanting crowd of 25,000 Ba'ath Party members that "War will continue, sometimes with rifles, other times with rocks; sometimes through demonstrations and other times in the form of an open military confrontation.''

Talk of territorial compromise, in this light, is absurd. The late Dan Laner, a kibbutznik and reserve general who commanded a division on the Heights during the Yom Kippur War, told me that the question of Israel's strategic depth is crucial: "On the Golan, the only conclusion possible is that the less strategic depth one has, the greater the importance of every yard of such depth.''

Laner, a leader of the forces against any withdrawal from the Golan, did not believe that the occasional dogfight or riot in the Druse villages meant anything in terms of war and peace. But he was concerned about Syria's growing military strength; and Assad's economic and political worries could lead to confrontation. "Whenever the Syrian government is in trouble internally, the easiest thing to do is to warm up the border.''

Forty years after the War of Independence, as the Palestinian uprising flared, fleets of tanks, batteries of artillery and the main armies of both countries remain poised along the basalt ridges of the starkly beautiful Golan Heights. In these volcanic hills enshrouded by fog, strange and terrible war seems to be an immutable fact of life. Sometimes it seems that all civilization has become a thin crust waiting in fear for this volcano to erupt.

V

THE PARENTS SAT in a semicircle on their children's little wooden school-chairs one evening in the early autumn, at a meeting with the new teacher. The head of the parents' class committee, a social worker who canvassed our opinions about holding a series of sessions to discuss mutual problems with our kids, communication gaps and the like, did most of the talking. Israelis love this sort of thing, and it sometimes seems that every other person is a psychologist. The analysts even peddle their medicine on a weekly television hour that should drive any balanced person up a wall.

At our kids' somewhat special school, where a large number of parents are pipe-sucking psychologists, we are expected to participate in many activities; shirkers are made to feel low: they're called "hitchhikers," parasites taking advantage of the school's excellent reputation while doing nothing themselves to enhance it. Some parents simply don't care, but an impressive number are extremely active in the various class and school committees. My wife and I are probably somewhere in between. She spent a year teaching English there twice a week on a voluntary basis. For several months, I taught English to fourth-graders and drawing to first-graders. One of us always goes on the monthly Saturday day trips with one of the kids. We go to parents' meetings regularly and take part in other activities. With three or four children at the school, that can be quite a demand on one's time. But given the terrible condition of Israeli education, we feel there is really no choice but to lend a hand—or a shoulder, as they say in Hebrew.

However, there are limits. Feeling exasperated as the social worker droned on about the need for these mental touchy-feely sessions, while the parents discussed what kind of expert should coordinate the project, I finally burst out, "Who needs it? Why do you talk as if sixth-grade kids are from another planet, as if none of us can possibly remember what it was like to be eleven years old? What's the problem? What's so hard to understand about them?"

Shocked silence followed. Finally, one woman said that the children of today are very different: they don't heed authority the way we did— we sabras and you immigrants alike. The kids talk without restraint and aren't at all intimidated by adulthood, as we were.

Of course, there are major problems in Israeli schools: violence (a great deal of hitting and kicking), and so much noise in the classrooms and hallways that it is amazing the kids get any education at all. But what really bothered me was that all of these busy people were willing to find a few more precious hours every month to attend jawing sessions about Relationships and Communication. Haven't we enough demands on our time? Not everyone feels that way. One policeman and his wife, who have children in my fourth-grader's and first-grader's classes, volunteer for everything and have become fixtures at the school.

The school itself—Givat Gonen, in Jerusalem's Katamon slum—is a rare success story in the increasingly bleak landscape of Israeli education. Unfortunately, this singular success may be no more than an aberration, for the entire educational system is beset with problems aggravated by budget cuts that spell a mortgaging of the nation's future. In the past, schools in the poorer neighborhoods have been able to soften the blows of yearly education budget cuts by obtaining funds from other ministries, social welfare institutions, even banks. But the wells have all nearly dried up, even for the most needy or deserving of schools.

Givat Gonen has become well known throughout Israel because of the dynamic leadership of its principal, Yael Benyamini Levine, a tough, no-nonsense educator. She created a neighborhood school with liberal, labor-movement values in the heart of a slum whose Sephardi residents are Likud loyalists. About half of the nine hundred children at Givat Gonen, who travel to the school from all over Jerusalem, are from Ashkenazi families that represent Israel's liberal elite: professors, writers, those numerous psychologists, journalists, physicians and other professionals. The other pupils are local kids whose working-class parents have become as fiercely loyal to Levine as they are to Likud.

Levine, who in 1986 was awarded Israel's prestigious Golda Meir Prize for outstanding contributions to Israeli society, is a Palmach veteran who has spent thirty years trying to raise the educational level of Jerusalem's poorest neighborhood. In 1981 Levine and a few concerned parents, disturbed by the deteriorating conditions in the neighborhood, the drugs, crime and family violence, decided to transform the local primary school into a showcase for integration and parental involvement.

THE POLICY OF INTEGRATING ISRAELI SCHOOLS originated in 1968. The idea was to bring children from poorer neighborhoods, whose populations were mainly of North African origin, to schools in mostly Ashkenazi, middle-class neighborhoods. But at Givat Gonen, Yael Levine reversed the process. By working a sixteen-hour day for years, this extraordinary educator forged Givat Gonen into such an exemplary school that privileged families were soon elbowing each other in a race to bring their children to Katamon.

Just how desirable has the school become? Some better-off families have actually moved to Katamon to get their children into the school, upgrading the neighborhood and raising the stature of local residents, who are immensely proud of their now famous school. Each year, another grade is added at Givat Gonen, and by 1990 it will be a first-to-twelfth-grade school.

Levine feels that the school's most important achievement has been the integration of social classes. "This was our primary aim, and it goes on all the time, both among the children and the parents," she told an interviewer. "It's a very hard and educational encounter for everybody." Levine's ideological approach is to instill a love of Zion by refusing to hide the truth about its conflicts and doubts, teaching Israeli history in a way that encourages pupils to explore complexities rather than accept dogmas. The religious schools get their views across very effectively— through their own ideological prism. Givat Gonen, and the growing number of other schools that are following its lead, tries to provide a humanist secular alternative. But for some parents, Levine's concern that only highly motivated teachers join the staff, and that the educational standard is kept high, is more important than any ideological slant.

Levine and her staff do not censor texts or stop children from saying whatever they want, including expressing hatred for Arabs—an increasing phenomenon. But they seek to maintain a climate where, in the long run, children are educated to tolerance and coexistence. "One of the reasons why socialists have had less success than the religious with the younger generation is that we haven't reexamined our history and principles and asked how they apply to realities today," Levine has said. Current events—politics—are supposed to be stressed in the school, and usually are. But there was surprisingly little discussion of the Palestinian uprising in its first months. Many of the children of socialist intellectuals may be turning away from their parents' beliefs. A growing number don't want to talk about Arabs, let alone study Arabic.

Israeli parents are allowed to determine 25 percent of the curriculum of their neighborhood schools, but this opportunity was rarely exploited until Givat Gonen set the trend. Now, a growing number of schools in mixed Jerusalem neighborhoods are following Givat Gonen's example. According to Noga Glick, a school consultant who is also one of the most active parents, the extraordinary level of parental involvement at Givat Gonen is a major factor in its success.

In many of the nation's school districts, "gray education" is creating an explosive social situation. Parents with money are able to pay for needed extra lessons and courses, while other parents cannot do so. There is less of this gray education at Givat Gonen because parents take up much of the slack created by reduced teaching hours, voluntarily tutoring students in a variety of subjects from English to computer programming. Every class has an active parents' committee, and the school has several parent-teacher committees, which plan monthly nature hikes and picnics, special study days, visits to industries and museums and daylong exchange visits with kibbutz children. The spirit of cooperation is emphasized, competitiveness played down. Homework is kept to a minimum, but the pupils, from first grade on up, are encouraged to work many hours outside the classroom on their "personal subjects" (anything they choose, from soccer to vampires to Israeli films to dinosaurs). This "individual thesis" idea has been popular and very successful. Encouragement comes not only from teachers, but also from the parents, who often get deeply involved in the projects.

"It's quite a sacrifice of valuable time for many parents. Everyday life in Israel is so much more complicated and time-consuming than elsewhere. Yet they find the time. But that may be because families here are generally more child-oriented than in the U.S.," says Glick, who lived in Philadelphia for several years. "The model set by Givat Gonen is being followed everywhere."

Integration in the lower grades at Givat Gonen is excellent. But in the higher grades the pupils tend to divide into outsider and neighborhood groups. Among the parents, an increasing number of local residents, like the aforementioned policeman and his wife, are becoming involved in classroom activities. However, many of the neighborhood parents are still shy about serving on the schoolwide committees, reluctant to express themselves in front of professors and the knowing psychologists. Nevertheless, the overall picture is a positive one.

Givat Gonen remains an exception in the reversal of the usual integration process of sending poor children to schools in better neighborhoods. Some Israelis feel that true integration will not be achieved until the Givat Gonen model becomes the norm. According to Moshe Mizrachi, chairman of the National Parents Association, ''real integration would be not simply bringing pupils from the Hatikah slum to North Tel Aviv, but also the opposite. I can't picture that being possible under current conditions in Israel.''

Levine, her devoted staff members and the more active parents at Givat Gonen worry about the ever-shrinking budgets. They must constantly fight for funds—from Project Renewal, for example, which helps deprived neighborhoods—to prevent the further paring of class hours, which have been at a ridiculously low level since the early 1980s. The situation in the last couple of years has become so bad that Education Minister Yitzhak Navon, who was Israel's fifth president, warned Prime Minister Shamir that the educational system was teetering on the brink of collapse. Treasury budget cuts deprived thousands of pupils of hours of vital teaching. And the parents of one million Israeli schoolchildren were growing alarmed about the deterioration of an already desperate situation.

Navon, according to some experts, was among the most ineffective education ministers in decades because of his inability to defy the budget-cutters, though he did inform Shamir before the 1987-88 school year began that further cuts would constitute a ''destructive blow'' that was ''unprecedented'' in the history of the country. Elementary schoolchildren, who finish school at twelve o'clock on most days, may be let out at eleven in the coming years unless parents all over the country follow the Givat Gonen example and volunteer to teach for forty-five minutes once or twice a week.

Experts believe that some one hundred and fifty schools will have to be closed down, and about six thousand teachers fired, with a freeze on hiring. The already overcrowded classrooms will be packed further, and, according to Navon, study will be rendered ''virtually impossible,'' particularly in poor neighborhoods and development towns.

CLASSROOM INTEGRATION on a national level has long been considered to be of vital importance, but many have expressed fears that Education Ministry officials may seek to end it. These officials have considered a controversial plan, under which junior high schools, and eventually primary schools, would take a minimum of 30 percent of disadvantaged pupils and then would be free to choose the rest of the school body. Parents, too, would be released from the present restrictions under which they may only choose from schools in their immediate neighborhood.

Although Navon says "we're not giving up on integration," several education experts have said that they don't believe this. Eliezer Shmueli, who until 1986 was the longtime director-general of the Education Ministry, put it this way: "I am very much afraid that soon we will be confronted with new waves of school segregation in spite of the Ministry of Education's declared policy for integration."

The personable Shmueli was with the Education Ministry for thirty-five years, but left after a rift with Navon, whom he claimed was not functioning as a minister should. Shmueli, a Labor man like Navon, was instrumental in helping Yael Levine launch her school. Ironically, it was done under a Likud government and a religious Education Minister, Zevulun Hammer. When Labor and Likud formed the national unity government and a Laborite took over the Education Ministry, Labor-value schools no longer got enough support.

Shmueli told me that he was extremely pessimistic about the state of the country's schools: "The drastic slashing of learning hours is undermining our own future, because the less you learn the less you know." He described Israeli school integration as "a success story...60 percent of pupils are now in integrated schools. But now, ministry officials appear to want to reconsider it."

Shmueli himself does not attack Navon, but other critics have said that the minister has been passive in combatting gray education, and that it has mushroomed mostly during the three years of his tenure. Parents go into hock to provide their children with these extra courses, some of which are held at the schools: for example, a private English teacher may be hired by a small group of parents to teach their children, who already know much more English than the other children in their class. Parents are also barraged with requests for money for more supplies and activities, amounting in some cases to hundreds of dollars per year.

Slates of extra courses are offered by school-affiliated organizations, and many children feel deprived if their parents cannot pay for these extras. This is all aside from individual tutoring and courses that parents feel are necessary to fill the gaps caused by the very short school day: of the four hours most children spend in school, little more than two and a half are spent on learning. A middle-class family with two children may spend as much as $200-$300 a month per child for judo, computer programming, private music lessons, ballet, English, ceramics and so on.

Shmueli feels that the advent of gray education is a sign of "Thatcherism" in Israel, or of the American trend to let education "go to the markeplace," where the strong endure and the weak are allowed to perish. "Gray education is a threat to the fabric of our society," he says. "In terms of education, the rich will get richer and the poor poorer."

In the comming years, the beleaguered school system seems certain to be headed for frequent shocks, with strikes and sanctions by teachers who are saying that the red line has been passed and drastic action must be taken to preserve a basically decent educational system, one that allowed a Givat Gonen to blossom. Yael Levine's example has made educators all over the country aware that everyone, including parents, will have to work much harder to keep the schools from collapsing.

VI

EVEN IN THE WORST of times, a huge number of Israelis read; and they encourage their children to acquire the book habit early on. In the land of the People of the Book, there are some eighty publishers—the highest number per capita in the world—and despite economic hardships Israelis are still buying impressive numbers of Hebrew children's books. This literature has become far less provincial in recent years, but it still heavily reflects the heritage of a war that has lasted since independence was declared, and which has only been punctuated by the *intifada*.

Israel remains very much a child-oriented society, and books are introduced at an early age. In most Israeli households both parents work outside the home, and they send children as young as one year to day-care centers and prekindergartens. A large number of these tens of thousands of nurseries are in private homes. Others are in facilities run by municipalities, working women's organizations or other bodies. All have a "book corner," small libraries of colorful books for the two-to-five age group, and this is where bookworming often begins.

Many Israeli children's books have come of age in the last decade, outgrowing narrow national concerns, even dealing with the fact that 17 percent of Israelis are Arabs. Although it could be argued that Israel should stay hokey and unsophisticated and locked away in the 1950s, there is really not much that can be done to counter the trend: music, films, television productions, theater—all are getting much better as Israel grows older. Today's children's books are marked by mature and polished writing, more craftsmanlike, professional illustrations and a greater emphasis on universal themes.

Although the themes of Israeli children's literature have broadened, many still deal with the pressure-cooker pace of Israeli life: the army and the security situation figure prominently in the books Israeli children read. Former Defense Forces chief of staff Mordechai Gur is among the many ex-soldiers who write children's books, like his *Azeet, the Paratrooper Dog*, which has also been published in America. Dr. Uriel Ofek's *Smoke over Golan*, written after the Yom Kippur War of 1973, is about a boy who tells of his experiences when he finds his farm surrounded by those lovable Syrian troops.

Some commentators believe there are too many stereotypes in Israeli children's literature—Arabs are bad, women do housework—but this tendency is also changing. In an increasingly complex Israeli society, and in a world undergoing a technological revolution, the literature has to become more suited to the times. A growing number of Israeli books are winning international recognition and awards. Nahum Gutman's *Orange Peel Patch*, published by Yavne in Israel and Dodd Mead in the U. S., has won a certificate of honor for its international merit. Writer Nurit Zarchy lost her father at an early age and was raised on kibbutz; these experiences are reflected in her many books. Her work is often cited as evidence that Israeli children's literature is finally outgrowing narrow patriotic confines.

Another exemplary author is Oded Burla, whose clever, funny nonsense stories, though written in Hebrew, are not tied to Israel. Among Israel's most popular children's writers are Yemina Avidar-Tschernovitz (who has published forty books), Dorit Orgad (whose animal stories are widely praised), Devora Omer, Galia Ron-feder and the late Leah Goldberg. In recent years some Israeli illustrators have also gained international recognition, following in the footsteps of such accomplished artists as Gutman, who has illustrated countless children's books since the 1930s. Among the best are Avner Katz, cartoonist Dudu Geva, Yossi Abolafia and Alona Frankel (whose book *Once Upon a Potty* was also a best seller in the U.S.).

Israeli kids are very "gang-oriented." The *hevra*, or gang, also figures very large in children's literature; the most successful books in Israel's forty-year history are Yigal Mossinsohn's *HaSamba* series about a gang of kids and their adventures stemming from the independence struggle. "Pucho"—Yisrael Wiesler—is a humorist who has written a successful book called *Methuselah's Gang*, the story of a group of kids who befriend a man with the longest beard in the world.

Today's Israeli kids are likely to be writing their own adventure stories on personal computers, carrying their disks to each other's homes and working on spy and adventure stories of their own. Times have changed in many ways, but "the situation," whether that means the Palestinian uprising or the threat from Syria, remains much the same as it has for forty years. An Israeli parent watching his eleven-year-old and his gang in the computer era still thinks about the war situation, about what will be in seven or eight years when his or her child is in the army.

Israeli parents, even the most primitive and warlike among them, pray for the day when their children will not have to kill or be killed anymore. The hope is that Israeli children in a few years time, when the third millennium begins, will read about their country's Forty Year War as past, and not present, history.

VII

DRIVING THROUGH the Judean Hills, descending from Jerusalem towards the small plain and the airport one late October day, I was awed and elated by banks of towering white clouds against the background of a blue blue sky. God, what a beautiful land it is. How happy it makes me sometimes. How I love this country like a fool.

I was ignoring the insane drivers, the bloody statistics that put Israel with Sri Lanka, Jordan and Syria as the worst countries in the world to drive in, with the highest rate of road accidents. I was ignoring the crash of stock markets around the world. I was going to meet some friends, an Ethiopian-Israeli and an American-Israeli and their daughter, all of whom had just taken a month-long trip to the States. A few hours later I was going to be among a large crowd welcoming two warm souls who had given me dinner in their Moscow home. Sometimes it is a pleasure to go to the airport.

It's a small international airport, quite human-sized. The security has been excellent since the massacre by PLO-affiliated Japanese terrorists in the early 1970s. Bright young men with walkie-talkies are everywhere. A grizzled old Jew waiting at the welcoming ramp with a big white cloth bag at his feet is asked four times in an hour if the bag is his. He complains about being asked so often, until a bystander puts him in his place.

No fancy or middle-class restaurants at this airport—just a couple of poorly run, outrageously expensive small cafeterias. The cashier ignores the customers as she twists her arm behind her head and dials a phone on a shelf behind her without once looking back. A marvelous performance. The surly service is a lot like Russia's. But then, why should she be nice? Why should she smile a plastic smile and say, "Have a nice day" or "Have a nice life"?

Five jumbo jets arrive at the same time, and at least two thousand chattering people crowd around the single welcome ramp leading out of customs. One of the jumbos, a Tower Airlines charter, disgorges three hundred black-garbed Hasidim carrying what seem like several thousand giant cartons and tens of thousands of bulging suitcases. It takes hours for them to get out of customs. "They're starting to check things real closely again," one waiting relative explains to her entourage. "A friend of ours brought a lot of new clothes for his eight kids—you can imagine— and they stopped him, and they tried to charge him an astronomical tax and he just couldn't believe it and just left all the clothes with the bastards. They're really cracking down again."

About twenty of the Hasidim carry a Torah scroll, and they start dancing and singing around it as it bobs up and down. What is so special about this Torah scroll? "It comes from Brooklyn, straight from the blessing of the Rebbe," a pimply young Hasid answers. It is holier than holy because it has been touched by *the* rebbe, the Lubavitcher, Menachem Schneerson himself, the aging rabbi whom tens of thousands of ultra-Orthodox Jews regard as the Mashiach—the Messiah. Does this mean that the great rabbi himself will be coming to Israel? A knowing snicker flashes across the adolescent face as it nods up and down. "Ha, ha—don't worry, He'll know when it's time to come," his head nods.

Mualim, an army reserves buddy who works at the airport, is watching the Torah dance from the little Avis office, where he's charming the pretty attendant and telling her how I was always taking notes for a book while we "fought in the foxholes of Lebanon." He is a masterful fibber, a good singer and a joker with a foul mouth. "That's what we get every day at the airport," he says, "the *dossim* [religious people] come with their nine kids, and Ciccolina arrives on the same plane and exposes herself at the Wall. Pure insanity in this country."

The next jumbo is full of secular teenagers, who emerge after the first-class passengers: a couple of Jerusalem millionaires—he's puffing a pipe, she's clinging to her furs—lead the children of Israel to the taxi stand or parking lots. Sitting on the *barzilim*, the iron railings leading from the customs gate, is a healthy group of about fifteen teeming teenagers waiting for friends who have been on some exchange program in America. They are young and vibrant, cheeky and sexy, wearing hats and tennis shoes without socks and hitting each other with the hollow-plastic hammer noisemakers that usually proliferate on Independence Day, shouting and giggling, banging tambourines and singing, touching each other constantly; and just about everyone seems to get a kick out of it.

Little kids break through the angry ushers guiding the passengers out and rush to the embrace of grandparents arriving from magical New York with dozens of presents. "What did you bring me?" Shouts and hugging and kissing punctuate the continuous roar of this crowd of Jews, and a few Arab families. It's Baghdad, Singapore, the Last Judgement, as the returning Israelis and the visitors pour into the Holy Land.

Five hours after I got to the airport my friends finally arrived—everything was late because of the five jumbos and the tougher customs posture. I didn't mind waiting for them at all.

Richard T. Nowitz

VIII

URING THE YEARS between the Lebanon war of 1982 and the Palestinian uprising in the winter of 1987–88, Israel's huge foreign press corps did not have that much to write home about. Of course, there were a number of short-lived sensations, like Operation Moses (the rescue of thousands of Ethiopian Jews) and the dramatic homecoming of Anatoly Natan Sharansky. But many veteran correspondents felt that the Israeli news business was a bit slow, and that the people in Chicago and Liverpool and Hamburg and Milan were not much interested in Soviet-Jewish emigration, or Israel's economic problems.

When Prime Minister Shamir addressed the hundreds of bookpeople assembled for the thirteenth biennial Jerusalem International Book Fair in April 1987, he said that there are a thousand good subjects in Israel that lend themselves to book-length treatment. But in his own personal view—from a man who doesn't read "any books," as he once told me in an interview—the best possible subject was a hope: "The exodus of the Soviet Jews." Although the subject is certainly not as sexy to newsmen as the revolt of the stone-throwing Palestinians, it is nevertheless of great importance in Jewish and Israeli history (when the state came into being, half of the cabinet was born in Russia); and the story of Soviet Jewry tells us as much about Zionism and Israel as any other issue.

Permit me to confess that I am an avid fan of Natan Sharansky. He is in a league by himself, a compact powerhouse with a razor-sharp mind, a warm heart and a quick wit—a rare and refreshing combination. In ten or twenty years, he could conceivably become one of Israel's leaders, and despite his distaste for politics and his attempts to stay neutral in the polarized Israeli society and the contentious world of Jewish politics, within a few years he could very well represent Israel as ambassador to the U.S. or the UN or, for all we know today, Soviet Russia.

Yet some Israeli VIPs feel that Sharansky probably *was* an American spy, as the Soviets had charged, or that he was "a coward," as one leftist journalist, Haim Bar-Am, wrote, or that he was so feeble-minded that his wife Avital, whose politics appear to be nationalist-religious, had immediately turned him into a ventriloquist's dummy: "I don't like such Russians," the sabra director-general of a key ministry told me over dinner one night. "I don't like him or his wife."

During a 1986 visit to the USSR I told a religious Jewish leader in Leningrad, a follower of the Lubavitcher Rebbe, that I didn't think most Israelis cared about the fate of Soviet Jews, and that this seemed especially so among leftist-liberal Israelis, although there were many exceptions. I then related to him some of the attacks on Sharansky for allowing his wife to put a yarmulke on his head. My Leningrad interlocutor was shocked by what I said. "It's a sickness," he said, "a disease."

Several Israeli journalists have told me, "Soviet Jewry is boring." Or, "There are just as many horror stories about capitalist countries." One colleague in the media, contemptuous of my reports about the repression of Soviet Jews, tried to get his superiors to send him to the Soviet Union to report on "all those Jews who want to stay." He told me that, in contrast to his feeling about the Jews in the USSR, he "sympathized" with Ethiopian Jewry, "but it's all Zionist hype about Soviet Jews." Yet this comment was from a man who really is not sure that Israel should exist at all. In the wake of the Palestinian uprising, many Israelis and good friends of Israel abroad were asking how anyone could support Soviet Jews when Israeli Jews were denying basic human rights to the Palestinians of the territories, and while Israeli Arabs were second-class citizens in every way.

Several Israeli journalists have said to me that most of the Soviet Jews are "dropouts" anyway, that only 20 percent of those allowed out choose to go to Israel. And those that do come "all end up voting for Herut or Kahane, in any case." Although there is some truth to this appraisal, it stems mostly from ignorance. Some of the Russian immigrants join kibbutzim, despite the hatred for socialism they have learned from first-hand experience. Others retain a humanist, centre- or left-oriented philosophy. It is ridiculous to believe that they all end up in Brighton Beach, Brooklyn—about half the engineers in Israel are immigrants from the USSR: over 200,000 Russian Jews are here, and they are vital to our existence.

In America a few years ago, a founder of the New Left, now a comfortable and pompous Marxist professor at a major university, told me about his "Jewish consciousness" circle, part of the *havura* movement that includes hundreds of Jewish cultural or neoreligious groups. His Berkeley circle, made up of a score of widely published leftists like himself, brought Cambodia and Cuba into the Jewish Question at every opportunity. But when it came to Soviet Jews, well, that was "an establishment issue—we're far too sophisticated to go out and demonstrate in the streets about something like Soviet Jewry."

A good many American-Jewish and Israeli leftists feel this is the wrong way. Some people on the left are every bit as devoted to the cause of Soviet Jewry as any religious or nationalistic Israeli. Not every leftist is too "sophisticated" or too pro-Palestinian to ignore the fact that there are, after all, as many oppressed Soviet Jews as there are Palestinians. Dedi Zucker, a "Peace Now" activist who became a member of the Knesset from the liberal-left Citizens' Rights Movement, says that for Israel there is nothing more important than the issue of Soviet Jewry, that it is time that the left overcome its prejudices (which may stem from the era when Stalin was an admired figure among "progressive" Israelis) and understand that the freedom of Soviet Jewry is a central issue in the continued existence of Israel.

After about a year in Israel, Natan Sharansky, the man who never yielded to the Soviet authorities, knew that his battles were far from over.

When fame comes to someone who has offered a moral example to the world, it automatically invites attack, entrapment, intrigue. It can come from ostensible friends, as well as from obvious enemies: an Israeli reporter who distorts and misquotes; an American-Jewish organization leader who uses the magic name to raise funds but lets the word out to fellow bigshots that "Sharansky's too outspoken"; an Israeli government official who tries to dampen efforts to intensify the public campaign for Soviet Jewry;

a PLO surrogate who tries to co-opt the language and leadership of the struggle for human rights.

But Sharansky is unflappable. He really seems to be the essence of the "indomitable spirit" he has been called so often and enthusiastically. He is the most focused person I have ever met, and he will not be diverted by what Nietzsche called "flies in the marketplace," petty people who try to impede a man ennobled by a higher calling. Sharansky, since rediscovering his Jewishness in the early 1970s, has had a mission: he remains determined to make the issue of freedom for Soviet Jews not a narrow concern of world Jewry but a problem the whole world must face. That is why he concentrates on the half million Soviet Jews who wish to emigrate, not just on the thousands of actual refuseniks or the famous activists whom Gorbachev freed when he launched glasnost.

Yet there will always be people who try to trip Sharansky up. In mid-November of 1986, just after Avital gave birth to the Sharanskys' first child, an Israeli Arab journalist, Adil Abu Raya, phoned Sharansky several times at Jerusalem's Misgav Ladach hospital and asked him for a five-minute meeting with a "colleague" of his to discuss "a human rights case," a deportation order against East Jerusalem editor Akram Haniye. Sharansky, though his privacy was being violated, finally agreed to receive a packet of information about the case from Abu Raya and his colleague—after Abu Raya had said to him, "What's the matter, you don't want to meet with me because I'm an Arab?" After Sharansky consented, Abu Raya asked if he could also bring along a journalist from the mass-circulation daily *Ma'ariv*. Sharansky said he wasn't giving a press conference, merely receiving material.

The next day, the Arab journalist and his colleague came to Sharansky's office. The colleague turned out to be Faisel al-Husseini, considered by many to be one of the main PLO political leaders in the territories. Sharansky, still new to Israel, did not know his visitor; nor did his name ring any bells. Husseini, whose father was the Palestinian military chief during the War of Independence, says he told Sharansky right away about his political viewpoint, that he supported "Chairman Arafat and the PLO."

According to Husseini, Sharansky then said that Arafat was not a man of peace, citing the PLO's terrorist actions against civilians. According to Sharansky, Husseini had said that Haniye, the editor, was connected to the moderate part of the PLO. "I stopped him and said there are no moderates in the PLO, and cited the PLO Covenant..." When Husseini asked him about the deportation order against Haniye, Sharansky said he wasn't familiar with this ordinance. There was nothing else to talk about, and the encounter soon ended.

But the PLO man and his intermediary had not come for nothing. (Husseini told me later that he went to see Sharansky because it was "important for me to learn about the leaders and heroes" of the Jews.) This visit was a publicity stunt, one that probably had been planned in advance. Sharansky realized immediately that the PLO "was trying to use me," and the next day he issued a sharply worded statement saying he would never have met with anyone identified with the PLO, which he called "a criminal terror organization dedicated to the destruction of Israel." At the same time, far-right nationalists like Rabbi Haim Druckman, who never called Sharansky to ask him about the incident, were telling the press that Sharansky had done a deplorable thing, meeting with the enemy.

Reaping the publicity bonanza, Husseini issued a statement to the press, deriding the internationally acclaimed human rights hero, saying that he was in reality a hypocrite, a little nothing. Husseini's ringing phrase, "Great man turns small," was picked up by sympathetic Jewish pro-PLO headline writers who saw in it some profound, masterly assessment of this greatly overrated Russian Jew.

Sharansky's overly strident language in condemning the PLO apparently provided some critics (usually the ones who couldn't care less about the repression of Soviet Jews, and never have cared) with mud to sling against him. They never condemned the so-called moderates for setting a trap, for using human rights in as cynical a fashion as the Soviets use the words "peace and freedom." Rather, all the blame fell on Sharansky.

"I've always thought, and still do, that we have to have normal contact with our neighbours, to discuss mutual issues: between right and left, religious and secular, Arab and Jew," Sharansky told me. "This was a disappointing experience...the most disappointing was not Husseini...but the behavior of Abu Raya, who's not directly connected to the PLO. The moment he had an opportunity for contact, he tried to use it to promote the PLO...

"And that's a real problem; on the one hand we must have normal contacts [with the Palestinians], on the other we should do nothing to help an organization with terrorist aims by giving them a publicity opportunity."

But Sharansky related the incident to the similar way the Soviet Union tries to use the democratic institutions of the West. The PLO would now claim to be fighting for human rights, and would find many outlets inside and outside Israel for the latest fashion line.

The attempt to co-opt the human rights struggle by authoritarian people who pretend to believe in democratic principles is not new to anyone who has lived under a communist regime. Husseini was trying to maintain that he, like Sharansky, was a human rights activist too, concerned only for the freedom of the individual. "What's important out of all this,"

Sharansky said, "is not to let the PLO get away with this misuse of the language" of humanitarianism.

He expressed regret that the situation now made it far more difficult for him to learn about the Palestinian position. Dialogue is essential, he said, but not with terrorists. He had fallen into a publicity trap—exactly what he has been warning the West about Gorbachev.

The right and the left attacked Sharansky over the encounter with Husseini, a range that in his eyes is "good—it means you are going your own way and not following after one or the other...The left and the right feed arguments to each other." One article by an establishment pundit will appear, saying that Sharansky is irritating the USSR too much, hurting chances for renewal of relations with Israel. Then another article will say he has become part of the establishment and isn't with the activists anymore.

Because of Israel's particular circumstances, "everything is black and white. I think it's a very serious problem, between the parties, religious and secular. People want to speak and not listen." He was surprised by the extent of the prejudice, the hatred in everyday Israeli life. Recalling all of the criticism directed against his wife because she is religious-nationalist, he said, "I can say that to the credit of the religious people, no one...has tried to put a *kippa* [skullcap] on me." The pressure from the secular people has been as strong, or "even greater." He lives in the Israeli goldfish bowl but remains unflappable. At a dinner at the King David Hotel in Jerusalem, where he was one of the speakers, Sharansky joined a small number of people who, before eating, washed their hands and said a prayer. No one else at his table did so, but they all whispered about how religious he was becoming.

THERE IS A DIFFERENT KIND OF SNIPING at Sharansky as well, stories from simple people who think he's getting $3,000 a month from the Jewish Agency, or $1 million or $6 million for writing his book. Is it anybody's business at all how much he got for his book contract? "No," says Sharansky, "it's nobody's business...It's much less than was written in the papers but, of course, much more than I used to get as an engineer in the Soviet Union. I don't get money from the Jewish Agency; I don't get money from President Reagan, as one Israeli newspaper reported. I use the advance money on my book to live on and to finance my activities." In order to maintain his independence he pays for his own trips and does not accept money from the government or Jewish organizations. He turned down a million-dollar offer to do thirty or forty lectures. "It's much more important for me to live with my wife and my family here in Israel. For those lectures and talks I have given, I did not make one dollar, because I'm not making a business of Soviet Jewry.''

He worked very hard to complete his book, but the Sharanskys' baby, Rachel, interfered a lot: Sharansky, in between recalling how he felt in the prison punishment cells, changed diapers and tended to the baby as most new fathers do. ''Of course—I do everything.''

His private life is his private life, and he wants to keep it that way. A few days before our long talk, some very important American had called to say that he would be in Israel soon and that he wanted to see Rachel. Avital, who spoke to him, said, ''Rachel isn't giving any interviews.''

Sharansky remains very upbeat about Israel, despite its obvious drawbacks and problems: ''The main thing for me is that I live in a state of Jews, which is an absolutely free society; I enjoy every day of living here, whether I was criticized on this day or not.''

''But shall we come back to Soviet Jewry?'' Sharansky keeps prodding. Everything we've been talking about so far is, indeed, peripheral—he wants to talk about Gorbachev, not about himself as a ''personality.''

One of the few issues on which Israelis of various persuasions seem to be united, Sharansky says, is the belief that the ''dropout'' phenomenon— Soviet Jews opting for America—caused the Soviets to close the gates as the 1980s began. ''So the Israeli government's position has been that we must make it clear that we are not for free emigration but only emigration to Israel. This argument, that the Soviets closed the doors because of the 'dropouts,' always irritated me, because it's just what the Soviet Union wants us to think.'' Allowing people to leave the USSR—a country where people are told what to read, what to write, what to think—is such a big threat that, by comparison, where a Jew goes—to the Middle East or to Canada—is much less important.

If it were just an academic question, a theory to be debated, Sharansky says, then it wouldn't matter, but officials draw serious conclusions, determining Israel's policy with an emphasis placed on combatting the dropout phenomenon. When Sharansky speaks out against this policy, he is attacked as a ''bad Zionist.''

The dropout phenomenon does influence Soviet policy, ''but not in the way the Soviets, along with many of our politicians, the Jewish Agency, etc., are saying...It's quite natural that Israelis don't want to demonstrate for Jews who don't want to come here.'' But the question requires reexamination. What can Israel do to reverse the dropout rate? First of all, ''change the image of Israel among Soviet Jews,'' Sharansky says. Soviet Jewry activists have come to feel that American Jews, and not Israelis, are at the forefront of the struggle. The Israeli government makes some de rigueur statements from time to time, Sharansky feels, but this is nothing but tokenism.

He gives an example: Hundreds of Soviet Jews have received Israeli citizenship—Sharansky himself was made a citizen in 1974—and the Knesset Judiciary Committee has stated that these Jews are full citizens in every meaning of the word. This citizenship has always been extremely important to the struggling activists in the USSR. "But the reality is that our government does not want to do anything that might irritate the Soviet Union." He displays a letter from the Ministry of the Interior's Department of Population Administration to a Haifa lawyer explaining why a request to issue Israeli passports to the Boris Chernobylsky family has been denied (Chernobylsky, a leading Moscow activist, is a former "prisoner of Zion" who was still struggling for an exit visa.) The ministry official, Y. Kahana, stated four reasons, including "concern for the foreign relations of the State that might be impaired."

But shortly after the release of Ida Nudel, Sharansky and three other ex-prisoners of Zion—Yuli Edelshtein, Yosef Mendelevich and Victor Brailovsky—appealed to Prime Minister Shamir to emphasize repatriation, that Soviet Jews be accorded the same status as the Soviet "Volga Germans" who were being repatriated to West Germany. Shamir's apparent acceptance of this position was of enormous significance to the movement, since it appeared, for the first time, to be a deviation from the course set by Sharansky, Nudel and Vladimir Slepak in the 1970s: putting the emphasis on human rights and the Helsinki Accords— reunification of families, and the right to leave any country and the right to return. Now, a new focus had emerged: repatriation, which the younger generation of refuseniks had been pushing for.

In attracting Soviet Jews, Israel can't compete, in a material sense, with the U.S. "But Israel is the spiritual home of the Jews, and Soviet Jews must feel that their home is concerned about them," says Sharansky. Israel can also help reverse the dropout trend by undertaking some basic reforms. "The Jew from the Soviet Union who leaves that awful bureaucratic society and decides to come to Israel" should be spared the bureaucratic monsters that await him at Ben-Gurion Airport. Absorption should be on a personal level, family "adopting" family, and the red tape must be eliminated. He has seen close up how difficult it is to get Israeli institutions to reform themselves. Criticism has been voiced for many years, and nothing has changed. "But something must be done."

"The road from Moscow to Israel must be made smoother." He feels that independent groups led by former refuseniks, like Jerusalem's Soviet Jewry Education and Information Centre, headed by Yuri Shtern and Yosef Mendelevich, are on the right track in devising new approaches towards absorption, "but unfortunately the authorities do not cooperate with them."

Sharansky feels that the Israeli government's philosophy towards the Soviet-Jewish struggle is fossilized, that the general attitude was forged in the pre-State era of Aliyah Bet, when survivors of World War II were brought to Palestine clandestinely, in the early years of massive immigration. "Quiet diplomacy" was the watchword, and this approach remains dominant. "Any suggestion to increase the public pressure campaign today is met with expressions of concern about rocking the boat," Sharansky says. The Israeli government approach appears to him to be an attempt to placate the Soviets, to say, "Look, we don't want to interfere in your internal affairs," and then to expect the Soviets to reciprocate by easing the curbs on the Jews. The Israeli government doesn't seem to understand that the only approach that will work with the Soviets is to "show strength," to mount a campaign to link international economic and other agreements to the granting of freedom of emigration for Soviet Jews. That, in Sharansky's view, is the only course of action to follow. "Gorbachev realizes, much better than did his predecessors, that only Western help can save the Soviet economy." That's the lever. Israel does not have enough power for the "quiet approach" to work. "We don't have arguments that will persuade the Soviet Union. Whatever we may tell them, they know that it is very serious to let Jews go," that it is a threat to the authoritarian system.

That is why the Israelis do no more than pay lip service to the citizenship issue; that is why the government doesn't cooperate with the activists. Six months before the release of his friends Ida Nudel and Vladimir and Maria Slepak, Sharansky speculated that most of the eleven thousand known refuseniks would be released during the year marking Israel's fortieth birthday and the seventieth anniversary of the Bolshevik Revolution. The Soviets would get the U.S. trade agreements they are looking for, diplomatic ties between the Soviet Union and Israel would be resumed, and the USSR would be invited to participate in an international peace conference on the Mideast conflict.

Sharansky himself believes that the trade restrictions should be reviewed and lifted in accordance with Soviet compliance on the basic human rights question of freedom to emigrate for Soviet Jews. The first *quid pro quo* on the part of the U.S. should be to lift the Stevenson Amendment, a relatively minor bar on the granting of trade credits to the USSR (the Soviets under Brezhnev found this congressional measure particularly irksome). If the Soviets allowed sixty thousand Jews to leave, then the Jackson-Vanik Amendment should be lifted for a year—the late Senator Jackson himself suggested that figure.

WHEN SHARANSKY was a member of Yuri Orlov's Helsinki Watch Group monitoring Soviet compliance (or rather, noncompliance) with the 1975 Helsinki Accords on human rights, he never signed petitions about how the Soviet system should be changed, but only about violations of human rights: as a Jewish activist, he wanted only to leave the Soviet Union, not to reform it.

"On the other hand, as part of the new freedom that my Zionist beliefs brought me, I felt free to express sympathy to those other people whose rights were being violated. Now that I'm in Israel, I still hold that view. I realize that the State of Israel, as the state, cannot take absolutely the same position. Nevertheless...I saw in England and elsewhere in Europe that the campaign for Soviet Jewry didn't reach beyond the Jewish communities. They are afraid to collaborate on this issue with anyone not Jewish."

It must be made clear that this is not a narrowly defined issue, solely a Jewish problem, but a world problem, Sharansky emphasizes. Of course, there are other oppressed minorities in the USSR—Sharansky worked for them and wrote about them—but the Soviet-Jewish issue is one of massive proportions. "And we must be ready to speak to the world about it."

Sharansky does not believe the Russian people will ever follow the path that the Sakharovs and Orlovs have taken. If they ever do attain freedom of choice, they are much more likely to pursue Solzhenitsyn's vision of a neo-Slavophile, neo-Christian, theocratic Russia. This is a *genuine* "internal affair" of the Russian people, Sharansky says.

It must be shown to the West that the best barometer of Soviet sincerity in international accords is the fate of some four hundred thousand Jews who have begun the emigration process and who are not allowed to leave. Instead, Sharansky says, we have the situation where the Jewish world "tries not to rock the boat," to speak to the Gentiles only in the narrowest of contexts, "like asking for mercy."

"We do have such friends as Secretary of State Shultz, but we must be able to go further...We must say that there can be no trust between East and West until an understanding is reached on the human rights question, the Jewish question."

Israel must speak out. "As Secretary Shultz once said to Avital on a quite concrete matter, 'But you demand from me what even your government does not do. The American government cannot do more than the Israeli government does on this issue.' And that's a good example. There must be a change of policy." With Sharansky leading the charge, supported by the other heavyweights—Vladimir Slepak, Ida Nudel, Yosef Begun, Victor Brailovsky, Yuri Edelshtein, Dina Beilin—a change of policy is entirely possible.

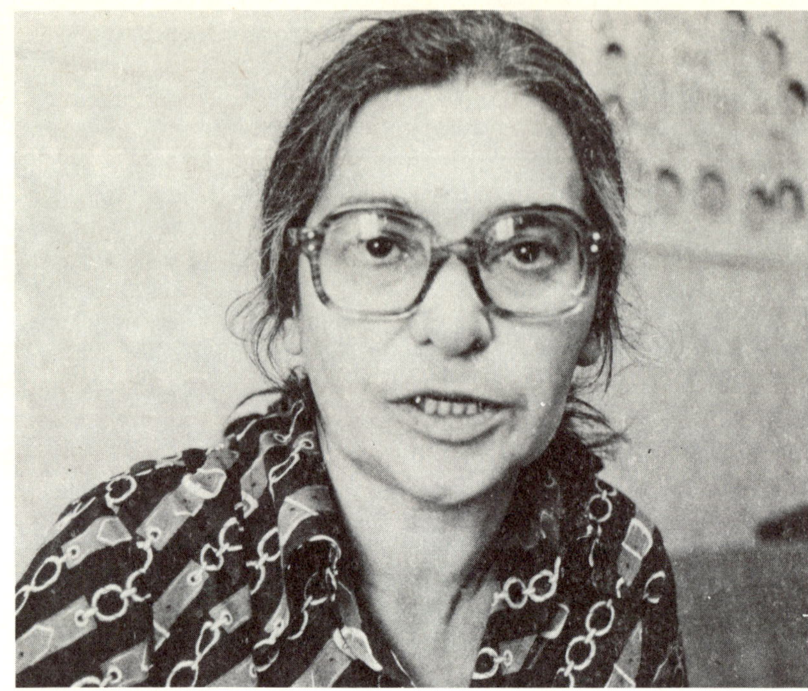

IX

WHEN IDA NUDEL, the "angel of the refuseniks," was released by the Soviet Union in mid-October 1987 and was en route to Israel, thousands of people awaited her arrival at an airport that has witnessed countless Jewish dramas. Ya'acov Fridman, the only child of her only sister, ran up to a journalist who had written extensively about the refuseniks, clasped his hands over his head and exclaimed: "We won!"

Ya'acov, who is in his mid-twenties, his mother, Elena, and her husband, Aryeh, had campaigned relentlessly for sixteen bitter years for the reunification of their family, and when Nudel arrived on Armand Hammer's private executive jet, Elena was the first up the ramp to greet her sister. Nudel's emotional arrival was later described as the first major event in the build-up to the celebrations of Israel's fortieth birthday. But, perhaps as a commentary on the true taste of life in Zion, Israel Television and most Israeli radio stations were not there to cover it—a journalists' strike had shut them down a week earlier.

However, many other Israeli journalists and a couple hundred representatives of the world media were on hand to record the warm homecoming and to hear Armand Hammer claim all the credit for rescuing the heroine. The eighty-nine-year-old tycoon, the son of a communist, knew and did business with Lenin in the early days of the Soviet regime. He is still going strong. Hammer told the journalists assembled at the airport Immigrant Absorption Hall that three weeks earlier he had met with Soviet Foreign Minister Eduard Shevardnadze in New York, who "asked me to go to Afghanistan to help get a settlement of that problem. I said I'd gladly go, 'but first you've got to give me your promise—give me Ida Nudel.'" Whereupon the easygoing Foreign Minister reportedly replied, "I promise to!"

And *voila*! Of course, Hammer made no reference to the Fridman family or the hundreds of housewives and students who had labored tirelessly on behalf of Nudel and other refuseniks. Nor was U.S. Secretary of State Shultz given any credit, even though the concurrent release of Nudel and other leading refuseniks, such as Vladimir Slepak and Victor Brailovsky, seemed obviously timed to coincide with Shultz's important visit to Moscow and the upcoming Reagan-Gorbachev summit.

Hammer went on to explain how he was upholding his part of the bargain—he was off for Pakistan and talks with President Zia ul-Haq in his quest to bring peace to the troubled area. Of course, there were not a few giggles at this display of megalomania. But the ancient ghetto institution of *shtadlanut*—Jewish merchant princes approaching the Gentiles on behalf of the miserable Jewish communities—is so ingrained, even after forty years of Jewish independence, that Hammer's chest-thumping was taken as gospel. The *Jerusalem Post* headlined its page-one story "How Hammer clinched the deal." (In the same issue, a profile of an Anglo-Jewish philanthropist, Maurice Wohl, was headlined "Rebuilder of Jerusalem," as if he were God himself.)

Hammer and the billionaire Bronfmans of Canada have replaced the Rothschilds as the leading practioners of *shtadlanut*. But their actual contribution to such issues as the rescue of Ethiopian Jews or the release of Soviet Jews remains an open question. Hammer would say later that the Kremlin had told "everybody," including himself and Teddy Kennedy, that Ida Nudel would never be allowed to emigrate. "They were so determined. I don't know why they wanted to punish Ida."

Jane Fonda, who helped bring Nudel's case to world attention, was a study in contrast to Hammer. Self-effacing, she spoke to the point, recalling that she was first made aware of the case in 1979 by I-WIN (Israeli

Women for Ida Nudel), and noting that Nudel fought for all Soviet Jews, that she was literally "the little guardian of the prisoners of conscience" who kept in close touch with all of the Jews imprisoned for wanting to leave their country and live in Israel. "She's little and she's beautiful, but she's also a strategist, one of the leading strategists of the Soviet Jewry movement...I want to thank her for teaching me one very important thing: never lose hope, never lose hope."

Prime Minister Yitzhak Shamir and his rival, Foreign Minister Shimon Peres, also spoke, paying tribute to Nudel's courage and vowing never to abandon Soviet Jewry; but anyone aware of the increasingly complex conflict between Jewish and Israeli interests on this issue took it all with Pliny's grain of salt. Several minor figures also spoke—a disapproving moan swept the room when Arye Dulzin, the much-criticized head of the Jewish Agency and the World Zionist Organization, rose to speak—and then, finally, it was Ida's turn.

She appeared to be overwhelmed with happiness and relief, quite different from the exceedingly brave but depressed and desperate woman I had interviewed for ten hours in Leningrad just over a year earlier. What a difference a year of *glasnost* seemed to make!

No one believed the Soviets would finally release her. As she spoke to the journalists and two hundred invited guests, her voice cracked, and she stumbled over her English, lapsing at one point into Russian. She did not share the easy public manner, quick wit and fluency in Hebrew and English of her close friend, Anatoly Natan Sharansky, who, in any case, is considered a unique figure in the movement. But Ida Nudel's spiritually powerful presence, her warmth and intelligence, had made her every bit as special as Sharansky; and these qualities came through now, at her moment of triumph. She had defeated the KGB and the repressive regime that had tried to crush her in Siberian exile. "For me, it is the moment of my life," she said. "I'm here, a free person among my own people."

Her main point was that hers was one small victory in the big struggle involving the fate of hundreds of thousands of Soviet Jews, and that she had 'just begun to fight.'

Her first thanks were extended to her family—her sister, brother-in-law and nephew—who "fought through the long years of my resistance side-by-side with me." She also thanked the people of Israel, and the governments of Israel, the U.S., Britain, France, Germany, Norway, Sweden and Australia, for their efforts on behalf of Soviet Jewry. "I would like to thank every boy and every girl, every man and every woman...on behalf of those Jews who are persecuted in the Soviet Union and other countries, who want to live in dignity..."

Without any doubt, Elena Fridman, Aryeh and Ya'acov deserved to

Without any doubt, Elena Fridman, Aryeh and Ya'acov deserved to be at the head of the list. Their constant campaign—picketing in front of government offices, traveling around the world trying to drum up support—had disrupted their lives for sixteen years. They were often in despair, not only about Ida's fate but about theirs too: they could not lead normal lives as long as the Soviets persecuted Ida. They trusted not in the princes of their people, who only provided token support. In reality, they could only count on a handful of steady friends—such as Hana Rabinovitch, a Jerusalem rabbi's wife who worked assiduously on Ida's behalf, or Raya Jaglom, a tough Jewish organization professional—a few activists, and themselves. This was their night, too.

After the press conference, Nudel appeared at an outdoor rally before a crowd of about five thousand Israelis, who had waited for hours to see her. Unlike the larger, mostly religious-nationalist crowd that had received Sharansky in early 1986, this cheering audience was more representative of the House of Israel: religious youth and kibbutz members, Sephardim and Ashkenazim, middle class and working class. They sang patriotic songs, including "Gesher Tsar Me'od" ("A Very Narrow Bridge"), which has become the theme song of the Soviet Jewry movement with its line "and the main thing, the main thing, is not to be afraid..."

There was more than a measure of corn, and several of the numerous speakers and singers at the rally—including the mayor of the modest town of Lod, where the airport is located—were less than distinguished. But Ida Nudel, a big-city person who is extremely intelligent and sophisticated, knew that this was only one face of the Israel she had been longing to get to. She must have known that the wolves would also be roaming around; and if she could read the mass-circulation *Hadashot* ("The News") the next day, she would have learned that the popular columnist Dan Ben-Amoz had decided that she and her sister were not Jewish according to Halacha (Jewish law). Ben-Amoz, not known for impeccable reporting, wrote that Ida's mother was not Jewish, or so he had been told. This was pure nonsense, simply another example of the destructive urges of a number of Israeli journalists, who have made a god out of iconoclasm. Sharansky, upon his big welcome to Israel, had gotten similar treatment from a more important columnist, Yoel Marcus of *Ha'aretz*, who wrote a nasty and uninformed piece about how Avital had instantly turned her poor husband into a religious-nationalist fanatic.

But Israeli viciousness as practiced by journalists and politicians looks like marshmallow pudding to a people who have been nose-to-nose with the KGB for so many years. Even the warmest and friendliest among them are very tough members of a no-nonsense breed. They already know that large segments of the Israeli populace are against the Russian Jews—

works at the airport waved his cup of coffee in the air and said just before Armand Hammer's plane touched down: "Do you think they would ever put on a big circus like this for a Syrian Jew?" I had heard this hackneyed tune many times before. A Moroccan-born sergeant in the reserves once told me: "When we came, they sprayed us with DDT. This Sharansky comes here and they treat him like the Messiah."

A sizable segment of the liberal-left establishment and media hates the Russian immigrants too, because so many of the former refuseniks are religious or vote for the right-wing parties. One shallow journalist I know told his editor that he didn't want to cover Ida's arrival because "it's all so predictable." Another journalist, who covers the West Bank and Gaza, said just before the uprising that he didn't know how to explain this whole business to his Palestinian friends.

Because of these and related phenomena, many kibbutzniks and liberal-left urban-dwellers made a point of showing up to greet Ida Nudel, to drive home the fact that there are a good number of people on the left who care about Soviet Jewry and that no party can claim an exclusive interest in such national issues.

The reclusive Menachem Begin, who brought the right-wing to power in 1977, said in a telephone interview (Begin, commendably, won't talk to journalists face-to-face) that Ida Nudel was "a great heroine," and that her triumph "heartened Jews everywhere, in Israel and the Diaspora." The struggle, he said, must go on until freedom is achieved for "every Jew who wants to leave the Soviet Union."

George Shultz, regarded by many Israelis as a righteous and warm friend, got an airport telephone call from Nudel, whom he had met in Moscow at the historic Passover seder he held earlier in the year. "I'm home," she told him, "I'm home." Shultz commented later that he was very moved. "Every once in a while something happens that is unambiguously good."

A FEW MONTHS BEFORE NUDEL'S RELEASE, I asked Natan Sharansky about his close friend's place in the Soviet Jewish movement. He knew her "from the very first days when I joined the movement in 1973, because she was already a well-known person—everybody knew that on anything concerning the problem of prisoners, you could get the information from Ida Nudel. She was not simply the source of all information about the prisoners of Zion. She was the one who almost every day was reminding us about the fate of our brothers who are in the camps, who are in worse situations than we are. And thanks to her activities, we felt ourselves obliged to do everything we could to help them. Our personal situations did not seem so desperate when compared to the situation of the prisoners.

"The influence of Ida Nudel was not only in practical terms—what she was doing for the prisoners of Zion—but she also created a special moral atmosphere in our movement. Ida, through people in the camps, tried to get information on new prisoners."

She discovered that the number of prisoners of Zion was double the sixteen or seventeen listed in the mid-seventies. Her activity led to the discovery of many "unknown Jews": a number of young Jewish boys from the provinces who had applied for visas, been expelled from the institutes of higher learning, and for this reason called to the army. They had refused to go, because if they did they could never emigrate to Israel. "These young Jews had been unknown to us," Sharansky said. "But she used all her connections to find out about them. She organized material help for their families, letters to them. What was important was that the atmosphere around them changed, and so they became more optimistic, and it was much easier for them to survive in the camps all these years. It was typical of Ida Nudel's everyday activity.

"She invented different ways to send things to the camps—two times a year, you can send a one-kilo parcel, but there's a very limited number of food items that can be sent. She was very inventive, finding new types of food from abroad that were unknown to the prison authorities—certain kinds of sweets, such as white chocolate. Minor things, but she made the lives of prisoners of conscience, the prisoners of Zion, much sweeter in direct and indirect ways. All this was very important.

"Many years after this, when I was in prison, I understood how important her activity was from the other side. She was sending me letter after letter, and I was regularly informed that one more letter from Ida Nudel has been confiscated. But even this information about confiscated letters was important, because it reminded me once again that my friends were remembering me. And she was constantly writing letters to the prosecutors and prison officials—even when she was in exile—about why her letters were stopped. And from time to time, letters from her to me did get through. In fact, with the exception of my mother and brother, the biggest number of letters I received was from Ida Nudel—and there's no need to explain how important these letters were."

Why did the Soviets, for so many years, prevent this fifty-six-year-old woman from emigrating?

"They do this to people whose very plight, whose fate, will frighten others, will discourage others from the struggle to emigrate. That's why they need the institution of refuseniks...But, of course, among the Jewish activists there are those whom they hate more, or less. Ida Nudel, whose contribution to the moral level of our struggle is so important, and who kept the world informed about the situation in the Soviet camps in spite of all the attempts the USSR made to mask the truth, to isolate the people in the camps from the outside world, was so big that of course they had special reasons not to like her.''

By the time Nudel was finally released, Mikhail Gorbachev had freed almost all of the score of prisoners of Zion, and many of these people were sent on to Israel. But the great fear among all of the leaders of the movement, including Nudel and Sharansky, was that once the 11,000 known refuseniks were allowed out, the gates would be shut tight on the estimated 400,000 Soviet Jews who want to leave. Sharansky and three other prominent ex-prisoners of Zion—Yuli Edelshtein, Victor Brailovsky and Yosef Mendelevich—appealed to Secretary Shultz to put the issue of Soviet Jewry high on the agenda of the coming summit talks. In a ringing Zionist declaration, they said that it was not a problem of ''family reunification'' but of ''the repatriation of a people, or, according to ancient Jewish tradition, the Return to Zion.''

These new immigrants to Israel voice sentiments that are often far from the feelings of the nonreligious sabra generations—the Israelis who were never in exile, who never roamed ''in the wilderness.'' The Russian Jews would not be deterred from their goal, no matter what darts were aimed at them by snide bohemian publicists, or secular humanists contemptuous of their Judaic roots.

In their unabashed message to Shultz, and to the world, the ex-prisoners put it this way: ''We, together with all the House of Israel, feel a national responsibility for the fate of our brethren in the Soviet diaspora. We have only recently parted from them, and we have suffered with them. We shall neither rest nor be silent until every Jew in the Soviet Union who asks to return to Zion is granted his request. They are our brothers and our flesh...All Israel are brothers and we are each responsible for the other.''

A MONTH AFTER NUDEL'S ARRIVAL, she was physically and mentally exhausted, and deeply worried about the fate of Soviet Jewry. She told me that the message she, Sharansky and others were trying to transmit was being ignored by many Jews in Israel and elsewhere, largely because of the strong desire to believe in Gorbachev and glasnost. Under glasnost the anti-Semitic Pamyat organization was allowed to flourish, even after a Leningrad Jew who was collecting material on Pamyat had been murdered.

But Ida realized that Western Jews were unresponsive to notes of alarm. She had just spoken from a TV studio in Tel Aviv to a convention of American Jewish leaders in Miami. They applauded half her speech. But when she sounded even a little bit like a ''Cold Warrior,'' there was no applause.

Top leaders of American Jewish organizations had been engaging in a whispering campaign against Sharansky, saying he was too radical, too "out-of-touch" with the positive developments in Russia. And Ida was beginning to feel the heat. In the Jewish world, "you're immediately categorized as being paranoid, or unrealistic, if you criticize Gorbachev too much."

She asked my opinion of Dr. Hammer. She said that he was insisting that she write a book and that it be handled by his agent and his publisher. She was suspicious of him, but felt that his help was probably necessary. I thought her spoon was long enough to sup even with the Devil. Shultz and the summit was the main reason she got out, she said. The Russians chose to implement it through Hammer.

She looked exhausted, but said that she could not stop to rest as long as friends like long-time refuseniks Lev Furman and Lev Shapiro and Yasha Rabinovich were still being turned down. (Furman and Shapiro were allowed to go to Israel in the summer of 1988.) Israel was everything she had dreamed about, and more, Nudel said. But she wanted a quiet life, somewhere in the country or on the seashore, with a feeling of space and privacy. Rehovot, where she lived with her sister's family, was not to her liking. She was going to join Sharansky in the demonstrations at the Gorbachev-Reagan summit, but she did not feel comfortable appearing publicly. She would go her own way.

The place of this extremely sensitive soul will be different from Sharansky's, or any of the other leaders of the movement, as she continues to lend great moral weight to what has become a lifelong cause. But she has lived in sadness for so many years, and her struggle against the authoritarian machine has taken such a toll, that despondency could cloud her redemption.

X

THE SYMPOSIUM on the Media and Arab-Jewish Co-Existence was held in Jerusalem in early March 1988, as the Palestinian uprising boiled into its fourth month. The event, staged at the Defense Lawyers' Building next to the Jerusalem Theater, honored Jewish journalist Danny Rubinstein of the Histadrut labor federation daily, *Davar*, and Arab journalist Qassem Zaid, of the Jewish leftist Mapam Party's daily *Al Hamishmar* (whose message still blares: "Workers of the World Unite!") for their "outstanding contribution in the media promoting cooperation between Israel's religious and ethnic groups."

Mr. Zaid, pleading illness, did not show up. Nor did Atallah Mansour, the token Arab journalist on the staff of Israel's most prestigious daily, *Ha'aretz*. His friend had died, the compere announced, explaining why the testy Mansour was not appearing with the rest of the pundit panel, as previously announced.

In fact, not one Arab was in the audience at this little play sponsored by Jewish-Israeli Let's-Have-a-Dialogue organizations like the Martin Buber Institute. One aspect of the problem is that "I-Thou" has become just "I."

Hannah Zemer, the editor of *Davar* who was one of the panelists, walked into the room with a chip on her shoulder, and went up to another panelist, Yossi Goell of the *Jerusalem Post*, challenging him to knock it off. Zemer, her blond hair swept back in a severe socialist style, exclaimed, "Why, there are people here I haven't seen in ten or twenty years," and greeted Goell in stentorian tones meant for all to hear: "I've been reading you and your fascist opinions."

Goell, a brave man with an encylopedic if flawed knowledge of Israel, reddened. He had been very much out of step with the far-left views of most of his colleagues at the Labor-oriented *Post*, and had written recently that the government should bar television cameras from the territories, because they provided—or rather, incited—cheap theater for the world, at Israel's expense. Pure fascist opinion-monger.

The symposium was dedicated to the memory of Gabriel Stern, a leftist Israeli journalist who tried to promote *sawa sawa*, equality between Jews and Arabs. He had believed that too much blood had been spilled by both our peoples, and that we had to talk more and shoot less. He was a leftist German Jew, and although he devoted decades of his life to the study of Arabic, his accent was so thick that nobody could understand him, recalled Danny Rubinstein, whose Arabic is very much up to par. But even without a thick accent, and despite his highly sympathetic view of the Arabs, Rubinstein's sentiments are probably as strange to Palestinian ears as were Gabriel Stern's.

Goell, the first to speak, defended his "fascist" positions, saying that he did not like preaching to the converted, and was trying to find a common language with Israelis who feel they have fallen between two stools (pun intended), the left and the right. "It says a lot that there are almost no Arabs here," he said, noting the obvious lack of I-Thou symmetry—in fact, there wasn't a single Israeli Arab or Palestinian from the territories in the audience. He said his background and beliefs came from the left, that he was in basic agreement with all these Buberites about demography and all, but that there was no one to talk to, really. The Jews were guilty of a lot, he said, but not of everything.

Someone in the audience rose to attack him, saying in slightly German-accented Hebrew that he had been reading Goell's articles in the *Post* with increasing disgust. "Goell is going more and more to the other side, so I'm not interested in his work." Someone else said that it was meaningless that there were no Arabs at this meeting, pointing out that at the Buber center, there were more Arabs learning Hebrew than Jews learning Arabic, and that Arabs *did* show up at coexistence sessions at Beit Hagefen in Haifa—at least, before the uprising, he might have added.

Hannah Zemer continued to hurl insults against Goell ("You shouldn't have the last word on anything, not with your perspective"), Danny Rubinstein told jocular stories (one about how to avoid the army reserves—become a Moslem), and Goell got lost in Zionist history and the rights of minorities.

And then the cares that infest the day folded their tents and silently stole away, like an Arab in the night.

THAT SAME WEEK in March 1988, Anthony Lewis, the Buberite columnist for the *New York Times*, found his Thou in Tunis. Lewis, and his colleague Youssef Ibrahim, encountered a smiling, proud and chatty Yasser Arafat, who was willing to make the "most unambiguous commitments yet to a negotiated peace with Israel." Arafat said he would accept a state of Israel living alongside the Palestinian state, "Yes...Definitely...Peace needs courageous men...Peace for both of us."

There was only one uncomfortable moment in this idyll: "He [Arafat] bristled at one subject brought up in the interview: the recent terrorist attack on a bus near Dimona, the Israeli nuclear center, for which his Fatah took responsibility. Mr. Arafat objected to the words 'bus attack' and said it had been aimed at the 'dangerous' Dimona facility."

Did Arafat really mean to defuse Israel's atomic weaponry arsenal? Not quite. His gunmen didn't know one bus from another on the Beersheba highway. The two women secretaries and the unarmed Israeli man who were gunned down by the terrorists were caught and killed by chance. Mr. Arafat is a liar, and always has been. I doubt that there are many Israelis who would be willing to accept Mr. Lewis's assurances that Mr. Arafat really means "Welcome! Welcome!"

THE SHUAFAT REFUGEE CAMP in northeastern Jerusalem is a grim collection of cinderblock buildings compressed into a few narrow streets behind the Coca-Cola plant in the adjoining Arab neighborhood of Anata.

It is one of about two hundred towns, villages, camps and neighborhoods that have been gripped by the *intifada* (uprising) since it began in December 1987. It started here when gangs of youths pelted the guards at the soft-drink plant at an intersection a little more than a mile away from the new Jewish neighborhood of Pisgat Ze'ev, which, like Anata-Shuafat, is across the Green Line, the pre-1967 border.

Shuafat and Anata were annexed by Israel along with the rest of East Jerusalem soon after the Six Day War, and today a good many Israelis regret that move. The eight thousand or so Arab residents identify completely with the PLO and the Palestinian nationalist revolution.

Jamal Awad, head of the camp's United Nations Relief and Works Agency branch, welcomed three journalists to the salon of his modest home, where his father, Mohammed, was talking to two Germans who said they worked for a women's rights group. The Awads retold the kind of story that had been recorded a few thousand times in three months; and much of it, if not all, was undoubtedly true. (What the Arabs omit to mention: the throwing of gasoline bombs and lethal rocks at Israeli travelers; the ravings of the *imams* in the mosques who whip the children into a frenzy with shouts of "Kill the Jews!")

The Awads say that they *could* understand when the security forces crack down on those who throw stones outside. What they couldn't understand was when Israeli troops stormed into their house and beat the elderly Mrs. Awad, and roughed up and threatened the children. The camp had become "hell," the Awads said, and they and their neighbors "need and want peace." Their anger was mixed with fear, and not only of Israeli force.

The Palestinian middle class has been totally radicalized, in part by the Israeli response to the uprising. Alleged collaborators—like the villager lynched in February 1988 or the Jericho policemen who was murdered in early March—are being tried by kangaroo courts, and the village headmen who worked with the Israelis for the last twenty years are trembling for their lives. People like the Awads will be taking orders from now on from young men with burning eyes and brimming hatred and a commitment to fight to the death.

The middle class can't say no. A Palestinian policeman I spoke to, Mustafa Adawi of the Dehaishe refugee camp, and hundreds of his colleagues throughout the territories resigned *en masse* two days after the Jericho murder and in response to a PLO demand transmitted in "Communique Number 10" of the Palestinian uprising.

"The PLO is the leadership of our people, and we will do what they want," Adawi said proudly. The policeman, fifty-two-years-old and the father of six, was not worried about the future. He said: "I have hope." Such apparent optimism, in the face of dark clouds of smoke wafting from burning tires and tear-gas canisters and smoldering molotov cocktails, seems entirely unfounded: perhaps it is only a reflection of the euphoria affecting the Palestinians, who have finally made it clear to the world that an equitable solution to the Israeli-Palestinian problem must be found. That new sense of pride that Adawi expressed could also be seen on the face of Wisam, a thirteen-year-old girl at one of the violent demonstrations staged in the Kadura camp in central Ramallah. She had the glow of revolution on her face. "This is our country," she told me in English, as other girls and boys and their mothers chanted in Arabic, "Don't want Mubarak or Hussein, just the PLO," and "Death to the Jews."

Troops from the elite Golani Brigade came sweeping down on them, with a flock of cameramen at their heels, and the rioters melted into the alleyways. An Ethiopian was among the soldiers. How was he handling it? He said he wasn't fazed, that he was doing his duty, that we all should be prepared for a long, draining, different kind of war.

Some observers have claimed that the daily confrontations with people who hate and insult you and who feel heady with the success of their revolt has had a pernicious effect on a large number of Israeli soldiers. A group of some five hundred Israeli professionals in the mental health services signed a petition in January 1988 saying that the Arabs in the occupied territories have lived in fear and humiliation for twenty years, and that the new repressive measures needed to control the hostile 1.5 million Palestinians were having a terrible impact on Arabs and Jews alike.

What everyone feared was that the constant confrontation would eventually lead to a bloodbath, a possible prelude to another war. Anything could set it off. The security guards at the Anata Coca-Cola plant, constantly cursed and harassed by gangs of Arab men and youths hurling rocks and burning garbage, could go berserk with their automatic weapons. Settlers who frequently brush with death when their vehicles near an Arab village could start killing Arabs indiscriminately, as they have threatened in the past. A trapped unit of soldiers could decide to blaze their way to safety. Another group of kamikaze PLO terrorists could infiltrate the borders and murder as many Jews as they could. Every day of the *intifada*, that eventual disaster appeared to grow closer.

The Gaza Strip, even Ramallah, were still relatively remote from everyday Israel as the uprising went into its fourth month, and some of the stark realities still hadn't really penetrated many Israeli homes, except on television. But Israelis are not insulated from East Jerusalem, with its Jewish and Arab neighborhoods often side by side—Shuafat is part of Israel's capital.

"The whole myth of Jerusalem being different from the West Bank is now out in the open for everyone to see for what it is," according to Meron Benvenisti, the leftist former deputy mayor of the city and now head of the West Bank Data Project. "For Israelis, it's like spitting in their faces. They're robbed of the illusion that Jerusalem is different."

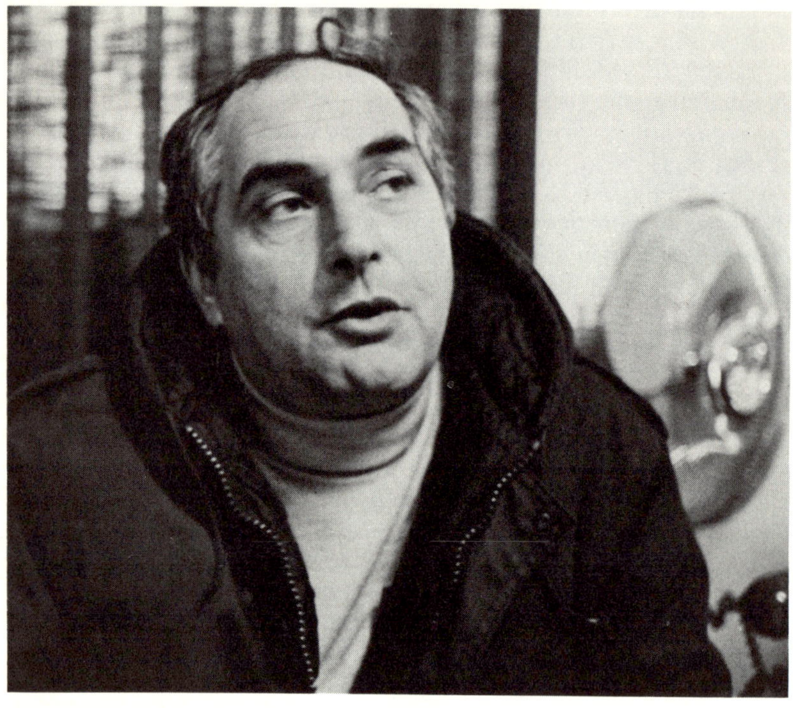

Louis Rapoport

XI

THE PALESTINIANS in the territories follow the orders of Faisal Husseini, a sly gray fox in his late forties who was put in prison three months before the big uprising began. He undoubtedly will be a key figure when and if there is a negotiated settlement of The Conflict.

Husseini is from a family regarded as noble by the Palestinians and ig-
nominious by the Jews. He is the son of Abdel Kader el-Husseini, the leader
of the Palestinian jihad (holy war) forces during the 1948 War of
Independence, who fought bravely and lost his life. Another Faisal Husseini relative and mentor was the late Haj Amin el-Husseini, the snake-
eyed Mufti of Jerusalem who preached the cold-blooded slaughter of the
Jews and was Hitler's honored guest during World War II as head of the
SS Moslem division.

Of course, it seems patently unfair to condemn a man because he may
be a descendant of Cain or Esau or Amalek or Haman, a reasonable person would say. But some observant Jews believe otherwise—King Saul
lost his throne because he refused the Lord's command to slay Agag, and
we are enjoined not to forget that. The righteous are glad when they are
avenged, when they can bathe their feet in the blood of the wicked. Heine
may have been thinking of Haman's ten sons when he said that the loveliest
sight imaginable would be to see his ten worst enemies hanging from a
tree in front of his house. None of this namby-pamby liberal stuff for
the Hebrew people.

A number of Israelis have defended Faisal Husseini as "someone you
can talk to." Many members of the vast Husseini clan are to be found
in East Jerusalem and throughout the West Bank. Yasser Arafat is a Husseini. A man with the doubly unfortunate name of Assad Husseini, one
of Faisal's innumerable cousins, is a handyman who is amiable enough
with his Jewish clients and who once told me, "It's just the politicians
who make the difficulties between us."

For every Jew who bends over backwards to portray Faisal Husseini
in a friendly light, there is a Jewish journalist in Israel or abroad who
will go to the other extreme. One American-Jewish editor, whose ignorance
about Israel is vast (he thinks the country is "very gentle"), shocked me
with a headline he chose for a story I once did about Husseini: "PLO
killer hiding behind the mask of human rights." Well, the PLO does
murder innocent people, and Husseini is one of Yasser Arafat's top
political lieutenants, ergo. . . So the editor weighed the evidence and convicted a man he had never even heard of before.

Husseini is hiding behind a mask, all right; but we will have to do a
bit better on the evidence before we hang him. It is more likely that we
will one day negotiate with people like Husseini and reach an accord.

IN THE YEARS BEFORE THE MASSIVE PALESTINIAN UPRISING, whenever
unrest increased in the West Bank and Gaza, the government often put
a number of Palestinian leaders under administrative detention. Faisal Husseini has spent months at a time in jail, but the authorities have never

been able to pin anything on him. An Israeli who works in the security forces once told me, "He is a real fox...a very dangerous man."

But some top Israelis (even members of the right-wing Likud) are inclined to feel that you have to talk to the enemy—not simply to know him better, but because one day you may be able to reach that elusive settlement with him. And this particular Palestinian leader appears to have such a career ahead of him.

Before his detention in the fall of 1987 and subsequent six-month term in the summer of 1988, Husseini headed the Arab Research Society in East Jerusalem, one of several such fronts that mask PLO activity in the administered territories and East Jerusalem. He would have been thrown out of Israel long ago but for the knotty legal problems—he holds automatic Israeli citizenship because he is a resident of East Jerusalem, which, unlike the rest of the West Bank, was annexed by Israel immediately after the Six Day War.

The weapon of deportation has been used regularly against Fatah members from the territories, as in one instance in May 1987, when two "student" leaders (men in their thirties who organized terror cells) were driven to the border south of the Dead Sea and sent across into Jordan—the kind of action that sends civil libertarians into a dither.

Of course, it is true that the Shin Bet, according to the Landau Commission report of October 1987, systematically lied to Israeli courts for sixteen years, and the organization has made many very serious mistakes (including such whoppers as the Nafsu affair, in which a Circassian officer in the Israeli army was imprisoned wrongfully for years); the allegations that the Shin Bet tortured prisoners have also proved to be true. But for the most part, the Palestinians whom the security forces deport are not exactly Gandhis and Martin Luther Kings—though the wiser Palestinians have cultivated those images. In any case, the security forces cannot deport East Jerusalemites like Husseini—"to our sorrow," as one agent lamented to me. But the Shin Bet can, and does, acquire three- to six-month detention orders under the Emergency Powers Detention Law of 1979, which replaced the British Mandate detention laws of 1945. In ordinary times, according to security sources, a total of about fifty Palestinians are under such detention. Since the uprising began, that figure has mushroomed into the thousands.

Trouble in the territories has always been likely whenever a nationalist Palestinian anniversary comes up: for example, the day marking a land protest and the death of six Arab rioters in the late 1970s; or on the occasion of one of myriad Israeli anniversaries, such as the events marking the fortieth year of independence. These calendar events have always been regarded as license for murder, as happened during the twentieth anniversary of the Six Day War, when an Israeli shopper in Gaza was stabbed to death, and an eight-year-old Jewish boy was brutally slain near the West Bank settlement of Elon Moreh.

The authorities could not link Husseini to these or other murders, but they maintained before the uprising that he was directly involved in orchestrating the curricula of violent demonstrations at West Bank universities. The Shin Bet said that he had a hand in other riots, as well, and that holding him in detention hampers the PLO's main local command structure—a sad joke in the light of the Palestinian uprising, which didn't need any Husseini or any PLO.

During one of his spells in prison, in the spring of 1987, Husseini got strong support from a group of Israeli intellectuals and Peace Now supporters, including writer Amos Oz and several Knesset members, who urged the authorities to release Husseini immediately or to put him on trial "if there is any evidence against him." In a newspaper ad, the leftist activists condemned "the use of administrative detention in general, and especially in this instance, when it is being used against a person who is publicly and vigorously working for a just Israel-Palestinian peace."

But not everybody on the left is enamored of Husseini. One prominent journalist who is very much in the peace camp and knows Husseini well told me: "He is not to be trusted." He said that the pro-Husseini advertisement was simply part of the left's infatuation with Palestinian nationalism. Around this time, Amos Oz himself lashed out at the left for its basically uncritical acceptance of the PLO as a potential negotiating partner, although he did not specifically distance himself from Husseini.

Nor was Husseini about to win any popularity contests with the average Israeli when he gave a newspaper interview in 1987 in which he compared the Palestinians under Israeli occupation to Europeans under the Nazis—particularly disagreable coming from a Mufti relative. These PLO people do tend to have a skewed sense of history, or of truth. They love to equate Israel with totalitarianism, whether of the Nazi or Soviet kind. Palestinian nationalism is so inextricably linked with Zionism that it fosters comparisons to the Exile, the Diaspora, pogroms, even the Holocaust. Outside observers who seek to be "evenhanded" excuse the Palestinian penchant for exaggeration by saying that this is a natural reaction of a people oppressed by a people that was always oppressed, or something like that.

Liberal Israeli backing for Husseini was no surprise, but in the early fall of 1987, Husseini got unexpected support from a prominent member of the younger generation of Likud leaders. Moshe Amirav, a forty-two-year-old man with impeccable right-wing Likud credentials, a veteran of three wars, met with Husseini several times in an attempt "to see if there is a common ground." Amirav, a member of the Herut Central Committee at the time, said to me, "I knew who he was, that he can go to Arafat and I can go to Shamir."

They did find common ground, according to Amirav. "He's a nice man, open and balanced, and you can talk to him." Husseini had fought with the Egyptians against Israel and hoped to throw the Jews into the sea, but he learned that that was not going to happen. "He's balanced now, a realist. He wants to reach an agreement."

Amirav was pressing for a temporary solution, some kind of autonomy that could be termed "almost a state." He knew Husseini was involved in distributing PLO funds and may even have a hand in the terror network. But Amirav is one of a small minority who feels that Husseini's generation and his own can make the breakthrough towards peace that both peoples really want. To his mind, the fact that Husseini comes from the Mufti's family doesn't really matter: the Mufti, and Husseini's father, obviously possessed "a certain kind of talent," which Faisal also shares. "Only he's not like the Mufti—he has much more balance."

When the Amirav story broke, Shamir and his people made vociferous disclaimers of any Likud attempt to negotiate with the despised PLO. Amirav initially got support and encouragement from many of the Likud people of his generation, including his close friends and Knesset members Ehud Olmert and Dan Meridor, two of the rising stars of the moderate right. However, it appeared that the old guard would not let up on Amirav until he was read out of the party. And that's what they did. In January 1988, Amirav tore up his Herut membership card after the party's high court stripped him of his seat in the central committee. He charged angrily that Prime Minister Shamir had led the party into an "ideological bunker" with far-right politicians like Geula Cohen of the Tehiya party and Meir Kahane of Kach. Amirav decided to join the new center party being formed around Professor Amnon Rubinstein's Shinui (Change) party.

Besides meeting with Husseini, Amirav also held talks with a prominent Palestinian intellectual, Sari Nusseibi of Bir Zeit University on the West Bank. Nusseibi's late father, Anwar, was a former Defense Minister of Jordan and head of a prominent East Jerusalem clan. When the reports of Amirav's meetings with Husseini and Nusseibi were published, anti-Arafat Palestinians beat up Nusseibi and broke his arm. The fact that none dared to do the same to Husseini was taken by some as an indication that he is indeed the number-one PLO man in the territories.

IN NOVEMBER 1986, Husseini launched a campaign that attempted to co-opt the human rights struggle for Soviet Jewry. He compared the Palestinians to Soviet Jews, staged more press conferences with weeping women begging for "reunification of families," and got considerable coverage in the media. He definitely showed talent, and continued that aping of Zionism that has marked Palestinian nationalism.

American Secretary of State Shultz, on his Middle East mission in October 1987, in those supposedly halycon days before the uprising, was pummeled with questions about Israel's policy of "impeding immigration to the territories." Shultz, who had become intimately acquainted with the problems of Soviet Jews over the years and openly aided the movement, totally rejected the new Palestinian line. He told a press conference in Jerusalem, "I don't know of any limitations on emigration [from the West Bank]...If you are inferring that what's the case on the West Bank and what's the case in the Soviet Union are similar, I certainly can't agree with that at all."

In August 1988 it became obvious just how important Husseini was. Prime Minister Shamir's people leaked the "Faisal document," a draft for a Palestinian declaration of independence. The bombshell came a few days after King Hussein renounced Jordan's claims to the West Bank, saying it all belongs to the PLO. Shamir said the leaked document showed "whom we are confronting, who is standing behind the bottle-throwers and rock-hurlers." In contrast, his Labor rival, Shimon Peres, called the leak "a stupid act." Husseini's supporters said that the leak was meant to further damage Husseini, whose re-arrest had now become a *cause celebre* among local peace activists and which the U.S. government condemned.

Without a doubt, Faisal Husseini will figure in future talks with Israel. When I met him in early 1987, he portrayed himself as "a dreamer" who pursues "peace and equality." He said he wishes for a "democratic, secular state" of Arabs and Jews in Israel-turned-Palestine—led, of course, by Chairman Arafat. But he knows this is just a dream, he said. "So the reality is to have two states. Jews have their state. Palestinians must have theirs. Borders are to be negotiated."

Unlike previous Palestinian leaders, Husseini made a point of publicly condemning terrorist murders of civilians, such as the slaying of a yeshiva student in Jerusalem's Old City, or the shooting of a tourist outside a Christian shrine. But Arafat himself will condemn such murders with one hand, while ordering more such attacks with a flick of the other.

The Husseini who uses the name Arafat has a lot to answer for. But Faisal Husseini defends the family honor and the memory of their mutually beloved relative, the Mufti. "I knew him well when I lived in Egypt for eighteen years. According to all the new research, there is no document showing that he was a Nazi agent," Husseini claimed. "He was with Hitler because he was against the British."

Not quite. According to Auschwitz survivors, Haj Amin el-Husseini toured the death camp with Adolf Eichmann and a suite of senior Nazi officials in June 1944. According to the Nuremberg testimony of Eichmann's aide Dieter Wisliceny, the Mufti prevailed upon Himmler to cancel a plan to trade some Jewish children for German nationals under detention in Allied countries. Faisal Husseini said that he had not heard of the non-Palestinian research into the subject of the Mufti, and did not believe that at the Eichmann trial documents were submitted showing that the Mufti proposed using Nazi extermination methods to rid the entire Middle East of Jews, including plans for the construction of death camps in Palestine to complete the Final Solution.

But then you can't condemn a man just because he is related to the Devil, or because his hands are the hands of Esau. It just would not be fair. And who is in a position to name Esau-Amalek-Haman today? (One of the 613 holy imperatives of Judaism is to "erase Amalek"—we are justified in seeking to hang those who desire to destroy the House of Israel.)

Esau was a man of uncontrollable appetite. The great question is, will he ever be satisfied with just a portion?

XII

HE IS THE MAN progressives love to hate. Army officers and the top fighters scorn him, but among the cooks and the drivers, long regarded as the lowliest army caste, he is the ironfisted rabbi on the white horse. When NBC wants to show how ugly Israel is, they have a ready-made symbol: Rabbi Meir Kahane, the pied piper who has promised to rid the country of Arabs instead of rats, the Jewish Frankenstein who will strike terror in Arab hearts and show no mercy to the bleeding hearts—those Jewish liberals and leftists whom he calls "dogs."

In the U.S., "Sixty Minutes" gave him twenty minutes, and *Newsweek* granted him its back-page interview to elaborate on his "ideas." In Israel, until the local media decided to stop playing him up in a secret "gentlemen's agreement" reached in 1986, Kahane had become an obsession. But the boycott appears to have had some effect, even more so in the conditions created by the Palestinian uprising: demagogues thrive on publicity, and Kahane is not getting the play he used to. The journalists have even ignored a High Court ruling that Israel Television must allow him to appear on news interview shows in proportion to his party's one seat in the 120-member Knesset. The media's ability to make or break a person has never been more apparent. Yet, Kahane certainly cannot be counted out altogether—not in a world of shocks and earthquakes.

Kahane still has an audience. Highly educated Israelis grow red in the face demonstrating at Kahane's street rallies, screaming at him, "Fascist, fascist, we'll never let you pass." But the mean, the stupid and the ugly, including virtually all of the country's taxi drivers, sing his praises, saying, "He's great—we have to have our Arafat too." (The taxi drivers, almost all of whom shamelessly cheat Israelis as well as tourists, are always willing to voice their political philosophy to any traveler. They call to mind an ironic passage in *Men at Arms*. "Always go to a taxi driver when you want a sane, independent opinion. I talked to one today. He said: 'When we are at war then it'll be time to start talking about war. Just at present we aren't at war.' Very sound that.")

Rabbi Kahane represents Israel's psychic abscess, with mainstream politicians on the right legitimizing his *outré* positions. Jewish fundamentalism is on the move, joining the worldwide march of reborn Moslems and Christians. Two years before Israel approached its fortieth birthday, the word "Kahanism" cropped up everywhere. Two years later, it was hardly mentioned, except to condemn mainstream right-wing figures like Michael Dekel of Herut, Knesset member "Raful" Eitan (a former chief of staff, who has compared Arabs to cockroaches and believes they should be shot for carrying a knife) and former army general "Gandhi" Ze'evi, all of whom say approximately the same thing Kahane says about the Arabs.

Kahane's showings in the polls in 1985 shattered the shopworn politicians of the religious establishment—he appeared to be twice as strong as the once all-powerful National Religious Party. The elitist journalists of the liberal media rushed to the defense of democracy: the rabbi's chauvinist yellowshirts, they thought, could win 5 percent of the vote in the next elections and conceivably be included in a rightist coalition government. "He's lowlife," his critics claim, an ex-informer for the FBI. But Ronald Reagan used to talk to the FBI, too, and that didn't stop him.

A squalid book in Hebrew about the rabble-rouser's seedy past, *Heil Kahane!*, sold briskly in Israeli bookstores when it first came out in 1985. But in the months leading up to Israel's fortieth birthday, he seemed passe—even after the Palestinian uprising, which one might think would swell Kahane's ranks. But the essentials of his platform have found a home in the Tehiya party, among a segment of the Herut party, and even with a cabinet minister, Yosef Shapira of the National Religious Party. The intelligentsia, the professionals and the kibbutzniks and the elite soldiers, call him "racist" and "Nazi," while many common people—*amcha* in Hebrew—call him "king of Israel," as they once called Menachem Begin and Arik Sharon. Where will it all end?

MEIR KAHANE, FORMERLY OF NEW YORK, with curly eyebrows, a beard fuller but every bit as ratty as Arafat's, a charming wife and four grown children who are part of "The Movement," did not wait for new elections to be called. The perennial campaigner for the premiership will do anything he has to do to get it, including infecting the souls of his fat bully boys with evil.

In an interview with me, the rabbi declared he has a good nose for evil: The "two evilest men in the Knesset," he mused, were Trade and Industry Minister Ariel Sharon (Likud) and Police Minister Haim Bar-Lev (Labor). Sharon is evil because he is Kahane's main rival and still way ahead of him. Bar-Lev, a cold and vain man, was for a while Kahane's chief irritant, a persecutor of good Jews, a man who tried to keep Kahane's thugs out of Arab towns. "Sharon is a bad person, utterly immoral, evil incarnate. So is Bar-Lev. But I would work with either one of them," the spiritual leader said cheerfully. In fact, he would join forces with *anyone*, (presumably even Satan) who agrees with his concept of a "Torah State," a country run strictly according to the Bible. No mistake about it, this is a man with a miserable messianic complex.

But since those heady days of 1985, when the polls were predicting that he would get at least 5 percent of the vote if national elections were held then, Kahane has been either co-opted or studiously ignored, and it now appears that he will be stopped short. But the people he represents are not going to disappear, and if he goes, they will be ready to rally behind some other, more formidable figure: "We need a dictator," is what they are saying.

AFTER ATTENDING one of Kahane's neighborhood street rallies and interviewing him in the Knesset, I could not help thinking of *Diary of a Man in Despair*, the compelling work of anti-Nazi German nobleman Friedrich Percyval Reck-Malleczewen, who was murdered in Dachau in 1944. Comparisons between Nazi Germany and anything Jewish or Israeli are usually obscene, but Kahane is a fascist, and nothing can erase that fact.

Reck-Malleczewen put it this way: "But suppose, now, that all of these things generally kept buried in our subconscious were to drive for emergence in the blood-cleansing function of a boil? Suppose that this underworld now and again liberated by Satan bursts forth, and the evil spirits escape the Pandora's box?"

In the early 1930s, as the fever started to take hold of Germany, Reck-Malleczewen was dining in a fashionable Munich restaurant. He was carrying a pistol—what a wise child of his times was required to do. Hitler entered, without his bodyguard, a "raw-vegetable Genghis Khan...I could easily have shot him. If I had an inkling of the role this piece of filth was to play, and of the years of suffering he was to make us endure, I would have done it without a second thought. But I took him for a character out of a comic strip, and did not shoot."

Kahane knows people want to kill him. He correctly says that the media whips up sentiment against him. Talking of himself in the third person, in a kind of "imperial He," the rabbi says that "the newspapers, television and radio incite against Kahane." He denies that he started it all by stirring up hatred against leftist politicians like Yossi Sarid (of the Citizens Rights Party), his favorite target for invective at street rallies. "I've never hinted that something should be done against Sarid," Kahane says. But in 1984 he wrote in his column in the yellow-hysterical-entertaining *Jewish Press* of New York that it was permissible to kill fellow Jews under certain circumstances. In the same article, he happened to mention Sarid and the leader of the CRM party, Shulamit Aloni. He said it was a religious duty to put some Jews out of their misery.

"I've never called for the killing of a Jew," he told me. "But in a war situation, and if they were traitors, well then, of course!"

He himself is not afraid of assassination, but he is "aware" of the threat: "The most I can do is to take care, to take precautions. There is incitement to kill me by the government, with the Army radio spewing forth hatred for Kahane. But I have my bodyguards." He said that during a rally in a Tel Aviv suburb the police were "clearly given orders to allow the demonstrators against us to come closer, people throwing iron pipes and rocks." In a future encounter, he vowed, "we will defend ourselves. We will use rocks and bars too. We have some very, very tough guys. I don't want to hurt Jews, but if the police don't hold back the leftists, we will—we can't allow them to break up our rallies."

Kahane has been very careful to keep within the law in voicing his support for random Jewish terrorism against Arabs. He will say it is wrong to commit these acts, "because the heroes who commit them will be caught." But he is within the law when he expresses approval with reservations. He told me once that Allan Goodman, his deranged follower who killed a Moslem guard on the Temple Mount, had done "absolutely the correct thing." He used the same words in support of a young soldier's attack on an Arab bus in which a passenger was killed. "It is absolutely correct to fire on an Arab bus. It is imperative to instill fear among the Arabs." But it is better if the government does it rather than individuals. "That's what Sharon did in Gaza [when the general used an iron hand to stop terrorism there in the 1960s]. It worked. Terror can work. If it is systematically done, and on a massive level, then of course it will be good, very good. It is morally obligatory to put terror in Arab hearts."

That is why many of the common people love him, while his enemies see a direct link with Hitler or Khomeini or Charles Manson, who hypnotized his followers into committing murders while he sat back with "clean" hands. Some of the men in the street think of Kahane as a magical being in the ghetto called Israel, a necessary evil who will strike fear into the enemy. The mass of Kahane's followers are of North African origin and are poor. They "know the Arabs," as they say *ad nauseum*, and they say that the only solution is to throw them out of the country: "Do away with democracy," they say, "Kahane is right—democracy is not a part of Judaism." There is even support among some intellectuals for the view that the Western Enlightenment tradition has no place in a Middle Eastern "Jewish state."

Doing away with democracy will be at the top of the Kahane agenda if he becomes prime minister or part of the government, he says. The first priority is to introduce the "Torah State," and the second is "removal of the Arabs."

Kahane, who probably believes he is the Awaited One of the Messianic Era ("Every Jew can have a special role in it if he wants to"), will change the entire character of the state. All state schools will become religious; secular parents will have to "convert" or fend for themselves. Judaism will replace such wasteful subjects as biology or literature. No secular thinkers or writers, no nonreligious ideas will be introduced to Israeli youth until after completion of high school. Women will dress "modestly"— no shorts or pants. Swimming pools will be sexually segregated. Anyone caught driving or lighting a match on the Sabbath will be punished ("just a fine, a citation" at first, he says. Probably crucifixion for second offenders.) Violators of any of the Ten Commandments will be treated severely. Intercourse with an Arab will be a prison offense. (Kahane, when asked about the many reports that he had committed adultery with his former secretary in New York, a Gentile who committed suicide, said: "You can't come out clean talking about mud; you can't win. It's not true about adultery. People lie about me." And Jim Bakker and Jimmy Swaggart, too.)

It will be a bad day for his opponents when Kahane takes power, he declares. "I expect the left to obey the law. If I'm in the government, we'll have the police go after them." He acknowledges that civil war is likely, but "that's the price we may have to pay."

He says he is not a prophet or a false Messiah. The spirit of Shabbtai Zvi (the seventeenth-century cabalist of Smyrna who proclaimed himself the Messiah) "is alive and sick. He was just a false Messiah," Kahane explains. "But we are definitely in the Messianic Era. The Messiah may come either with a great tragedy or not. It depends on us. It has to do with whether or not we obey the laws." He means the rabbinical laws. "We have to become holy."

Kahane is likely to make whatever big move he is planning during this fortieth year anniversary. He has even written a book about the significance of the number forty in Jewish tradition. Leave it to "Michael King," as Kahane used to call himself when he passed as a Christian, to try to co-opt this numerology in his quest for the kingship.

Kahane loathes the Knesset. "I hate coming here," he says. "They hate me here. I hate entering the building. But it's unavoidable. I have to use it. It's much faster to get to my goal this way."

In Jewish legend, the Golem, a subhuman creation of the mystical Maharal of Prague, eventually became a destructive force, threatening to destroy everything. Rabbi Loew barely succeeded in stopping his creature as it tore up the ghetto; but he did do so, removing the magic name of God from his mouth and thus turning the Golem into a mass of lifeless clay. The Jewish people were supposed to have learned from that never to make another Golem.

THE WORD "TRANSFER," which sent shivers through the Israeli political world even before the Palestinian uprising, was in the year leading up to the fortieth anniversary, on the minds of Israelis fed up with Arab terror: the murders of civilians walking in the Old City of Jerusalem, or the ritual murder of an eleven-year-old Jewish boy near one of the West Bank settlements. So Kahane is not alone in promoting the idea that the best way to deal with the Arab problem is to get rid of the Arabs, to send them to Jordan, which occupies most of Mandate Palestine, or to one of the score of other Arab countries, and to leave us Jews alone, without any more strangers at our gates.

Herut Knesset member and Deputy Defense Minister Michael Dekel, a leading proponent of accelerated settlement in Judea and Samaria, is one of those who believe that transfer is the only solution to the demographic nightmare facing the Jewish state. The West has a moral obligation, he told his fellow party members in the summer of 1987, to send the Arabs of Judea and Samaria to Jordan.

In reaction to Dekel's remarks, Knesset Speaker Shlomo Hillel, of Labor, told his countrymen that the transfer idea was not only undemocratic but also a threat to the moral existence of the State of Israel. Significantly, Herut dropped Dekel and another rabid extremist, Meir Cohen-Avidon, from its 1988 election list.

From the earliest days of Zionism, many have charged that the greatest mistake the Jews have made was to ignore the Arab presence, to pretend that they were not really there. Surprisingly, this may have been more true of Labor Zionists like Chaim Weizmann than of Revisionist Zionists like Ze'ev Jabotinsky, ostensibly the mentor of Dekel's Herut movement. In 1940, the year of his death, Jabotinsky clearly spelled out that "the process of Eretz Yisrael becoming a Jewish State may be fulfilled without uprooting the Arabs from their homes. Whoever claims the opposite (and such claims are widespread among the public) is completely wrong...If the Arabs would not decide themselves that it would be more comfortable for them to leave the country out of their own free will, they have no need to emigrate."

Dekel's statements raised a storm in the summer of 1987 because they followed on the heels of a similar statement made by the popular ex-general Rehavam Ze'evi (nicknamed "Gandhi"), the former chief of the Central Command (which includes the West Bank territories) and afterwards head of Tel Aviv University's Ha'aretz Museum. Advocating a Kahane solution, Dekel and "Gandhi" were backed by other voices in the Knesset when Deputy Speaker Cohen-Avidov, notorious for his loose tongue and fanatically right-wing politics, declared that he was "for the transfer of Arabs from all over the Land of Israel to Arab states." Cohen-Avidov added that the expelled Arab population should, "naturally," receive "proper compensation."

Knesset member Yossi Sarid, of the left-center Citizens Rights Movement, reacted by saying that "for all these years, the Arabs have been threatening to throw us into the sea. Now we are threatening to throw them into the desert." The transfer idea is repugnant to anyone who believes in democratic values. Unfortunately, the PLO and other terrorists have a symbiotic relationship with the Israeli far right. And if they continue to perpetrate terrorist outrages, or if the Palestinian uprising grows into a full-scale war, Kahane's solution to the Arab problem, the transfer of the million Arabs, is bound to win support from a significant segment of the population, whether he is around or not. This became more evident than ever in November 1987 when a cabinet minister, Yosef Shapira of the National Religious Party, proposed paying $20,000 to any Arab willing to leave the Land of Israel, and Arik Sharon of Likud, who is far more scary than Kahane, showed support for Shapira's position. Shapira's idea comes directly from the Thoughts of Kahane, who was more generous with Jewish money when he proposed a few years ago that every Arab who left should get $60,000. If that offer stands, tens of thousands of Israeli Jews may become Arabs overnight.

"Gandhi" Ze'evi sponsored a major conference on transfer as the Palestinian uprising intensified. Dozens of protesters shouted, "Fascism, fascism." Ze'evi, in a follow-up lecture to the conference, admitted that it was not clear yet whether a transfer was practical. But it was worth investigating, he said, because it was "Zionist by definition" and the most humanistic solution to the Palestinian problem. Out of deference to Holocaust survivors who abhor the word "transfer," Ze'evi said he preferred to talk about "the agreed-upon exchange of populations." By the six-month point of the uprising, polls showed that some 40 percent of the Israeli population favored a solution involving some form of transfer.

Despite all the hysteria over transfer, there may indeed be a mass moving of populations once a peace agreement is achieved and the repartition of what was Mandate Palestine takes place. Conceivably, the tens of thousands of residents of the Gaza hell-holes could be moved to Nablus, the largest city in the West Bank, or outside a Hebron divided between Israelis and Palestinians, or to Bethlehem. Jewish populations will also be transferred from settlements in the eastern half of the West Bank, which one day will become, together with Jordan, the new state of Palestine.

XIII

I T IS EASY TO SUGGEST that "the extremists of both camps" constitute the only real barrier to peace between Israel and the Arabs. Israel does have a few Kahanes, while the Palestinians, with their PLO leadership, have more. Obviously, the problem goes much deeper than that, beyond complexity. If only it were just a territorial dispute, and thus, solvable.

But anyone who is not a total pessimist will grasp for straws. That is why so many journalists and writers look for a story like Neve Shalom's, an Arab-Jewish "living experience" that tries to be very nice and to make everyone feel that as brothers and sisters we will work it all out, because we are all children of Abraham, or something like that.

No one has a more wishful eye than a journalist—one reason why media people are so distrusted. I know one Israeli writer of "think pieces"—what are known in the trade as "thumbsuckers"—who is convinced that the solution to our conflict is Jewish-Arab intermarriage. We will all simply disappear that way, meld into oneness. Or perhaps the answer is to make Nevada the Jewish State, as one cynical American leftist writer suggested?

I grasp for straws, too, even though I do not really believe that a solution is possible for years to come. But in the months before the great polarization set in as a reaction to the uprising, I kept looking for that upbeat story about Arabs and Jews solving their problems. One did occur in mid-1987, just as Israel began to celebrate the twentieth anniversary of the reunification of Jerusalem, a compromise in the new neighborhood of East Talpiot that at least hinted at eventual peace and good will between Arabs and Jews.

THE STORY REVOLVED around a dispute over land and trees: a Jewish National Fund forest of firs versus olive trees tended by Arab villagers. And it was the olive trees (which in Jewish tradition represent not only the dove of peace but also Israel itself) which eventually prevailed.

In terms of Middle East politics and the long and bitter conflict between the two peoples, the East Talpiot story may seem minor, or simply an aberration. But for many who seek a solution to the long conflict based on human terms, the saga of an olive grove in Wadi Zeitun was, at least for a while, a hopeful sign for the promotion of coexistence.

The story also serves as a microcosm for understanding the great changes wrought by the 1967 Six Day War, and the realities that have emerged: in Joshua's time, too, the allotment of the land and the subdivision into districts took many contentious years.

Part of East Talpiot, a five-minute drive from downtown Jerusalem, was no man's land until the war. But much of the six-hundred-acre tract, including three Arab villages, was ruled by Jordan from 1948 to 1967. Until the War of Independence the main village, Sur Bahir ("light-colored rock"), was a hotbed of followers of Haj Amin el-Husseini, the pro-Nazi Mufti of Jerusalem. There was a bloody history between these Arabs and the Jews who lived in the nearby neighborhood of Talpiot going back to the riots of 1929 and 1936. Nobel Prize-winning writer S. Y. Agnon, who lived in Talpiot, wrote about how the Sur Bahir Arabs destroyed his archives.

Jordan occupied the West Bank, which includes East Jerusalem, in 1948, and the only contact between Sur Bahir and Talpiot was a small amount of smuggling. The villagers were poor, and Jordan neglected them. Then came 1967 and the war that changed Israel and the whole Middle East equation. Sur Bahir, like the rest of East Jerusalem and unlike other West Bank areas, was incorporated into the unified city.

In 1970, 575 acres of the Sur Bahir tract were expropriated: five hundred for a new neighborhood, East Talpiot, and the remaining seventy-five, Wadi Zeitun ("wadi of the olive trees"), handed over to the Israel Lands Administration; but the Arab villagers were allowed to continue cultivating the olive trees and other fruit trees, pending further notice.

In the years after the war, government bodies, and the municipality under Mayor Teddy Kollek, ringed the newly unified city with a dozen new neighborhoods, almost completely surrounding Arab East Jerusalem. Several scattered Arab villages, like Sur Bahir, are now very much inside the city. In the years since the war Jerusalem has grown from a sleepy town of 200,000 into a sleepy city, more than doubling its population to about 450,000.

Some of the new neighborhoods were primarily designed for impoverished new immigrants—the gray, boxy high-rises of Ir Ganim, for example, have been compared to an East European socialist nightmare. At the other end of the spectrum is Ramot, where many individual houses go for as much as $250,000. In between are other new neighborhoods across the "Green Line" (the pre-1967 borders) such as Gilo, Neve Ya'acov, French Hill and East Talpiot, where a large number of the residents are young couples on their way up the economic ladder.

East Talpiot's multistoried apartment buildings—with a few bungalow villas interspersed (Israelis use the term "villa" to describe even the most modest five-room home)—form a semicircle around the slopes of two hills and a valley below. Of all the new neighborhoods, East Talpiot is the closest to the center of town and therefore considered a desirable place to live, with prices of three-room and four-room flats ranging between $50,000 and $90,000. It has a spectacular view of the Old City, rivaled only by the panorama from Arab East Jerusalem around the Inter-Continental Hotel. Mayor Kollek has built a long promenade on a wind-swept East Talpiot hill for local residents and tourists to enjoy the view.

Until the uprising began in December 1987, relations between the residents of East Talpiot and the Arab villages a few feet away were, for the most part, "correct," with little social interchange between the twenty thousand Jews and seven thousand Arabs. But "no amount of fine words will allow us to escape the fact that much of Jerusalem's Arab minority feels itself deprived and under occupation," Teddy Kollek said six months before the *intifada*. "Based on our own historical experience, Jews must always be aware and sensitive to these perceptions."

Increasingly, local Arabs found work in East Talpiot and throughout the rest of the city, and their family members used the modern facilities built by the municipality, such as the medical clinic and the Mother and Child Care center, the supermarket, the soccer field, the bank and, to a much lesser extent, the community center. All of the facilities have Arabic-speaking staff.

A certain amount of tension always existed between the two communities. According to Ephraim Huja, head of the neighborhood administration, Jewish and Arab children sometimes threw stones at each other on Palestinian nationalist days or after a terrorist attack. But meetings between the village *mukhtars* (those leaders who are now considered corrupt collaborators) and the East Talpiot officials were all that was needed to solve the problems, Huja said. "We have neighbors, and they are forever. We don't want a crisis, so we come to a compromise."

Of course, not everybody felt that way. A teacher's assistant, whose nursery school is just across the road from Jabel Mukaber, one of the smaller villages, told me in June 1987: "The Arabs create many problems, stealing and destroying our equipment. The *mukhtars* try to solve the problems, but the inner fears exist. I have them. I'm afraid not of these local Arabs, but of people from outside who will come and put a knife in my back." The woman, a Moroccan emigre, thought for a moment and then softened: "But when the Arab children walk by the road, singing songs that I know and like, and sometimes saying *shalom*, I feel that maybe it will all be all right one day. Maybe it will."

IN 1985 THE JEWISH NATIONAL FUND, with the agreement of the Israel Lands Administration, decided to build a park for East Talpiot residents in the seventy-five acres of land that the villagers of Sur Bahir cultivated. The olive and almond and fig trees were to be uprooted, the JNF decided, and replaced by a forest of firs and sites for picnic benches and barbecues.

The bulldozers arrived unannounced. The action aroused the ire not only of the Arab villagers, but also of several of the Jewish residents and community leaders. Teddy Kollek vowed to fight to help the Arab villagers, and the case went all the way up to the High Court of Justice, which ruled that the disputed acres belonged unquestionably to the Israel Lands Administration, which could do what it wanted with the land.

Meanwhile, a support committee was formed, led by Hillel Bardin, an American immigrant who works at Hebrew University, and Yehuda Litani, a journalist who is regarded as one of Israel's leading experts on the Arab world. Sur Bahir had articulate representatives of its own, including the *mukhtar*, Khader Dabash, and Hassan Abu Asala, a forty-three-year-old Jerusalem municipal planner.

In January 1987, sixty village-owned olive trees were uprooted by the JNF, and thousands of pine saplings planted in their stead. But the newly formed committee of Jewish residents of East Talpiot and nearby neighborhoods felt, according to Bardin, that "though it was legal, it wasn't decent." A peaceful demonstration by several hundred Arabs and Jews was held in the next month, with Mayor Kollek lending his support. "Neighbors are working together, standing together in what seems to be a matter of justice," he said. "I hope that we will succeed."

The Jewish supporters of Sur Bahir started an unprecedented petition campaign, with a favorable response. A compromise was soon offered: the remaining fruit trees would not be uprooted, and the villagers would continue to tend the trees on the seventy-five acres, with the understanding that they did not own this land. No JNF forest would be planted.

The compromise was accepted by the JNF and promoted by Kollek's office, but the Lands Administration balked. However, in late April 1987, after a drawn-out struggle, the compromise proposal was accepted by all of the parties involved, including the Agriculture Ministry, which oversees the Land Administration.

In the aftermath, a few voices warned that a dangerous precedent might have been set, but most people welcomed the compromise. Ephraim Huja said, "The government has the right to decide on land questions, but a few trees shouldn't destroy our relations with our Arab neighbors—this is a very positive development."

Khadar Dabash also saw it as a good sign, and Hassan Abu Asala said the villagers all felt very good about the decision, though it was "just one stone in the roadway—there's much that remains to be done, many problems, including a big gap in services."

Nora Malchek, cultural organizer at the East Talpiot Community Center, said she hoped that the improved atmosphere would encourage more of the Arab villagers to utilize the modernistic center, which offers a wide range of courses and activities. But she and other residents said that coexistence remained a very tender reed, and that the local Arabs were wary of publicity. "Someone wanted to do a film about what has happened here, but the *mukhtars* were afraid that it would be shown outside and would be dangerous. So the continuing efforts to bring the communities closer together are very low profile."

"It came out well, with the help of God, though we still have got to get the decision in writing," Dabash said. "We can continue working the land." He expressed his gratitude to Teddy Kollek and the group of Jewish supporters who had stood by the villagers. "We have only one desire—to be in this country in peace and quiet."

Yehudi Litani said a few months before the *intifada* that the East Talpiot story was unique. "The Jews who supported the Palestinians in this issue came from left and right, religious and secular. As a result of this show of support, social relations between us are very good—not at all like in other Jerusalem neighborhoods like Abu Tor or French Hill," where the hostility between the two peoples is severe.

Teddy Kollek was very pleased by the agreement he helped work out. "This land has been cultivated by Arabs for generations, and there was no real reason to take away their livelihood," he told me. "We have to find compromise in the city, to live together in tolerance, understanding and mutual respect, and this case is a classic example of how that can be done."

It did sound hopeful. I did want to write about it. Something positive *was* there. Decency. Fair treatment for the stranger at our gates.

But it was an aberration, wishful thinking. For only one "stone in the roadway" had been cleared. By the end of the year there were countless stones, even in East Talpiot, even in the heart of greater Jerusalem.

Youths from Sur Bahir started stoning the houses of their Jewish neighbors. At the home of Judy Segal and her family, who emigrated to Israel from the U.S. after the Yom Kippur War, the shutters were closed and the Segals stayed away from the windows. "We kept hearing the glass breaking," she told a reporter after fifty Arab youths pelted the house with hundreds of stones. Even after the border police came, the kids kept coming back, taunting the police to chase them. Four of Segal's neighbors on Meir Naqqar street, just across from Jabel Mukaber, also came under attack.

The Segals are leftists who support Peace Now, "but it's easier to be leftist when people aren't throwing stones at you. I have no hatred for the Arabs. I would be willing to give back territory for peace. But in the meantime it has to be made clear to them that this cannot continue," Segal said.

Police later went on a rampage in Sur Bahir, smashing furniture and roughing up people. The police spokesman, Rafi Levy, said that "those who take part in disturbances have to take into account the fact that the police will respond...The adults of Sur Bahir should control their young people, and then no one's property will be damaged."

Hillel Bardin, who had worked so hard to find a common ground with his Arab neighbors in East Talpiot, was in despair, saying, "I am opposed to violence, and I wish there was a nonviolent path which could give the people of Sur Bahir what they want."

Teddy Kollek stood amid the shards of glass and the wafting smoke, looking desolate, bitter and exhausted. He looked into the Israel Televi sion camera, swept his arm across the vista of East Talpiot, and said, "Coexistence is dead." Later, after he had recovered his composure, he denied that he had said the words the whole nation heard. He meant "almost dead." And that is what it was.

Richard T. Nowitz

XIV

AN ICONOCLASTIC FRIEND of mine believes that we live in a Godless theocracy, what Ben-Gurion, the atheist socialist, set up when he made his deals with the religious parties in the summer of 1947. What we are moving towards in the postdesert generation, according to just about everybody, is a theocracy that dispenses with the atheism and brings back God. Needless to say, there is much handwringing about all of it.

I am a secular Jew in my mid-forties, a believer for whom the Jewish religion has always been remote. But the increasingly popular religion of "secular humanism" strikes me as pitiful and basically empty, and some of its practioners are every bit as sanctimonious as the worst of the observant Jews. I have great respect for Judaism and its more enlightened followers, and little regard for the trendy Israeli yuppies who hate everything related to the religion that kept our people alive through the millennia. Too many of them are shallow and vain people who preach humanism but do not follow a cardinal rule, the guiding principle of Judaism: to fight for life; to save a life.

And though I do not want a yeshiva on my block—my wife and I were ready to man the barricades when the black hats tried to invade our neighborhood—I cannot bring myself to march with my fellow secularists in the widening *Kulturkampf* that is certain to contaminate our lives. I will not join my closest friends who come to Jerusalem from Tel Aviv on a Friday night to demonstrate secular solidarity by going to a movie downtown.

I want to be buried as a Jew, not as a bohemian.

I am perhaps overly proud of my roots. I can say to anyone who insults my people what Disraeli once said to an English anti-Semite: "When your ancestors were brutal savages in an unknown island, mine were priests in the temple of Solomon." My father's great solace was that he was a descendant of Aaron, a *cohen*, a priest in the temple of Solomon. These things do rub off. The dictionary defines the very word "theocracy" as government or political rule by priests, specifically, "a state so governed, as the Hebrew commonwealth before it became a kingdom." From what I have seen of our modern political leaders, priests or even kings do not seem any more outrageous—a holyman wearing an ephod of gems around his neck has as much credibility in my eyes as the Speaker of the Knesset or the head of the Defense and Security Committee.

So I have a soft spot for the Jewish religion, even though I will always feel an outsider to it. The penitent movement, the "possessors of the answer," will never grab me. But I can admire, from afar, someone like Uri Zohar, the one-time king of Israeli bohemia, the brilliant comedian/film director/*hashishnik* who is now a black-hat rabbi.

But it is not for me. But I do know that a Jew sometimes needs his religion.

The religion and its houses of worship are obviously of great importance

tance in the everyday life of many Israelis, an aspect of our lives that I was almost forced to learn about. A few years ago, I suddenly had to find a shul. I had just learned that my ailing father had died in Los Angeles, shortly after making a request over the telephone. "Say Kaddish for me, son. Promise me you'll say Kaddish."

I had a vague idea that Kaddish was a prayer for the dead; I did not know or understand that it is the prayer through which the parent's soul benefits from a surviving son's piety. I also knew that there were about a dozen synagogues within five minutes' walk from my door in Jerusalem's German Colony neighborhood; but I did not feel I could just walk in to the Moroccan shul or the Persian one or the *haredi* (ultra-Orthodox) yeshiva on Rachel Imenu Street. The little synagogue that I finally found, Ezrat Israel, is just one of about eight hundred shuls that serve Jerusalem's three-hundred thousand Jews. A closer look at Ezrat Israel, set in a humble white little house on Rehov Hildesheimer (the tiny street is named after the founding rabbi of the Agudas Israel movement), helps reveal the unique nature of Israeli synagogues, and how they differ from American Jewish houses of worship, for example. The differences go beyond the fact that American synagogues have cantors and Israeli shuls do not, or that rabbis do not play a central role in Israeli services, as they do in American rites...

IN MY GRIEF AND CONFUSION about how and where one says Kaddish, I turned to a neighbor, the son of a Bronx rabbi, who told me to start by getting a prayer book and *tefillin* at Schneiders' in the Mea She'arim neighborhood. The man also explained to me what the words of Kaddish meant, and that I would be reciting it four times at the morning service, as well as during evening services. He told me to come to the little Ashkenazi synagogue on Hildesheimer, where "they'll take care of you."

Like the other synagogues sprinkled around the neighborhood, Ezrat Israel is an unpretentious house of prayer. Set a few feet off the street, down a walk lined with cypress trees, it was a stark contrast to the big Conservative synagogues frequented by my father, or the country-clubbish Reform synagogue in Beverly Hills, where I grew up. I had never been inside an Israeli synagogue. My neighbor wasn't able to come that first morning, but the old men in the shul (there were no young congregants there in 1980) were very helpful when I told them that I wanted to say Kaddish. As they wound the *tefillin* down my arm and fixed the other phylactery on my head and guided me through the service, I felt like a helpless child.

Different members of the congregation drifted over to my pew whenever the Kaddish was about to be recited. I was baffled by the prayer—a song of praise for God without any mention of a departed loved one; a simple reaffirmation of the existence of God; and a hope for peace for all the house of Israel, and that the Messiah will come in our day. It is an eternal prayer, in both stormy and tranquil times. I did not really understand it, but I would never forget the kindness of the congregants throughout that time.

I have gone to the same shul every year since to say Kaddish for my father. No one has ever made me feel uncomfortable; no one has pressured me to come more often. Because of that, I found myself going there on special occasions, and I appreciated the place and respected the congregation.

But I remained a secular Jew who is a believer. In an age of increasing religiosity, I subscribed to what the poet Emily Dickinson once said: "Some keep the sabbath going to church; I keep it staying at home." But I realized that there was also a need for public prayer, and, somehow, I began to understand the institution of the *minyan*, and why the Mishnah set a quorum of ten men over the age of thirteen for public worship. At this time of increasing conflict between secular and religious Jews, I found myself sympathetic to those who want to bridge the growing gap between the believers and the nonbelievers.

WHEN I FIRST WENT TO EZRAT ISRAEL, it was a tiny, cramped place whose congregants were all elderly. But in the last five years, the synagogue has reflected the general changes in our southern Jerusalem neighborhood: more young and middle-aged professional people, including many from English-speaking countries, have moved into the German Colony, which is rapidly becoming gentrified.

In 1984 the synagogue's drab building was renovated to accommodate the growing "Modern Orthodox" congregation. The far more spacious and comfortable shul now became a very mixed congregation: well-to-do and poor, government officials and cobblers, Holocaust survivors and sabras, an Ethiopian Jewish Agency worker studying to become a rabbi, Natan Sharansky (who has since moved from the German Colony but still comes to the shul occasionally), and the famous Talmudic scholar Rabbi Adin Steinzalz, whose epic work has been compared to Rashi's, the greatest commentator on the Talmud in the last one thousand years. Yet, this medium-sized shul is just one of hundreds of similarly humble synagogues that harbor the dialogue between the individual believer and his Creator.

The *gabbai*, or sexton, of Ezrat Israel, Thomas Wisell, is a successful businessman who emigrated from Sweden in 1980. He has seen it through its rapid growth and the changing composition of the congregation.

"At Yehuda Halevi synagogue, around the corner, there are sixty to seventy families of more or less the same background: professional, young thirties, modern. Here, at Ezrat Israel, there's much more of a mix: top government officials, security guards, young and old, Sephardi and Ashkenazi," says Wisell. "It draws a more disparate crowd because of what I think is its very special atmosphere." The reconstituted synagogue holds a Kiddush every Shabbat and a Devar Torah, inviting newcomers. "Now, we have a lot of bar mitzvahs. Five years ago, there were none."

One of the regulars at this house of prayer, lawyer Gedalia Zisquit, says that the shul is not at all similar to the Orthodox synagogues he attended before emigrating to Israel from Florida in the late 1970s.

"In America, the synagogue serves as a center for the community, in addition to its religious function. Here, the synagogue is basically a place to pray. You don't need the community because it's all around you. Here in Israel, you live in a Jewish framework, and don't need the shul to express your Jewishness on a social level." Of course, on the religious level, "an observant person cannot function as an Orthodox Jew without a community of worshippers."

Zisquit usually prefers going to Friday night services fifty feet down the street from Ezrat Israel, at a second-story shul overlooking the busy thoroughfare of Emek Refaim. Most of the congregation at this synagogue, which is flooded with light flowing through ornate Oriental windows, is comprised of Persian Jews. But the service is not much different from that at the Ashkenazi shul on Hildesheimer, and Zisquit likes dividing his prayer time between the two shuls because the other, too, is "a warm and inviting place."

He says he would also feel comfortable praying at the Jerusalem Great Synagogue, a twenty-minute walk from the German Colony toward the center of town. This huge and lavish synagogue, completed in the mid-1980s, appears garish and ostentatious to some Jews who think it "too American." But Zisquit is not bothered by the opulence of the two-thousand-seat shul. "Judaism doesn't preach that kind of modesty. It doesn't bother me at all."

According to the late Maurice Jaffe, founder of the Jerusalem Great Synagogue, the massive shul was built to replace an improvised synagogue in the entrance hall of the adjoining Hechal Shlomo, seat of the Chief Rabbinate, where the services were always overcrowded. One critic of the lavish adjunct, which rises like a giant monolithic carbuncle on Hechal Shlomo's neck, was reminded of the axiom coined by a medieval poet: "No sooner is a temple built to God but the Devil builds a chapel hard by." But the big synagogue, which also includes a huge banquet hall and an auxiliary "pocket shul" favored by former chief Sephardi rabbi Ovadia Yosef and his followers, is considered a success story. The shul attracts a wide variety of Israelis, as well as Jewish tourists from abroad, who may feel more at home in an ambience marked by silky Italian marble floors and glittering crystal chandeliers.

A Jerusalemite never has to walk very far to find a synagogue, and the variety is staggering. But in contrast to the multitude and variety of synagogues in older neighborhoods around the city center, there is a severe shortage of shuls in the newer, outlying areas; and in this age of renewed religious belief, it is a big problem. Jerusalem is becoming, increasingly, a "religious city," and many young secular residents are moving to Tel Aviv, where it is not considered desecration to go to a restaurant on Shabbat.

According to Sevanah Meryn of the Jerusalem Municipality, the synagogue shortage is acute. In one section of sprawling Ramot, in northeast Jerusalem, makeshift synagogues have been installed in bomb shelters and rented cottages. Similar situations have been reported in half-a-dozen other new neighborhoods.

Many religious immigrant Jews still long for the synagogues they left behind. The Moroccan community of Har Nof, another of the new Jerusalem neighborhoods, built a cultural center and synagogue and recreated the interior of its new shul based on one in the old country. Rabbi Shlomo Dayan organized the transfer of the Toldot Yitzhak Synagogue of Tetuan in Spanish Morocco to the hilly neighborhood in Israel's capital.

The original synagogue was built by Rabbi Yitzhak Ben-Walid (1767–1870), a leading halachic (Jewish law) authority in Spanish Morocco and a miracle worker revered by Jews and Gentiles alike. The community brought from Tetuan thirteen large Torah scrolls, big glass oil lamps adorned with silver, the rabbi's chair, the tiles of the floor from the rabbi's study (which form a Star of David) and other artifacts. "We want to preserve the warmth of the original building," Dayan said.

Perhaps it is a trend: the Lubavitcher rebbe's followers have also constructed an exact replica of their spiritual leader's Brooklyn headquarters right here in Israel, and if American Jews ever decide to immigrate to Israel in significant numbers, they may recreate their houses of worship in the place where it all began. The country-club synagogue of Short Hills, New Jersey, right here beneath Mount Zion.

According to Jewish tradition, God himself prays in Jerusalem; this city is the most important place where a Jew can pray. It is written that, "When one prays in Jerusalem, it is as if he prays before the Lord's throne, for the Gate of Heaven is there, and it is open to the voices of worshippers." Although one might suspect that He prays on the Temple Mount, it is entirely conceivable that He is the tenth man, hustled in from the street, making the *minyan* at Ezrat Israel. After all, according to His book, He looks just like us.

XV

Yehuda Amichai is an earthy, sad-eyed man whose work might seem, to the casual reader, to be marked by an obsession with God. But for this sensual poet of the land, the word "God" is just a convenient name for describing that unknowable, hovering mystery, what Dylan Thomas called "the force that through the green fuse drives the flower."

Amichai (the word means "my people lives") is a man of strong convictions who believes that the conflict between religious and secular Jews is Israel's greatest internal problem. Born in Germany in 1924, this singular

Hebrew poet came to Palestine in the mid-1930s. He has no patience for the nationalist camp—they were and are "fascists" to his mind, and he characterizes their greatest poet, the late Uri Zvi Greenberg, as a blusterer, ornate icing on a Mussolini wedding cake. The secular socialists, on the other hand, have always been the backbone of the renascent Jewish homeland, Amichai believes.

Amichai, who until recent years never experienced financial security, now lives in a recently remodeled Jerusalem house in the completely gentrified former slum of Yemin Moshe. From the windows of his house he can see Mount Zion, the Old City wall, a purple haze over the Valley of Kidron, and the ravine called Gehinnom in the Bible—Gehenna, or hell. But he treats this heavy historical view with the same scepticism and irony that one senses in his poetry.

In his book *Songs of Jerusalem and Myself*, Amichai, who came to Jerusalem over fifty years ago, wrote a poem called "I've Been Invited to Life" in which he said: "I sign the guest book of God: I was here, I stayed on, I loved it, it was great, I was guilty, I betrayed, I was much impressed by the warm welcome in this world."

Jerusalem for him is the "port city on the shores of eternity," and it represents both pain and peace.

Although Yehuda Amichai's first language was German, he was brought up in an Orthodox-Zionist home and learned Hebrew at the Jewish state school he attended in Wurzburg, in south Germany. His father and six aunts and uncles all came to Palestine during the first two years of Hitler's reign. Yehuda had great respect for his merchant father, and though he would soon break from the religion, as so many members of his generation of young Palestinians did, he knew that something of the tradition would be carried on, a sort of spiritual DNA. In a poem called "My Child," he would write: "My father's movements in prayer/And my own in love/Lie already folded in his small body." His father's life and death are a powerful component of Amichai's work.

Did he stop being a believer when he broke with the religion during his teens? There are "different kinds" of belief, says Amichai. "Believing means that there must be some kind of power about which we'll never find out, and that's it. I just don't want to spend much time thinking about it."

Amichai characterizes the prevalence of God in his poetry as utilitarian and symbolic. "I use it as I use 'father' and 'mother' instead of saying 'the supreme power' or 'supreme intelligence'—this kind of silly bending over backwards to avoid saying 'God'—I use it in the way I called my father 'abba' and didn't call him 'a genetical machine for providing semen from past generations to the future.'"

Critic Aloma Halter has written that "God is always hovering over Amichai's prose, charging even the most secular subjects with the particular intensity of the inverse; religion brought in to evoke the ultimate in sanctity or blasphemy. There is a tendency to use religious imagery and metaphors as tailors use interfacing to stiffen collars and cuffs, putting it in wherever the material might develop an ungainly sag."

Though every schoolchild knows that the earth revolves around the sun and not vice versa, we still say, "The sun is going down into the sea." According to Amichai, "There are two languages: one as things seem to us and the other of knowledge." He is a grounded man who uses everyday life and language to weave a complex vision of this still new nation with its Biblical roots. While a tourist visiting Yemin Moshe may be awestruck by the historical importance of the physically unimposing Mount Zion a hundred yards away, Amichai lives here and sees different things. "Most of the time when I go out I see I have to take laundry in; or when the children were small, the diapers; or I'd see that some stones were loose, and the paint is cracking on the fence...but sometimes, I do have a feeling of really seeing Mount Zion and the Old City wall and everything. But I'm a very down-to-earth person." (Vladimir Slepak is a kindred spirit. When the ex-prisoner of Zion and longtime leader of the Soviet Jewry movement arrived in Israel in late 1987 and was asked, "What next, Mr. Slepak, what are your plans?" he answered, "I plan to take a shower.")

Three hundred yards from Amichai's balcony is yet another stage, the Mount of Olives and the Valley of Kidron, the place of the resurrection of the dead at the End of Time. Amichai has written a poem called "Resurrection," that evokes something of this backdrop:

> Afterwards they will get up
> all together, and with a sound of chairs scraping
> they will face the narrow exit.
>
> And their clothes are crumpled
> and covered with dust and cigarette ashes
> and their hand discovers in the inside pocket
> a ticket stub from a very previous season.
>
> And their faces are still crisscrossed
> with God's will.
> And their eyes are red from so much sleeplessness
> under the ground.

And right away, questions:
What time is it?
Where did you put mine?
When? When?

And one of them can be seen in an ancient
scanning of the sky, to see if rain.
Or a woman,
with an age-old gesture, wipes her eyes
and lifts the heavy hair
at the back of her neck.

(translated by Chana Bloch)

Does Amichai see the End of Time in a literal sense? "I think the end
is endless," he says. "It's either a big black hole or a big white light or
both together. But it's totally meaningless, because even if someone would
explain it, I wouldn't understand it. Because we can't name it or phrase
it or imagine it..."

There is a great tiredness in his beautifully rendered poetry, with its
particularistic insights ("people here live inside prophecies that came true")
and expressions of hostility towards those whom he does not love, like
"the black crow people from Mea She'arim" (the ultra-Orthodox
Jerusalem neighborhood).

The poet, who joined the British army in 1942 and worked as a Haganah
gun-runner and agent of "illegal" immigration in the years before the state
came into being, says of the rival and much smaller Irgun Zvai Leumi
(and the Herut-led Likud political party it later spawned): "I loathed them,
and it has never stopped. They were just a bunch of lousy terrorists...They
never had the staying power of kibbutzim, who could fight for months.
The best of them were naive and brave people, and the worst were just
a bunch of cowards."

Amichai is totally negative about the legacy of Ze'ev Jabotinsky, founder
of Revisionist Zionism, who engaged in "bravado acts instead of everyday life." And to his mind, there is nothing redeeming about Greenberg,
the greatest poet of nationalist Zionism. "He's a typical fascist poet. His
poetry is like the buildings of Mussolini: garish, glorious, pompous and
hollow."

Nor does he have kind words for any of the religious parties. His father
was a member of the religious-Zionist Mizrachi, what later became the
National Religious Party. It was a positive movement in its prestate days,
Amichai says, but it deteriorated into something beyond contempt. "The

National Religious Party today is somewhere between Gush Emunim on the one hand and the most horrible petite bourgeoisie on the other.''

Amichai believes that the greatest problem in Israel is the increasing enmity between the religious and the secular. (Some critics have attributed Amichai's tremendous popularity in Israel to his ambiguous attitude towards Judaism.) He is not sanguine about ameliorating the conflict: ''There is no solution.''

Critic Michael Hamburger has written of Amichai: ''Although he is steeped in Jewish scripture, he cannot accept the certainties of an exclusive faith. For Amichai, therefore, to be an Israeli is quite as difficult as to be a Diaspora Jew. . . Amichai does not preach or prophesy, but his ironies and his gift of total recall provide a corrective to every kind of national complacency and intransigence.''

He is a poet of ripe grapes and warm lips, a ''taster of pain,'' in his own phrase, and an eloquent chronicler of Jerusalem, this ancient-modern city, and the journey of its residents. Jerusalem changes ''and I change too,'' he says. ''What I see is also a change in me.''

In the jungle of Israeli poetry, some of the young lions are out to eat the old man—to denigrate Amichai. They say his best work was done years ago, and that the days of youth are ''worth all your laurels.'' Undoubtedly, it is not equitable that in the international literary world he is the only Israeli poet who is famous. But the best of the young lions will get their turn one day; in the meantime, the older lion remains in the streets, and he goes on.

One day, world-wide fame may also come to several members of the two generations of accomplished Israeli poets post-Amichai, and there are many to choose from: Meir Wieseltier, Dalia Ravikovitch, the late Dan Pagis, Harold Schimmel, Mordechai Geldman, Maya Bejerano, Aaron Shabtai, Ayal Meggid, Yair Hurevitz, Israel Pincas, David Avidan. But the giant's robe will hang loose upon all but one or two of them. In youth, he took more chances, the younger generations of poets say. But that is the nature of youth. Amichai, talking about his days in the Haganah, said that he recalled that time as ''very adventurous—but when you are in your twenties, you see no dangers.''

Poetry, Pablo Neruda once wrote, is ''a deep inner calling in man; from it came liturgy, the psalms, and also the content of religions.'' The heavy Judaic content in Amichai's work attests to that. In his short story ''The Times My Father Died,'' Amichai wrote: ''In the synagogue they have a pair of lions holding up the tablets over the holy ark. Even our laws, too, can only be protected and upheld by wild animals.''

He, too, can still roar. Even though there may be some truth in his critics' claim that his "best work is behind him," Amichai must know that his life's work comprises a rich legacy for his people.

He is also not sitting on his laurels when it comes to politics. Amichai was abroad when the Palestinian uprising began in late 1987, and when he came back to Jerusalem two months later, the city, he said, seemed like a nostalgic memory in pastel colors. In the city he left, he and his family would take long walks in the Old City a few hundred yards from their home. Now, it was dangerous to go there. All the shops were closed. It was a different Israel.

Amichai joined with other left-wing writers—novelists Amos Oz and A.B. Yehoshua and journalist Amos Alon—in an appeal to American Jews to not be afraid to criticize the Israeli government, to speak out at this turning point in Israel's history. He also spoke at Peace Now rallies, calling for immediate talks between Israelis and Palestinians and a territorial solution to the long conflict. When asked by a local Jerusalem newspaper how he and his fellow writers could invite American pressure on Israel, Amichai responded: "We work according to our beliefs. The involvement of writers and intellectuals is an accepted phenomenon in Israel, and generally not just an ornament. It seems to be completely legitimate...I'm not a politician; my involvement now is because it is impossible to remain silent."

It seemed to me that there was also a note of enjoyment in the pain, something I could easily understand. For as Ilya Ehrenburg once said in a very different context, "There are days in the history of one's people which cannot be understood from what one is told. They have to be lived through."

XVI

THEY'RE LEAVING ON A JET PLANE and don't know when, or if, they'll be back again. "Where are you going?" the gatekeeper asks. "Away from here," is the classic answer. But why is it that so many Jews decide to leave Israel?

In this country, no topic generates more heat than what arcane Zionist terminology labels *yerida* (descent), going away, or "down," from Israel. You had better be careful if you believe it is nothing more than a basic human right to leave your country. Of course, we are not the Soviet Union, which signs accords guaranteeing this right but allows only a handful to leave. But we *are* prisoners of Zion in the philosophical sense, for any Jew who leaves our country is termed a "descender," or the droppings of some hideous crawling thing, or "fallout of weaklings" in Yitzhak Rabin's estimation (*nefolet shel nemushot*).

Before going any further in this mine field, let me come to my defense by averring that I love Israel with all my heart, that I would sell sandwiches in the park on Shabbat before I would leave for economic reasons, that I, too, believe that immigration is the lifeblood of the country and that emigration is hurtful, and that I am ultimately highly optimistic in my belief that within a few years of Israel's fiftieth birthday, Israel will be a nation that has attracted more than half the thirteen million Jews of the world, instead of one-quarter as at present—despite the bleak prospects of today. But in the Zionist world, if you do not see anything wrong in an Israeli leaving his country for another, you are considered an outlaw.

In 1985, when I wrote a long article in the *Jerusalem Post Magazine* defending people who feel they must leave Israel, the resultant furor was simply amazing. The editor must have foreseen the flak, running alongside my article a carbuncle piece with an opposite view to my own. It began, "If *yerida* is a disease of Israeli society, most concede that a deepening economic recession will inevitably be accompanied by increased emigration, just as the flu brings with it fever and weakness." But my question was and is, Who is really sick here?

Soon after my article appeared, an employee of the Jewish Agency, that quasigovernmental company which systematically defrauds the Jewish people, wrote a rejoinder, saying that his sabra children read my words, and "their comments were too strong to print in a newspaper." He scoffed at remarks that Israel should strive for normalcy, saying, "No, Mr. Rapoport, we are not living in the post-Zionist era. We are, thank God, alive and well at the beginning of the greatest epoch in our history, the Zionist epoch..." He went on to blame me for the loss of uncountable

Jewish souls: "No one will ever know how many people will leave Israel and run the danger of being permanently lost to the Jewish people as a result of Rapoport's article."

Another "rebuttal" by a local lecturer villified my "misguided" article for committing the sin of "legitimizing *yerida*"; and one of many irate letter-writers scoffed at the notion that a typical Western immigrant family with two children needed $1,200 a month to survive in Israel (my wife and I have four children, no car, live modestly, and figure we need $1,500 to $1,800 a month. The $1,200 figure I used came from the Absorption Ministry). The letter said: "We are a Western family. We bought a four-room apartment, new, in a new neighborhood, and are paying a mortgage. We drive a large family car seven days a week. We have all the electric appliances Americans are prone to. We are dues-paying members of two non-Orthodox synagogues and four organizations. We have subscription tickets to a concert series and a pool club membership. We have a wide circle of friends and entertain frequently [undoubtedly in tents on the lawn]. Hardly a week goes by that we don't give a gift to someone. We take vacations and do what is comfortable for us—not what is necessarily thrifty. If we had an expensive month, we use $600 to live. We can't even begin to imagine what more one has to do in order to spend $1,200 a month." It was signed, "Satisfied *olim* [immigrants], name and address supplied."

Of course, the letter had to be a complete put-on—unless that mortgage is the most reasonable since the state was declared, food and utilities and medical care are free, and those six memberships are fantastic bargains; but the newspaper's letters' editor obviously took it seriously. Imagine, everything you want and need for you and your family and your house for under $600 a month! Who says the Messianic Era hasn't arrived?

Other letters suggested that those who were leaving the country should go to a military cemetery to see "the young people who died so that we can live. Don't we all owe them something?"

The reactions only strengthened my belief that such ideological baggage is bondage, and that too many souls wear blinders to avoid real life. Yes, it is true that millions of European immigrants to the U.S. returned to their countries of origin when life in the Golden Country proved too tough. And true, hordes left Australia. It is even true that hundreds of immigrants left our blessed land in 1939 to return to Poland and other countries on the volcano; and a large number of pioneers returned to Joseph Stalin's Russia to help build a "truer socialism" than what could be found in the kibbutzim of Palestine. Needless to say, they were the shipwrecked generation, among the first to be exterminated in Stalin's massive purges of the 1930s. And as one of my critics pointed out, many of the original *yordim* went back to the killing fields of postwar Germany after the State of Israel was declared, for one unhealthy reason or another. So what does it matter?

JEWS HAVE ALWAYS LEFT their homeland, in prestate Zionist days as well as later. But in recent years, the number may have been increasing, and the general situation has deteriorated in a broader, more disturbing way than in the past.

The numbers game is difficult and usually unenlightening. The government agencies that deal with emigration take years to come up with figures, and there are dozens of ways to interpret the fuzzy statistics. But a ballpark figure is that 350,000 to 500,000 Israelis, 10 to 15 percent of the country's Jews, live abroad, mostly in the U.S. Shmuel Lahis, the former director-general of the Jewish Agency who came up with those figures in a report in the early 1980s, came under vicious attack for trying to clarify the problem. Lahis, who heads a volunteer organization to combat emigration, is more sympathetic than most Zionists towards the so-called *yordim* on an individual basis, but he is one of those who talks about emigration as "a cancer."

There are various ways of categorizing the emigrants. A number of them hold dual citizenship, or have a close relative who is an American citizen, for example. Some have the professional qualifications required for a resident visa abroad. Others find a way around the rules, and get to where they want to go no matter what. It is usually not easy—the American Embassy in Tel Aviv has become very hard-nosed in recent years. Many Israelis who try to visit the U.S. for only two or three weeks, to see a lover or friend, are flatly turned down. When I tried to intervene with embassy officials on behalf of our babysitter, who wished to visit her American fiancé, I was told, "You'll only make it harder for her if you raise a stink."

According to officials at the embassy and at the American Consulate in East Jerusalem (which serves as a kind of "Legation to Palestine"), applications for visas have increased appreciably in recent years from West Bank and Gaza Palestinians as well as Israelis. But it can take several years to get a visa, unless an immediate relative holds American citizenship. What the State Department used to call a "quota" (the policy that held sway during the Holocaust) has now been euphemized into "numerical limitation," and no more than twenty thousand immigrants are allowed into the U.S. from any one country.

In the period leading up to the year of the uprising, other Western embassies, shipping agencies and aid organizations like the Association of Americans and Canadians in Israel also reported a sharp rise in the number of people leaving Israel, or getting ready to do so. But then, the old Israeli joke—"last one out of the airport turns out the lights"—will probably always be with us. Grizzled old-timers may shrug their shoulders over the fallen sparrows and point out that half the people from the Third Aliya period did not persevere in Palestine. Doctrinaire Zionists and pious commentators locked in a time warp may continue to contemptuously dismiss the emigrants as "descenders," materialistic weaklings using the economic or security situation to "slink out the back door," as one of them put it. But they are simply blind to reality, to the way real people live in real Israel. Life in our country has become so difficult for so many people—economically, socially and politically—that the negative, in their eyes, has started to outweigh the positive, and all too often they feel it just is not worth it anymore.

My INTERVIEWS WITH SOME OF THOSE leaving do not represent a cross section. All are Jerusalemites, and their situation is undoubtedly different from those in other cities, in the depressed development towns or on the bankrupt farms. What emerged after talking to many of those who were "going away" was a strong feeling that the terms, the very idea of *aliya* (ascent) and *yerida*, are inappropriate in the face of a national emergency, and that the "shame" associated with those who leave Israel is ridiculous. A fierce reappraisal of values and radical solutions appears to be the only way to stem what may become a flood of emigration.

The word "aliya" can be taken literally in some cases, such as the dramatic 1985 rescue and immigration of thousands of Ethiopian Jews who were otherwise doomed to die in the famine and pestilence of Northeast Africa, or Natan Sharansky's odyssey from Chistopol prison to Jerusalem. For them, and for many other Jews, Israel is indeed a miracle, and they *have* ascended. But for millions of Jews in the free countries of the West, the talk of ascent and descent is arcane.

A few years ago, the iconoclastic Israeli journalist Baruch Nadel wrote an article entitled, "The Day I Almost Left Israel." What stopped him at the last minute, he wrote, was the heady smell of orange blossoms that wafted his way as he approached the airport. But not long afterwards, Nadel, a man of the right who had been in the Stern group and eventually became one of the country's first investigative reporters (he exposed the scandalous "black money" situation that so plagued the economy), finally did leave Israel, orange blossoms notwithstanding.

Why do people leave? Is the situation really deteriorating? Should emigrants be regarded as scum, traitors? Is there a way to counter the trend?

Doctrinaire Zionists are classic Jewish mothers in their use of guilt. But it does not work anymore, even if it is true that there is no greater guilt than discontentment. It will not make people stay, it will not bring them back, and it will not entice newcomers.

Aliya and *yerida* were empty words for Eli and Nancy Turgeman (not their real names—almost all those I interviewed asked for anonymity, a measure of how much shame is attached to emigration). Until they finally departed for the United States, the Turgemans lived in a squalid, tiny three-room apartment in a drab housing project in Jerusalem's Katamon neighborhood. Constant shouting echoed in dusty corridors strewn with debris, penetrating the thin walls and doors of the cramped apartments.

Nancy, forty-one, came to Israel from the U.S. in the late 1960s, during the upsurge in immigration that followed the euphoria of the Six Day War. Eli, thirty-nine, was brought to Israel from Tunisia at the age of two. They have two small children. Economically, life was never easy for them. Neither of their families had money, and there was no income from land in the old town of Rehovot or a house in middle-class Kfar Saba. In Israel, most young couples get help from their parents. Interest rates are astronomical, and usually the biggest mortgage obtainable represents no more than 30 or 40 percent of the cost of an apartment. Many Western immigrants would not dare to live here without an outside income, trust funds, or a factory in the family. Yet one young university lecturer I know, who drives a $40,000 car and lives in a plush penthouse, fulminated in a newspaper opinion column against the traitor-emigrants who use the ''excuse'' of economic reasons.

Eli, a sensitive man who never finished high school, did mostly physical work in a printing shop—a seventy-six-hour week (thirty hours of overtime). His net salary for this grinding labor ranged, in a period of eroded pay, from $600 down to $400 a month. ''Every night, I'd come home exhausted. Eat and go to sleep. Not much of a life.''''But we managed on our income somehow,'' Nancy interjected. ''We never went out, took a taxi, or bought any fancy clothes. We had meat on the table once a week, never more than that.''

Nancy felt completely at home in Israeli society. Thanks to a religious upbringing and her own insistence on rarely speaking any English, her Hebrew was perfect. Her American background had been middle class, but years of poverty-line existence in Israel soon gave her the tired, withered look of those who ply the Number 18 bus between Katamon and the Mahane Yehuda market downtown.

Eli felt that what really broke his spirit was four tours of army reserves duty in Lebanon between 1982 and 1985, including a stint at the Ansar prison camp. ''It simply wiped me out. I felt I was guarding prisoners of war, not Nazi terrorists. They had no POW status, no status at all. I just said to myself, I can't do this again.'' Eli, who defined himself as in the center politically, was upset by the rise of Kahanism in the streets of his working-class neighborhood. The general shift to the right scared him, he said. For a still-small number of reservists, duty in the West Bank or Gaza is rapidly becoming something like service in Lebanon. It can be the last straw. Eli said he would never refuse to serve in the army. "It's better just to leave. The men who rule this country are totally insensitive to the people. But I believe I could somehow deal with all of the ideological problems if it wasn't for the economy."

The Turgemans wore the look of poverty, and hard luck plagued them in the year before they finally decided to leave. They lost a bitterly contested $1,500 lawsuit, and part of Turgeman's modest salary was attached. The bank subsequently lowered the amount allowed on their overdraft, and a big check to the local grocer bounced. It was an ugly business, a tense feeling even when the kids went into the shabby little grocery store to buy rolls and milk. "There were terrible pressures all around," Eli said. "We were running around like rats trying to keep things from falling apart. I wondered, is this life? If it is, life is not worth it."

Eli's parents and his eight brothers and sisters wholeheartedly supported his decision to leave. "If any of them had a way to get a visa to the U.S., they would go too."

THE ECONOMIC CRUNCH has hit professional people as hard as it has members of the working class. But one family that was all packed up to go a couple years ago somehow is still holding on, though it has been touch and go. Bill and Alice Cowan, who settled in Israel in 1971 upon completing college study, told me they were "just getting strangled."

The Cowans, who are entirely self-supporting, both work more than full time (as do most Israelis), and also are raising four small children. Bill was assistant teaching at Hebrew University—which is $100 million in debt and periodically firing whole blocs of scholars—and taking home a salary of about $375 a month. Alice, an independent teacher ("one of the few who pay taxes"), makes about $300. They get another $100 a month in National Insurance Institute allowances for big families. It has not been nearly enough: they were running short about $300 a month, the sum they pay for rent (they were robbed of all their savings and their dream apartment by a crooked contractor soon after they immigrated). "There is no such thing as a normal mortgage, so we don't stand a chance of ever buying a place," Bill said.

Because of the difficulty finding a long-term lease, they had to move every year or two, which created periodic havoc in their lives. They felt they could not work more than they already do, and they were not willing to stop declaring Alice's earnings to the taxman. "Unless you cheat, you can't make it,'' Alice said, referring to Israel's high rate of tax evasion. "And even if you cheat, it's hard. It eats away at you. Either you become tough and cynical, or you end up hungry and feeling you've been screwed."

The Israel they came to "doesn't exist anymore"—a commonly heard plaint of those who remember a smaller, more idealistic country—and they were distressed that the only Westerners who are coming to live in Israel are religious people. "They have a different way of looking at things than we do." But they did feel that at least some of the newly observant Jews who have come to Israel from Western societies share their democratic, humanitarian beliefs.

The Cowans felt that they were being squeezed out of Israel. They did not want to leave, and dreaded life in America. "This is home—not there...During all our years in Israel, even in the blackest hours, we never thought of leaving the country, not until [ex-Finance Minister] Aridor pulled the rug out and we couldn't pay for food."

They also felt that they were being deprived of a day of rest—no Sabbath in the Jewish state. "Saturday is the day for cleaning house, because there's no time during the week. Work-sleep, work-sleep, work-sleep. There's no time to ourselves, no strength left; and we're becoming incapable of joy," Alice said.

They see themselves as "sixties people," idealists who worked to change things. Alice organized a consumer boycott of the Supersol supermarket chain, for example. "What was important was how we lived," Bill said. "We never cared about money; it never was a problem until our subsistence level was undercut. Either you get crushed or you survive. We didn't leave when we were cheated by the system, or by the contractor—none of that was cause for leaving. You *can* fight the system and get the municipality to reopen a kindergarten—social problems can be dealt with. But what can we do as individuals about the economy?"

The economic realities were taking too great a toll. Alice: "I can't be a normal mother, don't have time to read to the children, and I'm angry all the time. It's not a way to live, and I'm sick of it. It's not living. But the main question is, am I ruining my children?"

The arguments of the generation that fought for independence ("We left comfortable homes and stuck it out through thick and thin") have worn thin. It is not just that the later generation is so much more materialistic. The Cowans were not asking for an American standard of living; they simply could not bring themselves to cut off music or language lessons for their children, who do not get a proper education in Israel's financially beleaguered school system. Yet when I wrote about them having a terrible time living on $750 a month, the indignant letters and contemptuous rejoinders came flying: "I don't know the Cowans," one writer rebutted, "but I do know that any Israeli family that can't make ends meet on a monthly net income of $750, which is way above the average family income, had no business coming here in the first place." This, from a Ph.D.

I did a little monthly budget of my own family's expenses. We, too, have four children. We do not have a car, as the Cowans do (that would cost roughly $150 a month, including gas, upkeep and insurance). Our mortgages come to $230 a month, as opposed to their $300 monthly rent. We pay $90 monthly interest on our overdraft (which is of average size). Medical-fund payments are $60 a month. We spend $200 on the extra lessons that have come to be called "gray education" (judo, ballet, English, art, music, exercise). Property tax (on a small Jerusalem apartment), public school fees and school supplies are another $70 a month. A municipal kindergarten for our youngest child is $90 a month. Utilities—gas, electricity and kerosene for heating during the bitingly cold Jerusalem winters—averages $145 a month annually. Telephone, not including long-distance calls, is $40. The eternal state tax on the television and our radio is $10 a month. Repairs to ancient plumbing and sewage system, and a perennially leaky roof, amount to $20 a month. Other than underwear, we buy all our clothes at a second-hand shop, but let's not include any money for that. Shoes, one pair annually for each adult, two for each child, $30 a month. Nothing for entertainment, eating out, swimming pool membership, birthday gifts, synagogue dues or catered black-tie affairs like those held by the family of the letter-writer who cannot imagine spending $600 a month; or for our babysitter. Nor do I include the brilliant leasing deal I made, in which I paid $160 a month for five years for a computer and printer. Or the dentist, who charges $400 per crown. The grand total of only the very basic costs comes to: $985 a month.

So there you have it.

Except for food, which costs an arm and a leg, another $100 a month per person at the minimum—$1,585. Even doing away with education and chicken, there is still no way to get that figure below $1,100 a month.

Or maybe the Cowans and the Rapoports should just move in with that family that does so much more in their lives on "far less than $600 a month."

THOUSANDS OF ISRAELIS leave every year for a period of study abroad, government or Zionist organization business, sabbaticals or just "a break" to earn real money. A good many, even some of the aliya emissaries, never come back. These people are often the cream of the crop.

Yoram and Maggie Harel returned from a two-year stay in the U.S. in the early part of the decade. Yoram, thirty-nine, was born in Jerusalem.

Maggie, thirty-eight, came to Israel in 1975 from New Zealand, describing herself as "a Zionist goy." Her conversion was not performed by an Orthodox rabbi, so they had to be married in Cyprus, traveling a well-worn Israeli route (not only are Conservative and Reform conversions not recognized in Israel, but *cohanim*, descendants of the priestly caste who comprise roughly 5 percent of the male population, are prohibited from marrying a divorced woman).

When I visited them, it was obvious that there were no economic problems here. The bright, attractive couple and their two children lived in a spacious, redecorated house in a mostly Arab neighborhood. Their Jewish neighbors were black-garbed Orthodox living in an enclave physically distant from the ultra-Orthodox stronghold of Mea She'arim, but spiritually very close.

"When we were in the U.S., I missed Israel," Yoram recalled, "but it was a shock coming back, when I suddenly realized what makes life so difficult here." It was not the economy. Or the army—Yoram was a major in a top fighting unit. But like Eli Turgeman, Yoram felt the Lebanon experience had changed his life. "I serve in the Israel *Defense* Forces, not in the Rearrange the Middle East Forces." He, too, felt that it was wrong for any Israeli to refuse to serve, whether in Lebanon or the West Bank. But his dissatisfaction was of a different nature than Turgeman's. "I'm not sure anymore if Israel is the answer. Zionist goals are not my goals."

Zionism, he felt, had been co-opted, or swept away, by those who believe in a Greater Israel or a religious Israel, who say that democracy is not really a part of Judaism, and who easily justify the subjugation of another people. "We Jews, who have been wronged by nationalism, are doing the same thing to our Arab neighbors. When you are in the army, and you are fighting, you have to believe in what you're fighting for. I had to ask myself, who is closer to being my brother, Arik Sharon or my Arab neighbors? There's no doubt in my mind—my Arab neighbors. I went to the Yom Kippur War from this house, and the Arabs came and wished me well. My *haredi* [anti-Zionist Orthodox] neighbors, of course, did nothing of the sort."

Maggie did not suggest that they leave; she felt it was not her place to do so. When I talked to them, they had not yet told the children, the hardest part. "The most positive reason for staying is that Israel remains a great place for children; the society is wonderfully child-oriented," Maggie said. "It's heartbreaking to have to tell them that we're going to leave. When we were in the U.S. for two years, the kids felt good saying that they are Israelis who are going back home in such and such a time. They have a tremendous sense of identity here."

Yoram, a professor of physics with broad experience in the computer industry, knew he would have no trouble finding work in the U.S. When he had made up his mind, they decided to sell the house (many emigrants hold on to their footholds in Israel for years, just in case) and not to store anything. "It's a very sad decision for me, and it's haunting me, as if I were on trial, justifying myself. Every time I have a pleasant day, I change my mind."

But the Harels had decided. They said that the only thing that could make them change their minds would be if Israel undertook a peace initiative and struggled to reach a settlement based on the principle of territories for peace. They voted left-liberal, for the Citizens Rights Movement, but were basically uninvolved politically. Cynicism won the day. A short while later, they moved to the Pacific Northwest.

Those people who feel they must leave for economic, psychological or other reasons cannot survive on hope; they feel they have no choice. It is a painful decision for most of them. Why should they also be burdened with guilt laid on thick by the self-righteous souls who think people are only looking for an "excuse" to leave. That attitude is almost Soviet: "We educated them, gave them everything, and then they spit in our faces and abandon us."

But if cynicism prevails among those leaving for political and social reasons, and the "good Israelis" leave everything to narrow power-brokers and zealots, this country will continue on a downhill course. The mythic "lights out at the airport" joke will never happen. There is no "escape" for millions of Israelis. But if the light of hope for a peaceful, viable, democratic country continues to dim, Westerners are not going to "ascend" to such a place, and it will be absurd to condemn those who "descend."

I know a veteran Israeli, a man who has devoted most of his years to the Jewish people, who is struggling with the question of whether to remain an Israeli. His feelings had nothing whatsoever to do with the economy, the horrible drivers, the maddening bureaucracy, the inefficiency or the everyday meanness some people encounter in the streets. He believes Israel is on a collision course with disaster, because the country's leaders do not deal with basic issues concerning national and religious identity, relations with the Jews outside Israel, and the Palestinian question. He has been on the verge of giving up for years now. "I told someone the other day that what I should do is stay at the airport, to catch people before they catch the plane out of here. People who talk about leaving Israel should either do something to change things here or they should leave.

"If I could stay at the airport and catch people—good people who aren't leaving because they want a bigger car or something, but because they're frustrated—and tell them, look, you are perfectly entitled to leave, but there's a bunch of us, ten people, who are trying to do something. Why don't you join us? But the fact is that people aren't ready for that, don't want to commit themselves to what is needed here—nothing short of a revolution.''

In his view, the entire approach to immigration and emigration is distorted, a product of Zionist mythologizing. If Israel were a normal country—and Zionism was once a movement to normalize the existence of a people made abnormal by two thousand years of exile—then immigration would no longer be called ''aliya,'' even if that word is supposed to imply transcending one's self. ''People still talk of 'ascending' to Israel, so it all becomes ceremony, something to do with religion. The whole notion of calling someone who emigrates to Israel an *oleh*, one who ascends, should be repugnant. It's racist in American terms. What kind of nation is it that vulgarly declares itself superior, that says if someone stops being an American and comes to Israel, he ascends, and if anyone leaves Israel, he descends? Some people left here and ascended, and others came here and descended.

''A former minister of education, a prominent Labor Party leader, once made a speech that the *yordim* are all traitors. I happened to see him two days later over breakfast, and I attacked him. I said that the very words 'aliya' and *yerida* are good reasons for leaving Israel—you don't need any more reason than that.''

Not everyone is willing to take a fresh look at the concepts that guide our society. But there are some people who are not content to let the old formulas go unchallenged without at least thinking about them. Something is obviously wrong if only sixty thousand American Jews have come to Israel since 1948, while at least six times that number of Israelis have gone to the U.S., the home of the largest Jewish population in the world, a land that has drawbacks of its own.

What would happen if, for example, a genuine land reform were enacted, if the land in Galilee and the Negev and the central plain were no longer held in trust for ''the Jewish people'' but made available cheaply to Israelis and Jews abroad who want to immigrate to this tortured but vibrant land? What if a unilateral Israeli peace initiative brought results? What if honest pay were accorded for honest work, a total reform of the inequitable tax system? What if parasitical institutions, whose only product is red tape, were eliminated? Perhaps hundreds of thousands would come, and tens of thousands who want to leave would change their minds. For Israel, despite all the legitimate complaints, is a glorious place to live, and it does seem to have a special future.

Immigration may still be seen in terms of aliya: fulfillment, integrity, idealism. But these qualities can be retained while we rethink what it means in the fortieth year of the post-Zionist era to come to live in, or to leave, the State of Israel.

XVII

RETURN. Not everybody is leaving: some are even coming back. Annual service in the army reserves to age fifty may be one of the major reasons people leave Israel (or why they don't come back), but there are many exceptions. Maybe it is even a trend: a growing number of the children of the "deserters" are coming back to Israel.

After two weeks of reserve duty, Zvi finally got a positive response from one of his fellow reservists: "You came back from America? *Kol hakovod!*" (more power to you). Most of the others said he must be crazy, and they meant it. At first, Zvi gave rather ordinary reasons for his return to Israel. Then, the real, and unexpected, reason emerged: he came back to do his army service!

Zvi's family left Israel when he was twelve years old, that special age when your gang is firmed up, when your parents start you on bar mitzvah instruction, when you are going to save Israel from her innumerable enemies with a complex computer game. Zvi's family settled in Los Angeles, the city of the angels, where they ran a nursing home. Brought up like most kids in Southern California, Zvi became a self-described "sports freak," a thoroughly Americanized high-school football star. But his English was always a handicap—he could never entirely shake that Israeli accent. When he went to California, he did not know a word of English; he started out far behind and never quite caught up. The young kid from Israel poured his energy into sports: basketball, baseball and, mostly, football. He became a varsity linebacker on the high school team, a tough position in a mean sport, the great achievement of his life.

A nonacademic business administration major, he attended a state college in the Valley, where he also played some football. "There were lots of Jews there, and a couple of hundred Israeli students; but that's where I ran into real anti-Semitism for the first time. I heard things from fellow students like, 'If you don't behave, we'll put you in the ovens,' or, 'I hope the Arabs kick the shit out of you.' It was all said in a kind of joking tone, which only made it worse.

"I wasn't a 'practicing' Israeli. I never thought about it until that time, didn't even know I could buy *Ma'ariv* on Fairfax Avenue until some Israeli students told me.

"My parents also didn't talk much about their years in Israel. They were members of a religious kibbutz, where my father was a top mechanic. They moved later to the religious enclave of Bnei Brak, near Tel Aviv, and finally left Israel in 1957. My father was influenced by his two older brothers, both of whom had gone to America from Czechoslovakia. They were successful in business and would send money to my folks—they thought we lived in tents."

Zvi's mother did not want to leave—"she loved Israel"—but his father was "fed up" and felt that he wasn't getting anywhere.

"I was twelve years old, but I knew I didn't want to leave, either. I tried to run away from the boat—two policemen grabbed me and dragged me back. My parents told me and my two sisters just forty-eight hours before our departure that we were leaving for America. I vowed I would come back.

"I arrived in America wearing a yarmulke on my head. Two months later, I took it off for good, and started adjusting to my new life."

Zvi did not pay any attention to what was happening in Israel throughout his high school years. He was "too busy with sports"—like the rest of the world. Yet he always felt he was an outsider. He couldn't keep up socially and never went to the de rigueur school proms. He spent all his leisure time watching television, in the years before MTV and fifty channels: a car commercial every ten minutes, the dealer's dog posing on the hood of Today's Special.

"The year 1967 was my first in college, and I started to take interest in news items about Israel. I was proud of Israel, and felt a part of it.

When the war broke out, I tried to volunteer. I wished I had been in the Israeli army—I got out of the American army by paying off a doctor, $700 for an asthma 4-F. But I wanted to fight for Israel.

"In 1970 I came to the country on a study tour, spent six months on a kibbutz and then returned to L.A. After I graduated in 1974, I started the process for returning to Israel as an *oleh hadash* (new immigrant). At first, the Jewish Agency representative turned me down, said the authorities couldn't help me because I hadn't served in the army. They said I had to serve three years in order to obtain full privileges. Then the rules of the game changed, and I only had to serve nine months, at my age, to qualify for full immigrant rights.

"I didn't mean to stay here after the army—I just wanted to serve and go back; but the privileges induced me to settle. So I did."

But for how long?

Zvi is boastful about his college degree; to an observer, he often seems immature and ill-educated, a spoiled kid. Summer jobs were always provided by his father, who sold the nursing home and became a well-to-do building contractor.

His fellow reservists think that Zvi is stubborn, that he simply feels superior: he seems to have an expert opinion on everything. He fullbacks his way through an argument with a religious kibbutznik in a nearby bunker, dominating the conversation as if all argument were football. At thirty, he is still a boy. "I wish I never had to grow up," he sighed.

Although he seems basically good-natured, he annoys many of the men in our unit. One of them, Eliezer, a loud, demonstrative character with an organ-grinder's moustache, a fruit-and-vegetable dealer who came to Israel from Iraq in the fifties, gets into a shouting match with Zvi. The vulgarity of Eliezer's first words to Zvi, concerning Zvi's wife, had shocked the Israeli-American. So did Eliezer's next words: "Over twenty years I've been in this shitty army. I'm sick of it. What's it like in America? I want to go there. Israel is a rotten country, rotten people."

Zvi, coloring purple, exploded, calling Eliezer "filth." A hot exchange followed, then silence.

That was during Zvi's first stint in the reserves following basic training, and he remained gung-ho for the first two weeks. Then, towards the end of the third week, he grew a bit more sloppy, but still was not as lazy as the next guy. He still angered quickly at those who complained they had had enough of the annual reserve burden.

Zvi had only been married for two months, to a Russian immigrant, and there were no children yet who were missing their father. Other reservists, who do anywhere from twenty to thirty-five years of reserve duty after three years in the regular army, scoffed at Zvi's gung-ho attitude.

Zvi maintained that he came *because* of the army, but he believed that army service is the main reason emigrants do not come back to Israel.

"My sister married an Israeli in Los Angeles. He can't come back here because he avoided the army. He went to the University of California instead of doing his service—he just didn't want to go in. But his own brother came back to Israel from L.A. in order to do his full three years, and when he finished, he returned to California: he just didn't want to feel like a deserter. And now, the two brothers hardly talk to each other anymore."

Zvi felt that one of the main reasons why Israeli men who left are permanently stranded in America was because of the restrictions on them on visits to Israel: "You're only allowed one trip back. After that, the army can draft you, even if you've acquired American citizenship."

Zvi had found a home in a Negev development town and worked in a hotel. He told me that he had never been happier. But he didn't exclude the possibility that he would return to the U.S. some day...

He seemed to me an odd mix of Israeli and American—a confused man; and many people sensed this. Every time they asked him, "What are you doing here?" he had to ask himself the same question. He had no more understanding of why he had come home than the dust that returns to the earth. Return is just something that has to happen, until the final return.

Richard T. Nowitz

XVIII

THE MOST POSITIVE SINGLE EVENT in Israel's fourth decade was the spectacular rescue of thousands of Ethiopian Jews from the pestilential refugee camps of Eastern Sudan. That dramatic story, which took place in 1984–1985, evoked Biblical themes, and reinforced the very foundations of the State of Israel.

But since those heady days, the road has been rough for most of the fifteen thousand Ethiopian Jews now in Israel, and their trials and tribulations are not likely to end soon. Over three years after Operation Moses, horror stories abounded: in one case, a deranged Ethiopian immigrant in Mevesseret Zion ("Harbinger of Zion"), near Jerusalem, committed suicide after a pharmacist in the local clinic refused to fill a prescription from a mental hospital because the proper stamps were not affixed to it.

In all, there have been about thirty suicides among this deracinated community, people traumatized and bereaved by the deaths of some three thousand members of the community in the Sudanese camps. But given this circumstance, as well as the severity of their culture shock and the terrible burden of separation from parents and children—ten thousand to fifteen thousand Jews remain trapped in Ethiopia—they have done remarkably well. The suicide rate, exaggerated in press reports, was in fact far lower among the Ethiopian immigrants than it was among the emigrants from Germany to Palestine in the 1930s.

The daily press also reported frequent displays of hostility towards the Ethiopian Jews by their Israeli neighbors in such locations as Petah Tikva and Beersheba, where, according to experts, the immigrants are concentrated in too large numbers. Hundreds of Ethiopian immigrants are now regarded as permanent social cripples, refusing to work or to attend retraining courses. But despite all the suffering, there is no question that the people who were once called *Falashas*, "strangers," or "exiles," feel that they are far better off than they were in Africa; they are persevering in Israel, as they did for thousands of years in exile.

It is axiomatic to say that every immigrant group has it rough, in varying degrees; and undoubtedly it has been far from easy for the black Jews who lived a backward life in the remote mountains of northwestern Ethiopia. But it is a mistake to listen only to the gloom- and doomsayers. This vibrant community has focused on the goal of Zion through many centuries of war, slavery and impoverishment. A rude neighbor or an indifferent clerk or a big gap in education is not the worst enemy they have had to face.

But certain problems persist, due, in no small part, to internecine battles in the bureaucratic immigration institutions, the coldheartedness of the Chief Rabbinate, and bitter intracommunal problems among the Ethiopian Jews. Many saw the Chief Rabbinate's requirement that Ethiopian Jews wishing to marry undergo a semiconversion ritual as insensitive, insulting and cruel. At one point, the rabbis actually appeared willing to reach some sort of compromise on the conversion issue, one the Ethiopians could "live with," just as the majority of Israelis have learned to submit to the injustices of a society where religion and state are not separated.

But a two-month-long sit-in demonstration opposite the Chief Rabbinate in Jerusalem in 1985 worsened relations between the religious establishment and the Ethiopians. And contrary to reports at the time—often by those who were mainly interested in using the Ethiopian case as a cudgel to bash the Chief Rabbinate—there was no groundswell of support for the Ethiopian cause. In fact, the opposite was true. A number of Israelis simply let their racism emerge. Others said, "They want to go back to Ethiopia? So go back!"

From the religious viewpoint, there was apparently a genuine argument that Jews who did not have Hebrew or the Talmud, no matter how observant they may have been, must adjust to modern Judaism. However, there was an obvious double standard in the rabbinate's full acceptance of intermarried Russian Jews who knew nothing about Judaism, or American-Jewish immigrants whose credentials were also not always kosher. But the obscurantist ultra-Orthodox were not the only ones saying that the Ethiopian Jews had to undergo ritual immersion ceremonies. Many mainstream intellectual Jews in the observant community also called for the Ethiopians to submit to rabbinical demands.

At one point, because of the Orthodox establishment's attitude, some of the more militant leaders of the Ethiopian community were threatening to secede from the Jewish people and become an outsider community like the Karaites or the Samaritans, heretical sects that reject the Talmud and rabbinical Judaism. Israel, they warned, would have a "black problem."

Among the Ethiopians themselves, the policy of some of their militants caused a schism. The "establishment" religious leadership within the community was shunted aside. The veteran Ethiopian immigrants, who did more than anyone to bring their people to Israel, were disregarded, dismissed as "tools of the Agency" or of special-interest groups.

Another important aspect of what appeared to be an emerging tragedy was the bureaucratic struggle between the Jewish Agency and the Absorption Ministry. Neither the Laborite Minister of Absorption, Ya'acov Tsur, nor Haim Aharon, his Herut party rival who headed the Agency's Immigration Department, made enough of an effort to bridge the differences between them in order to help their wards. The Housing Minister and Deputy Prime Minister, David Levy, was of even less help. The Moroccan-born Levy has frequently been accused of discriminating against Russian immigrants, as well as Ethiopian, for ethnocentric-political reasons. Thousands of Ethiopians were put into leaky caravan homes "temporarily"—a period that turned into three years. Only by staging angry demonstrations, in the classic Israeli tradition, and asking what had happened to all the millions of dollars American Jews raised for the absorption of Ethiopian Jews, did the Ethiopians manage to obtain a promise from the bureaucrats that permanent housing would soon be found.

According to one knowledgeable immigration official, the successful absorption of thousands of Ethiopians who arrived between 1980 and 1984 was facilitated by the Absorption Ministry's agreement to put everything in the hands of Jewish Agency social workers and their helpers. Many of these low-paid professionals are devoted workers, a world apart from the bloated Agency bureaucracy. Because of the monumental culture shock that the Ethiopians suffered, they needed the professional care of a trained social service staff. In general, the Agency's Social Work Department takes responsibility for the immigration of "high-risk" immigrants. In the case of the Ethiopian community, it was more necessary than ever to provide the immigrants with caring, professional guidance in obtaining housing, vocational training and employment.

But the successful policy was abandoned, as were the criteria set forth in an Absorption Ministry "master plan" calling for vocational training for all adults and establishing guidelines for permanent housing that would not concentrate large numbers of Ethiopian immigrants in one area or in "disadvantaged" neighborhoods. Suddenly, the Ethiopians were no longer referred for formal vocational training. Absorption centers were turned into permanent housing, and hundreds of Ethiopian immigrants were put in block housing in slum areas in Ashkelon, Afula and Beersheba. The result was ghettoization. Mayor Eli Dayan of Ashkelon was one leader who expressed his outrage at the government's indifference, and at the terrible price that human beings must pay because of bureaucratic infighting over funds and power. But the biggest problem of all has been the dislocation and suffering caused by separation from family members still in Ethiopia.

In August 1987, it seemed, for a moment, that the government was finally going to push the Ethiopians' cause. Prime Minister Shamir—who, along with his predecessor Menachem Begin, helped to orchestrate the rescue of roughly half the community of Ethiopian Jews—headed a group of luminaries who appeared before an assembly in Jerusalem of three thousand Ethiopians. He called for African leaders to press Ethiopia to free its remaining Jews, and vowed to put the issue at "the top" of Israel's agenda. Other speakers at the assembly, which was organized by the Ethiopian community, called for a massive campaign by world Jewry to push for the reunification of Ethiopian families: at least one thousand children now in Israel have parents living in Ethiopia who are not allowed to leave.

The assembly was the first to draw support from such a wide cross section of Israeli society: Knesset members from the right-wing Tehiya to the left-wing Mapam and Citizens Rights Party sat side by side on the rostrum. Hundreds of blue-shirted youths from the Mapam-affiliated Hashomer Ha'tzair/Kibbutz Artzi were bused in from all over the country, while soldiers, elderly Israelis and Orthodox youths were also in evidence. For a moment, it all looked impressive, even "historic," as some activists called it. But on the government level, nothing happened in the following months, and the issue was more or less left to the Ethiopians and to student organizations to worry about.

MOST OF THE THOUSANDS of Ethiopian Jews who arrived in the years before the airlift have made great strides adjusting to a foreign environment and been spared the radicalization affecting many of those who came shortly after disease wiped out their family members in the camps. Apparently this is also true of the small number of Ethiopians who have managed to get to Israel in the years since Operation Moses, as was the case with a twenty-four-year-old man whom I had last seen when he was thirteen, and who looked me up a few months after his immigration in 1986.

On my first visit to Ethiopia, he had guided me on horseback through the majestic landscapes of Falasha country north of copper-tinted Lake Tana, the source of the Blue Nile. In a book I wrote about the Falashas in 1979, I called him "Shimshon," and described how this bright young schoolboy wearing brown sackcloth clothes had queried me about why "the government of Jerusalem" didn't come to the rescue of his people. He was from a very poor family in one of the poorest countries in the world, yet he had learned English and some Hebrew through remarkable diligence and a fierce desire to get to Israel. His last words to me were, "Don't forget us," which is what the Falashas said to every foreign Jew who visited them.

It took "Shimshon" (he still does not want his real name used) a long time to reach his goal. He was conscripted into the Ethiopian army and sent to fight in the Ogaden desert. After army duty, when he tried to reach Sudan by foot, he was apprehended and imprisoned in Gondar for six months. Like hundreds of other Ethiopian Jews, he was systematically tortured there, turned upside down and beaten with a wooden cudgel on the soles of his feet until they turned into raw flesh. He laughs when retelling his story. "That's life."

Once in Israel, he was enrolled in a vocational school with immigrants from Europe, Asia and Africa. It was hard for him, very hard, he said; but the teachers were encouraging, and he felt that in time he would be able to adjust to this strange country. He told me that he never wants to see his name in print (an extremely rare and healthy reaction for a human being), that he does not want to get involved in the fractious politics that have divided the Ethiopian community. He is not a militant, nor has he been "paid off" to keep quiet. Although it has been far from easy for him in Israel, there have been no "surprises." All he wants is to study, to catch up. When he saw the personal computer in my house, his eyes brimmed with tears of wonderment and determination.

He is extremely shy, even by the standards of a community known for its shyness, and he is unusually intelligent. "I don't want problems. I only want to be 'clean,' to stay away from all of the controversy and anger. There are those among my people who can split hairs and tell stories up to the heavens. I've only been here a year. I want to learn, not to talk."

GIVEN THE LARGE NUMBER of depressing stories about the absorption of the Ethiopian Jews, it may be a bit hokey to go the other route and write about a success story, an Ethiopian who has pulled herself up by the time-honored bootstraps. But Esther Wube Hollander's story deserves telling. When I first met her in 1974, she was a twenty-one-year-old new immigrant working as a waitress, and an activist on behalf of her community. The late Gail Rubin (machine-gunned by PLO freedom fighters in 1977 while she was taking pictures of birds at the Ma'agan Michael nature preserve) photographed this stunning woman for the cover of a story I wrote in the *Jerusalem Post Magazine*.

Esther Wube, whose father was the kosher butcher in the town of Gondar in the heart of Falasha country, was nineteen in 1972 when she made her way to Israel with help from her sister, Rachel. Rachel, who had been one of twenty-seven young Falashas brought to the Kfar Btaya youth village in the 1950s and who stayed on to become a nurse, was able, with great difficulty, to obtain a tourist visa for her sister.

Esther finished an intensive five-month Hebrew language course at a kibbutz near Ashkelon and then went to live with her sister in Herzliya—not the beachside town of villas and luxury hotels, but the Herzliya of drab gray housing projects on the other side of the highway. She wasn't at all sure that she liked Israel, and actually planned to go back to Ethiopia after a few months, where most of her family remained. But her attitude changed. Gradually, she started to feel at home. Before too long she thought that "nowhere else *could* be home."

Having no money for study, she went to work in a light-bulb factory. The pay for this gruelling labor was $125 a month (fourteen years later, thousands of the new immigrants from Ethiopia were working for similar coolie wages, about $140 a month for a fifty-five hour week). After work every day, Esther, who had had two years of secondary school in Ethiopia, took evening classes. She became obsessed with learning and with earning enough money along with Rachel to bring their parents and remaining seven brothers and sisters to Israel—the classic immigrant experience.

After completing night school, she got a second job as a waitress in order to supplement her factory pay. She had learned that the situation of the Jews in Ethiopia was worsening. A massacre of about forty Falashas had occurred. Drought and famine had left two hundred thousand people dead in the provinces adjoining the Gondar area, where over half her community lived. The absentee landlords of Haile Selassie's feudal regime were increasing their demands on their tenant farmers, including the Falashas. Esther's reaction was to subordinate everything in her life to making money to rescue her family. Every weekday, she left for the factory before dawn and worked until late afternoon. After a one-hour break, she would take the bus to the Daniel Tower Hotel on the Herzliya seashore and work in the hotel's American-style coffee shop from six o'clock to midnight.

Esther became an activist in the small Ethiopian community (there were about a hundred and fifty Ethiopian Jews in Israel in the mid-seventies), trying to raise the consciousness of Israelis and Jews everywhere about the plight of the Ethiopian Jews. It was not easy. The Falashas were not hot copy for the newspapers, and very few people were interested. But eventually she and Rachel were able to bring over most of the members of the family.

In 1976 Esther Wube married a fellow employee at the hotel, Aaron Hollander, a skilled maintenance worker whose parents had come to Israel from Poland in the 1950s. At first his parents were adamantly opposed to their son marrying a black. For their part, some of Esther's Ethiopian relatives and friends told her she was crazy to marry a Pole. However, acceptance from both sides was not long in coming and was reinforced with the birth of the couple's two children.

In the next few years, Esther started to work in the accounts department at the Daniel Towers, eventually rising to an executive position as department manager. In the summer of 1985, she was selected as one of Israel's representatives at the world conference on women, which convened in Nairobi. On this, her first return to Africa, she became the target of vicious verbal and physical attacks by some Arab delegates at the convention. At one workshop, when an Iraqi accused Israel of being responsible for the Iran-Iraq war, the diminutive Israeli delegate shot up from her seat and shouted, "You're lying! You're killing yourselves in your own war." A fracas followed, in which she was pushed and shoved by Arab women, and only the presence of an Israeli security man saved her from further harm. Throughout the conference, Esther was regarded by the other Israeli women on the team as a guiding light.

The family members whom she helped bring to Israel became some of the leaders of the protest strikes against the Chief Rabbinate. But Esther tried to stay independent and objective about the contentious issues still facing her community. She volunteered her services whenever she could find free time from the demands of her job and family. She remained critical of government planners who are ignorant of the special problems faced by the Ethiopians. "The bureaucrats are always pressuring the new immigrants, and the people have lost all faith in the Jewish Agency," she said. The tendency to concentrate immigrants in a small number of locations means that "many Ethiopians are afraid to leave the absorption center, to interact with Israelis."

That most of the immigrants can find only menial employment bothered her less. "What's wrong with sweeping the streets? That's what many of the immigrants from Europe had to do in the 1950s."

She described the overall absorption of the young people, many of whom are in top army units, as "magnificent." "They learn Hebrew very quickly, and they somehow overcome the prejudice that they encounter. And as far as the rabbinate goes, well, all the people of Israel now realize the truth about that particular institution: all politics and no religion.

"But the overall situation is much better than it was. The immigrants are getting good guidance; they're relating to the country, and the country is relating to them. Many problems have been solved."

But despite her basic optimism, she never stopped being outspokenly critical of the government at important junctures in the story of the migration of "the lost tribe of Dan." More can be done, she has always believed, to reunite the Jews still in Ethiopia with their families in Israel.

Knesset member Tamar Eshel, a women's activist who has served as leader of the Public Council for Ethiopian Jews, has singled out Esther Wube Hollander as a person whose "example can be a message of hope to millions of refugees of how people can rebuild themselves, how people of different cultures and backgrounds can live together, creating a new society where a woman can find her rightful place." Jews outside of Israel have also recognized Esther's contribution to her people. Canada's largest Zionist organization, Hadassah-Wizo, has established a scholarship fund in her name.

For every such success story, of course, there are many failures that go unrecorded or unnoticed. But as another veteran leader of Israel's Ethiopian community put it, "We can teach our people a great deal, spare them a lot of the pain that we suffered trying to win acceptance in Israeli society. And it's a different Israel now as far as we're concerned—the attitude toward us is much more positive. We are survivors."

XIX

J EWISH SAGES have long considered the ideas of national freedom, restoration and ascension—immigration to Israel—as a prelude to the Redemption. The story of Exodus is etched in the Jewish soul, and most Israelis, for all their complaining about newcomers, basically believe that the ingathering of Jews is the lifeblood of the nation.

But there is a persistent feeling that Israeli political leaders only pay lip service to this notion. It sometimes seems that the immigrants get here in spite of, rather than because of, the government's efforts. And many Israelis do not believe in the "lifeblood" notion at all, or they feel that the Arab-Israel conflict, our intense intracommunal problems and relations with the Arab minority must take priority on the national agenda.

Without question, some Israeli officials are fiercely committed to bringing Jews, especially those in countries of distress, to their ancestral homeland. Israel has risen to the occasion when the call comes—as with the ingathering of 100,000 European Jewish survivors in the first days of the state, the Magic Carpet airlift of Yemenite Jews in the early 1950s (which the Yemenite Israelis still call "the time of our redemption"), the mass airlift of 121,000 Iraqi Jews in 1950 and 88,000 Rumanian Jews around the same time, the reception of over 150,000 Russian Jews in the 1970s, and the Operation Moses rescue of thousands of Ethiopian Jews from one of the remotest corners of the earth in the first half of the 1980s.

In retrospect, it seems remarkable that Israel was able to absorb such large numbers of immigrants when it was still struggling in its infancy, while the far richer, rapidly industrializing Israel of today seems to have just as many problems handling only a fraction of the number of immigrants, and at enormous expenditure: the estimated cost of absorbing 15,000 Ethiopian immigrants over a five-year period was $300 million.

The times have changed in other ways, too. Some observers feel that, in the postdesert generation, fewer Israelis really care that large numbers of Jews in the "lands of distress" are still waiting for their Passover. The whole immigration issue appears to have been relegated to the province of religious Israelis, and to the wealthy and sentimental Jews of the United States, England, France and other Western countries. Some kibbutzim do get more involved in issues such as Soviet Jewry; and there will always be secular, veteran Zionist activists trying to keep the old traditions alive, like Lova Eliav (former Labor Party leader, writer and promoter of humanist values) or Abie Nathan (owner of the "Peace Ship") or the much younger Dedi Zucker, the center-left parliamentarian who believes his constituency does not pay enough attention to nationalist concerns. But they seem to be part of an ever-shrinking minority.

In contrast, most observant Jews in Israel and all over the world continue to believe that the time will come when even the safest and most comfortable Jews of other lands will join in an inevitable reunion in their homeland. Until that messianic flood, there will always be Jews who feel that it is essential to prod the Israeli government and world Jewish leaders to rescue those of their people who are still in bondage.

THE REDEMPTION FROM EGYPT, and the final Redemption, are part of the same historical process, wrote Rabbi Avraham Yitzhak Hacohen Kook, perhaps the leading spiritual figure in modern Judaism. The "mighty hand and outstretched arm" which brought the Jews out of Egypt was evident throughout the ages, Kook believed. He said that the Jews who listened could hear the humming of the wheels of deliverance as the Lord gathered together the dispersed of Israel.

Many believing Jews feel that the mostly secular movement called Zionism was and is part of this historical process; and in every immigrant from every country of the earth they see the beginnings of the fulfillment of Isaiah's prophecy (11:11–12): "And it shall come to pass in that/day,/That the Lord will set His hand/again the second time/[the first was the Exodus] To recover the remnant of His/people,/That shall remain from Assyria,/and from Egypt,/And from Pathros [Upper Egypt/Sudan], and from/Cush [Ethiopia], and from Elam [Kuzestan, between Iran and Iraq],/and from Shinar, [Babylonia, today's Iraq] and from/Hamath, [Syria] and from the islands/of the sea [the Mediterranean lands]." God will "assemble the dispersed/of Israel,/And gather together the scattered/ of Judah/From the four corners of the/earth."

Since the return to the land of Israel began a century ago, and especially since the state burst into being in 1948, this ancient prophecy has appeared to be coming true. It is not an exile's wild dream of hope: a walk down any street in Israel will inform the most casual of observers of that verity. But it seems particularly true when one walks through a bustling Israeli absorption center, such as in sprawling Gilo, a beehive of ugly modular apartments thrown together on a windy Jerusalem hill. Redolent of cooking smells from dozens of little kitchens, the center swarms with families from the four corners: Syria and Iran, Soviet Georgia and France, Ethiopia and Morocco, the U.S. and Kurdistan, Argentina and South Africa.

Gilo, and scores of other such absorption centers, serve as way stations for immigrants, a place where they can learn Hebrew for up to a year, live rent-free and receive subsidies for food and other expenses. Often, they go all but unnoticed by the neighbors who surround them, people too busy hustling for a living, discussing cinema and Hebrew literature at wine and cheese parties, cursing soccer players, worrying about the children's schooling or listening to the latest "King of the Cassettas" rendering his Mideast-Greek musical lament. But from time to time, "Passover" hits nearly every Israeli Jew—not just the religious and the nationalists—engendering a positive response: when the news broke about the airlift of the Ethiopians, even the most ignorant and racist elements of the population, such as the taxi drivers, were at least momentarily thrilled.

According to government statistics, the total number of new immigrants to Israel in recent years has averaged about fifteen thousand per annum—probably less than the number of veteran Israelis who are emigrating. Nevertheless, as Israel entered its fortieth year, and in the light of glasnost, there were especially heightened expectations for the release of thousands of Soviet Jews, besides the well-known leaders of the refusenik movement. This was especially important because Israel sees the two million Soviet Jews as its last main source of immigration. Moshe Arens, a former defense minister and a leader of the Likud, termed it "the last reservoir from which Israel can draw sustenance. We need Jews. It is our most important issue, our very future...And we're not doing all that we could."

THE REDEEMED OF THE LORD do not always come singing unto Zion. There are angry, often vicious splits among most immigrant groups—whether Russian, Ethiopian, Iranian. Rivals sometimes slander each other, hinting that their counterpart has a KGB background or is mentally unstable. One leader of the religious revival among Soviet Jews, Ilya (Eliahu) Essas, who arrived in Jerusalem in 1986, is widely mistrusted by the broader activist movement, partly because of his close links to World Jewish Congress president Edgar Bronfman and the establishment American Jewish leadership, as personified by Conference of Presidents leader Morris Abram. Bronfman and Abram traveled to Moscow in early 1987, and Abram called for the "redemption of the Jews who stay in Russia" in addition to massive emigration. But the activists feel that there should be no diffusion of goals; world Jewry should focus all its energies on the emigration movement, and not on trying to improve conditions for Jewish religion or culture in the USSR.

To many in the movement, Essas simply lacks the credibility of Sharansky or Vladimir Slepak, Nudel or Yosef Begun. But when I spoke with him, as he was holding forth at a dinner at the King David Hotel, he also appeared to agree with the activists in focusing on the emigration issue, which for him meant also attracting more American Jews to Israel. "Exodus means a very real thing in every generation," he said. "Also in this one. American Jews shouldn't rely on their seeming security, the tranquility of their situation. Exodus is a complex of spiritual and physical factors. We aren't free until we are in Eretz Israel—and there, too, we must work on ourselves.''

His view had its antecedents; it is classical Zionism, whether of the secular or religious variety. Rabbi Yehuda Alkalai, a spiritual founder of modern Zionism, wrote in 1843 that ''we, as a people, are properly called Israel only in the land of Israel.'' Redemption would come slowly, and not through miracles but through the efforts of the Jews themselves, who would organize, learn Hebrew, choose leaders ''and leave the lands of exile.''

That is what increasing numbers of Jews have been doing over the last century, a very fast time frame in terms of Jewish history. Of course, it was not fast enough for millions of European Jews, and that apocalyptic experience will never leave the Jewish consciousness. No matter how inappropriate it might be to compare the situation of the Jews of any country today to the Jews of Nazi Europe, the fears of Iranian, Ethiopian or Russian Jews are not difficult to understand.

When some eight thousand Ethiopian Jews were rescued in 1984–1985 from the Sudanese camps where three thousand of their family members died, most of the survivors translated their salvation in terms of the Exodus and the final redemption. ''These are the things of Moses,'' one of their elders said in wonderment at the time. According to Rahamim Elazar, a veteran leader of the Ethiopian community in Israel, because only half the Ethiopian Jews were rescued in Operation Moses, ''our task is not finished. *Aliya* is a major commandment, and our people feel that very strongly. They came here, even on foot.'' They would not stop pushing until their government gave ''top priority to the problem of the divided families.'' Once the remaining Jews were brought to Israel, it would truly be possible to speak about Redemption, he said.

The year leading up to Israel's fortieth anniversary was also a momentous period for the remaining thirty thousand Jews of Iran, with a few thousand managing to buy their way out. In the years immediately after Khomeini's revolution, when there were 100,000 Jews in Iran, only a handful opted for Israel. Many of them were wealthy, and they preferred Beverly Hills to Beersheba, especially after hundreds of them who had put their capital into Persian carpets were discouraged from coming to Israel by suddenly prohibitive Israeli taxes on imported carpets. But Israel put the blame for the dropout rate on the Iranian Jews themselves, and said that their attitude had adversely influenced some of those Israelis who work, in the shadows, for Jewish emigration. A high-ranking government official told me, ''After so many Iranian Jews rejected Israel, there was a definite loss of enthusiasm about helping them.'' This source also said that at no time in the Irangate arms deals with Iran did Israel raise the issue of Jewish emigration with the Khomeini regime.

Yet despite the past history, a growing number of Iranian Jews seek to make their home in Israel. Most of the remaining Jews in Iran are from a different stratum from the earlier emigrants—the lower middle-class and working class, and ''a large number of them apparently have a preference for Israel,'' according to Tel Aviv University professor David Menashe, an Israeli who was born in Iran.

''We are not doing much to bring them here, or to absorb them when they get here,'' said Menashe, who formerly headed the Association of Iranian Jews in Israel. ''The Jewish Agency and the Absorption Ministry don't have a proper policy. And unfortunately, the Iranian community here is weak and divided—they don't do much to help their brothers to come here.'' Nevertheless, a sizable number, many of them young, began arriving in Israel in 1987; and suddenly, Farsi could be heard at absorption centers around the country.

Despite the fact that the Gulf War made a sizable Jewish exodus more difficult, it could be done with the will and the money. But in fact, a large segment of the thirty thousand remaining Jews prefers to stay in the land where Daniel was cast in the lions' den and the handwriting appeared on the wall—''the days of your kingdom are numbered.'' The reluctance of many Iranian Jews to leave that country has a precedent: 2,500 years ago, when the Persians conquered Babylon, a large number of Jews declined the chance to return to Jerusalem. There is even a much older precedent: the Jews who did not wish to join the Exodus, preferring the fleshpots of Egypt.

Professor Menashe feared for the fate of the community in post-Khomeini Iran. ''There were twelve executions of Jews in recent years, and this is horrible; but tens of thousands of Moslems were executed at the same time, and the persecution must be kept in perspective. But it is really dangerous for the Jews to stay there. The revolution is not over, and in the turmoil and economic unrest that is coming, the Jews may become victims.''

Menashe said that the Iranian immigrants who came to Israel forty years ago are still the butt of jokes, and that like most other immigrant groups—the Indians, the Georgians, the Moroccans—they have traveled a tough road. As Golda Meir said, ''Israelis love immigration but not immigrants.''

Though most immigrants to Israel from the lands of distress seem to know all about the problems and the roughness of the road, they still come. Haim Burshtein, a young penitent Jew who had been a thorn in the side of the Leningrad KGB before they finally let him and his family go in early 1987, watched the sun going down over the Judean Hills from his bungalow in Mevasseret Zion ("Harbinger of Zion"), a big absorption center near Jerusalem. "Here at Mevasseret," he told a visitor, "I see the ingathering of the exiles. It is wonderful to be able to celebrate our first Passover in freedom. But we cannot rest until freedom has been realized for other people, too." Despite all the political bickering and intramural hatred, the long mysterious Exodus goes on.

Richard T. Nowitz

XX

DAILY LIFE IN ISRAEL is the greatest pleasure and a thousand pains, a battle between love and hate, a comedy and a madness, an illusion and a play of passion. Sometimes, it all seems like an idyllic Jerusalem courtyard of olive, pistachio and fruit trees, with black asps concealed in the sinewy bark—all within a few minutes walk from the massive stone walls of the Old City...

On a crystal-clear Indian Summer day in late November, the trees in the courtyard of Haim and Molly Hilbi (not their real names), in an old quarter of new Jerusalem, the valley of Rephaim (Emek Refaim), are only half naked from the first rains, but every cool breeze on this sunny autumn day sweeps hundreds of crinkly leaves from the branches onto the flagstone and greenery of the yard. Two other families share the big, divided house, built in the heart of the little valley by Greek merchants a century ago on the edge of the German Colony, which was started by a Christian messianic sect in the 1880s. (The grandchildren of these Germans became Nazis and were shipped back to Hitler by the British army.)

The Hilbis, secular people who immigrated from Canada in the early 1970s, bought two small rooms in the house in 1976 for $29,000 and eventually increased their space to five small rooms by building up and digging down. Haim, an unemployed journalist, believes his property will be worth a million dollars by 1993, as the millennial fever builds. Another family, wealthy young religious immigrants from the United States, bought three rooms in the house for $75,000 in 1983 and, with another $70,000 or so, turned it into a three-floor, six-room cottage, worth at least $350,000 in 1988.

The building has an interesting history. The family from the U.S. replaced an immigrant family from Yugoslavia, a couple of partisan fighters who, after the war, emigrated to Israel and eked out a living by sewing clothes or working in construction. The Hilbis replaced a Moroccan family, a mother and her twin children, after the mother committed suicide in the house. Her grown daughters, who were not on speaking terms with one another, were glad to sell the apartment.

In the wake of the 1948 war, the neighborhood was inhabited by poor immigrants, many of them European Sephardim; Jews from the Kurdi regions of Turkey, Syria and Iraq; and a few Ashkenazi Holocaust survivors. Sometimes, they hated each other as passionately as the twin sisters from Morocco, whose husbands handled the sale of the dead mother's apartment.

Because of some slight in the distant past, the Bulgarian family who lived on the east side of the big house did not talk to the Yugoslavian family on the south side of the house or the Kurdi family on the bottom floor of the house on the opposite side of the courtyard. People in a third house on the south side of the courtyard—families of superior-feeling immigrants from Switzerland and Shanghai—also would have nothing to do with the Kurdish family, with its ten desperate people crowded into three small rooms. Another Bulgarian family, living on top of the Kurds, did not get along with their Oriental brethren either. The matriarch of this small family had a sophisticated theatrical background, spoke many languages, read *Elle* and *Vogue* and displayed Picasso prints on her walls—a Sephardic snob, the Kurds called her, one who saw life "with a narrow eye." Neutral observers could understand why she hated her neighbors, and vice versa. She was cursed, in any case, with a forty-year-old daughter who had returned to her mother after a vicious divorce. She was a psychologist, a loon who never emerged from her room in daylight, and made her seventy-five-year-old mother's twilight years into hell on earth.

For a decade, the Hilbis got along well with most of their squabbling neighbors, except for a French nun, the daughter of a Jewish mother, who bought a basement room in the house and who was regarded by her Jewish neighbors, except for the Kurds, as cold and calculating—and not at all nice, despite her fixed smile. There had been many disputes among them over blocked sewage pipes, who was responsible for cleaning the passageway, and other issues.

In 1987 war broke out between the Hilbis and one of the eight Kurdi children, the one who inherited her family's house and was raising a much smaller family of her own in the three rooms. This neighbor—by most standards, slothful, ignorant and superstitious—resented the Canadian immigrants, and she let it eat away at her. Her children threw large stones at the Canadian children, and at the child of another nearby neighbor.

Ever since the younger people moved in around the courtyard, it had been relatively free of the hatred that the 1948 families had felt for one another. But the Kurdi woman and the Bulgarian intellectual had never gotten along; and now, the Kurdi, married to a Basque who had converted to Judaism, had declared war on the Hilbis as well. Her *causus belli* was a house key. For years, the Hilbis had kept a spare key to their door in her house, in case one of their five children was locked out. One hot September day, the Kurdi woman, Yaffa ("beautiful," one of those unfortunate Hebrew names like "lucky" or "gentle" that never seem to fit the person so named at birth), shrieked at Mrs. Hilbi that she was sick and tired of being at "the beck and call" of the Hilbis' irresponsible children, and gave her the key back, spiced with some rude remark.

The real cause for Yaffa's anger was her pregnancy with an unplanned third child, and the need for her, because of the general financial crunch, to start a nursery school in her home for five children. This situation had brought her to the verge of hysteria—she did not like children very much, and she liked work even less. So she spread her bile around the beautiful courtyard, which visitors thought so idyllic. Her children threw more stones at the Hilbis' kids and rubbish on the Hilbis' patch of land. Other neighbors, hearing the angry exchanges, tried their best to ignore the situation, but as the venom spewed forth, there was a definite feeling that paradise had been violated. It had reached an absurd point, a page out of Thomas Berger's *The Feud*. There was nothing funny about it. Yaffa and the Hilbis projected pure hatred every time they passed each other, and the kids were constantly at war.

JUST AFTER DAWN ON THIS NOVEMBER DAY, Haim walked the family dog down Hazfira ("the Clarion") Street, stopping at Adi's, the local grocer, to buy milk, cottage cheese and rolls for the kids' lunch. Adi, who opens at 5:30 A.M. and closes at 8:00 P.M., introduced Haim to the couple who would be running the small *makolet* for the next month or so, while Adi and his family took it easy in Tiberias, and maybe in France for a week or more. Adi made it clear to Haim that his replacements would, as he always did, act as bankers, so that Haim could always cash his checks for a hundred shekels or more above his purchase, one of the reasons why Haim patronized the easygoing Adi, whose shelves sometimes displayed mice droppings and whose cottage cheese was often spoiled, and did not limit himself to the cheaper and far bigger minimarket on the main steet a block away. But the minimarket was also an inviting place. It was run by two men in their early thirties: Dudu, a burly bear of an Ashkenazi man, and Eli, an extremely friendly Jew of Moroccan origin, both of whom worked hard from 6 A.M. to 7:30 P.M., hoping to make enough in five years to retire, if they did not die of heart attacks first.

Their workers were excellent, a good team of two young Israeli Arab men and three Israeli Jewish women. During the Palestinian uprising, Eli drove his Arab workers home every night. They were stopped several times. One army officer refused to believe that Ahmed had not taken part in a stone-throwing incident in Abu Tor, the mixed Jerusalem neighborhood, on the previous night after 10:00 P.M. Eli assured him that Ahmed worked like a dog thirteen hours a day, and was not about to go out late at night to join the *shababa*, the unemployed youths who have led the uprising. Eli and the officer argued for an hour before Ahmed was finally allowed to go home. Both Eli and Ahmed told Haim Hilbi that everything was going to be all right, "Everything is going to be all right," they both said.

MOLLY HILBI GOT UP LATE—6.15 A.M.—made herself a cup of filter coffee, read the front page of the paper, and then set about waking the kids and getting them dressed for school. Once Haim arrived with the rolls, Molly made the kids' "ten o'clock snack" (*arohat eser*), stuffed them in their bulging school backpacks, and served breakfast. Haim put on the Army radio station, whose genial breakfast host has become an Israeli institution. Alex Ansky's homey comments on what is in the morning papers are interspersed with good music and "Good Morning Israel" banter. The phone rang—a crossed line. The Hilbis' eldest daughter, nine-year-old Carmit, listened to the conversation between two women and giggled. One of the women heard her and demanded, "Hang up!" Carmit said, "Then send me a cake." "What kind do you want?" one of the women asked. "Chocolate." "I'll send you two." In order to clear the line, all parties agreed to hang up at the same time. It worked. Haim picked up the phone and called Mr. Cohen, beseeching the old man once again to come patch the leaky red-tile roof before the second rains came.

As every newcomer to Israel soon finds out, getting decent service is a problem. It is very difficult to find someone who will really fix an appliance or unplug a blocked sewer or repair the washing machine. The country is full of individuals who buy a wrench and pass themselves off as plumbers. "Contractors," with their teams of Arab workers, will promise to finish a job in two months at such-and-such a price, but five months later, with the price doubled and rising, the job will still not be completed, and the houseowner will be beside himself. (From my own experience, I would advise one never to hire a playwright moonlighting as a "contractor.") The Hilbis, because of differences with the neighbors, once tried to get a private water meter installed—a seemingly simple task. But after many exhausting visits to the Kafkaesque water company, the payment of a big deposit and the near-destruction of their kitchen by a plumber looking for a nonexistent pipe, they just gave up. On the other hand, the roof maven, Mr. Cohen, never overcharged them and sometimes even managed to stop the leaks. But his wife would not always let him out of their house on Emek Refaim street, fearing that he was too old, at seventy-four, to continue this sort of work. He was in great demand, since he was intimately acquainted with most of the temperamental tile roofs, as well as the oft-flooded basements in the low-lying neighborhood.

When Mr. Cohen showed up later that day, Hilbi watched the spidery old man in the greasy old cap scramble up a home-built ladder to the heights, a second-story man, a Willie "the Actor" Sutton look-alike vaulting onto the roof. Cohen replaced two of the fragile tiles, scampered back down and charged Hilbi the equivalent of nine dollars, materials included. Some roof repairers, as likely to break a dozen tiles while fixing two others, would charge ten or twenty times as much. God bless Mr. Cohen.

Hilbi had just read, in a consumer-protection column in a local newspaper, what struck him as a classic example of the syndrome of uncompleted jobs or jobs poorly done, an instance that every Israeli could swear happened to him at least five times a year. In February 1986, a couple ordered a large bedroom cupboard from Yehuda, a private carpenter, and made a down payment. It was to have been completed and installed in their home no later than May 20 (the simplest order often takes three months to fill), but after six months, Yehuda had still not completed the job, and told the couple that he had no workers. They found a worker willing to help Yehuda; together they installed a half-completed closet. More time passed. Yehuda promised he would finish the job.

Thirteen months later, the couple wrote to the consumer columnist, who approached Yehuda. He should have been guiltridden, but he spoke as if the problem were someone else's fault, employing a philosophy that the customer is always wrong. Yehuda said that he really wanted to complete the job but had a bad back and no workers to help him. More months passed. Finally, the couple took the case to small claims court. The judge ordered Yehuda—who did not appear in court—to pay the couple the equivalent of $1,500. The couple was advised to hand-deliver a copy of the judgment to Yehuda and to tell them that he had a week to pay up, or else. When this produced no results, the couple filed a complaint with the government agency that executes court judgments. Weeks went by. There was no word from Yehuda. Eventually, the couple was told, the file would be passed on to the police. In any case, they would never see their money again, and they would have to find another way to complete that cupboard.

Of course, there are good, honest craftsmen, too; people like Mr. Cohen, who never show greed. Born in Jerusalem, he had always been a worker, one of those living on the edge of poverty. Hilbi, who had learned much about the neighborhood through the years, greatly appreciated the wiry, wizened Mr. Cohen.

In the days of old, the valley where these people, and I, live was lush with fields and plantations. During the harvest seasons, the peasants gathered their crops and walked to the Temple about a mile away to offer a tithe and thank the Lord. The poor, people like Mr. Cohen, came after them to pick the grain that had escaped the attention of the farmers, as God rustled the tops of the mulberry trees. To this day, "Like a harvestman in the valley of Rephaim" is a Hebrew expression for a poor man who here and there ekes out a living, replacing roof tiles...

Richard T. Nowitz

XXI

THE SETTING, at least, was perfect.

When Bob Dylan, pulse of the universe, began his encore at the foot of Mount Zion on the eve of Israel's year-long fortieth birthday party, he started playing his best-known Jesus song; and God pulled the plug on an otherwise successful evening. The electricity shorted "Slow Train Coming," and the concert that began with a bang ended with mutterings about typical Israeli inefficiency.

To his fans, Dylan is undoubtedly an angel and a genius, Rimbaud and Shakespeare, harbinger of redemption; and the gods obviously love him. But the ancient people he was born into—not the Hell's Angels and Jack Kerouac—has this problem about Jesus, and not a few bad memories from the two thousand years of hate and persecution by those who believe in false Messiahs.

In any case, most Israelis, even artists and intellectuals who have lived in America, did not appear very interested in Dylan's first public appearance in Israel. "This is for you guys from America," an angry young

Israeli poet told me at the Jerusalem municipal swimming pool. The poet, perfectly bilingual, knew that many of the best writers and poets in the English-speaking world put Dylan in a class by himself. But "his work doesn't speak to us." Since Dylan unquestionably has universal appeal, I wondered if this Israeli distance might have a particular ancestry. Two of the greatest American poets, Dylan and Allen Ginsberg, are both Jews whose travels eventually brought them to apostasy, to pantheism or Christianity, a journey that does not wash well in the renascent Jewish homeland.

But for a small number of Israelis, Dylan's appearance, just as the Jewish new year began, did generate the kind of excitement that he has sparked around the world for over a quarter of a century. They were joined by some of the people who loved Dylan from the sixties, those who, like him, felt that they "saw and not just heard that the flying saucer had landed."

In Jerusalem, Dylan was playing at a site associated with Pontius Pilate—the rock quarry turned amphitheater known as the Sultan's Pool—beneath an outsized full moon hanging right on top of Mount Zion, which is really just a little hill dominated by the crosses of Christian churches. I took my harmonica-playing eleven-year-old son to see him there, fifteen minutes' walk from our house.

Dylan's appearance, a few yards from the prophesied site of the Last Judgement, was awaited by an audience of nine thousand, with another couple thousand nonpaying fans observing from the bushy terraces snaking up Mount Zion on one side of the valley and the posh Yemin Moshe neighborhood on the other. His Jerusalem appearance was preceded by a concert in Tel Aviv two days earlier, before forty thousand people (or 1 percent of the nation's population). The Hebrew-language newspapers panned his Tel Aviv performance, complaining about his scratchy voice and "nasal monotone," with *Hadashot* terming the whole evening "B-O-R-I-N-G."

The gossipy dailies, whose hungry reporters could not get near Dylan, said he was a rude egomaniac, that he stood up Shimon Peres and Teddy Kollek, that he hardly acknowledged the room-service waiter, and that he committed various other terrible crimes against all classes of society—in short, that he was a snob. Dylan refused to give any interviews during his brief Israel tour, but the papers were full of quotes from people who said they knew him back in Minnesota or Greenwich Village. The talented TV entertainer Gidi Gov wrote a very funny satire on the journalists who had staked out Dylan's hotel and interviewed the room-service waiter. A few papers mentioned Dylan's Jewish roots and his identification with Israel.

The only Israeli periodical that got a word out of Dylan was an English-language right-wing monthly, *Counterpoint*. When asked why he didn't meet either Kollek or Peres, Dylan answered: "How come I never met with Mayor Daley or President Nixon?" His interlocutor also wanted to know why Dylan didn't sing one of his first songs, "Talking Hava Nagilah." Dylan said, "I started singing it when I first heard about this tour, and I've been singing it ever since. I'm singing it right now. You just can't hear me."

In the U.S., Dylan has sometimes been viciously attacked for being a "Zionist." Supposedly, he wrote "Neighborhood Bully" in defense of Israel when it was being villified for the Lebanon war. He has visited Israel many times and brought his son to the Western Wall for the boy's bar mitzvah ceremony. Quoted as saying that Israel is one of the few places left in the world where life has any meaning, he is said to own an apartment in Jerusalem. He apparently became involved with the Lubavitcher Hasidic sect in Brooklyn after the ardor of his conversion to Christianity cooled. But reports of this mercurial artist's "return to the Jewish fold" might be premature.

MOUNT ZION WAS CRAWLING WITH PEOPLE who did not have to buy a ticket (at twenty dollars each) yet had just as good seats as the paying audience, who were gathered inside the amphitheater beneath a stage decked with huge speakers and banks of drums and keyboards, all connected to some mysterious electronic source.

Tom Petty and the Heartbreakers, Dylan's backup group, warmed up the audience from beneath this tower of electronic musical equipment, which looked like some kind of rock-age Golem. Then Dylan came on, opening with "The Times They Are A'Changing." He looked like a beggar of Jerusalem, very ragged indeed, with long hair and fuzzy beard, singing one of his immortal songs. In the early part of the evening the full moon rose effortlessly, haloing the stage.

The high point of the concert, for some at least, was Dylan's rendition of his classic "Like a Rolling Stone." When the crowd joined in, on the line "no direction home," I broke into uncontrolled weeping, clutching my son and crying like a baby. Dylan's voice reverberated, a tremelo, a complete unknown. "Like a Rolling Stone" brought a great roar from the crowd, and he coasted from that peak. Mingling new songs with the old, he sang from the heart; he was playing to an audience that related the lyricist and his guitar to King David and his harp, and not a few of those listening to him had always thought that Bob Dylan was the spirit of Elijah, if not the Messiah himself.

Black singers dressed in white robes accompanied him on his last songs.

And as he approached the end of the program, he sang, "You gonna need to serve someone—it may be the Devil or it may be the Lord, but you're going to need to serve somebody." But how many Lords? Christians use the word Lord to refer both to God and to the Jew they regard as the Messiah. To Jews, this is polytheism. An old acquaintance of Dylan's, Tuvia Haim Ariel, a repentant Jew, said that Dylan is a Jew representing a country that is mostly Christian. "The first and only Jewish hero that he heard of until the age of ten was J. C., King of the Jews."

Dylan had obviously taken his audience into consideration. Knowing it would be offended if he included many songs from his Christian-convert period, he saved Jesus for last. My boy was falling asleep and had school the next day, so we walked out just before the end and went over to the nearby Cinematheque and its cafe for hot chocolate and apple pie, where we could hear Dylan as clearly as from inside the quarry-amphitheater. We heard him begin his encore, which was suddenly squelched by the power failure, and we watched as the bewildered but mostly satisfied crowd poured out of Sultan's Pool.

AMONG THE NEGATIVE REACTIONS to Dylan's Israel performances was that of Shalom Hanoch, one of the country's leading folk-rock singers who has tried his best to look just like Bob Dylan, while writing puerile songs like *"Mashiach lo ba"* ("The Messiah doesn't come.") He told an interviewer that he was disappointed, that he had "lost patience" with Dylan (for tarrying so?). Rivka Zohar, another popular singer who had recently returned from a heroin-addicted life in New York, also said that she was disappointed. But Shlomo Artzi, one of Israel's most popular "serious" singers, said that he had a great time listening to Dylan. Journalist Yuval Levi also had good things to say about Dylan in a local Jerusalem newspaper, *Kol Ha'Ir*. And songwriter and TV compere Ehud Manor, probably Israel's leading expert on popular music, described the concert as a very emotional experience for him. He said that those who expected to see a Madonna-type were necessarily disappointed. Dylan, he added, was a "suffering, interesting man," a performer whose music and lyrics have helped to change the world.

In any case, the powerful force called Bob Dylan, a completely American product, has a special attachment to Israel that appears to be very strong. And he is unlikely ever to forget his appearance in Jerusalem, a city that has long suffered a bad press for how it treats prophets.

Israel Press and Photo Agency

XXII

SUCK-CESS, ISRAELI-STYLE, may spell exile, wealth, sex, trade in death, power and dubious fame. For my generation—people as old or a little older than the state—success has a different ring to what it meant to the generation of Moshe Dayan and Yigal Yadin. One story in this context, about a man who transformed his arms profits into the ploughshares of cinema art, provides insight into the wider phenomenon. But we should view it through the special lens that shows there is nothing more feeble than this species, which believes it will never suffer evil as long as the gods provide success and man's work flourishes.

For years, Arnon Milchan's conscience tortured him—not because of the fortune he made in arms deals, but because of his role as the mysterious Israeli moneyman in what became known as South Africa's "Muldergate" scandal. The manipulation of "information" by authoritarian forces, working on a grand scale in the 1970s, he told me, taught him a life lesson. We were sipping daquiris at a luxurious hotel in Taba, a small slice of Eden on the Egyptian-Israeli border, and his statement reminded me of the clear enunciation of that idea in *Brazil*, one of the better films he had produced.

Newsweek always favored the adjective "shadowy" when reporting on Milchan, and the media have often portrayed him as a "mysterious arms merchant," or elusive "Israeli millionaire-playboy." He is close to major political leaders, famous actors and artists. His name has been linked to the alleged smuggling of atomic timers—known as krytrons—from the U.S. to Israel, and he acknowledges that it was he who laundered vast sums of money in the information scandal that rocked the South African government in 1979. (He also drove the getaway car in a scene in *Once Upon a Time in America*, Sergio Leone's champagne-flight spectacular about Jewish gangsters—another Milchan production.)

Milchan has led a life that seems tailor-made for the movies. Before I met him, I imagined a Fitzgerald character, a Jay Gatsby or Monroe Stahr. Or someone cut from the same cloth as the enigmatic figures in a Le Carré novel. But Milchan surprises—the mystery man turned out to be an exceedingly personable, warm spirit, exuding boyish charm alongside the expected dynamism. Yet he is, no doubt, as cunning as they come, and behind the *hamische* but sleek exterior, the waters run deep indeed.

A healthy-looking sabra in his early forties, Milchan lives in Paris but spends several months in Israel and the U.S. every year. Although he made his first fortune in agricultural chemicals and now distances himself from the weapons trade, he undoubtedly continues to be well acquainted with that shady, big-bucks world. But in recent years, the shadowland that has come to obsess him is the world of film, and he has proved to be an adept cinema businessman, who apparently also possesses rare artistic sensitivities. He is seen by some as a sophisticated counterweight to another Israeli who splashed in Hollywood, Menachem Golan.

"The big question is, where does Milchan really get his money from?" one knowledgeable Tel Aviv journalist has said. Another Israeli journalist said it is impossible to know how much Milchan makes, but "it's in the tens of millions per year."

CONTRARY TO POPULAR BELIEF IN ISRAEL, Arnon Milchan did not inherit his fortune. Although he is a tenth-generation Israeli (the Gavriellis on his maternal side, the Shlanks on the paternal), and therefore well plugged in to the Old Boy network, he built his fortune from scratch. But he did come from a well-off, supportive family, owners of citrus plantations and prosperous small businesses.

Milchan's parents sent their only son to England for his education, which included his first exposure to anti-Semitism and expulsion from school at Hertfordshire. He later attended City of London College, the London School of Economics and the University of Geneva, but his main interest at that time was soccer. He returned to Israel and became a sports instructor in the army. The highly competitive young Milchan played center-forward for one of the top clubs in the country, Tel Aviv Maccabi, and was good enough to make the national soccer team.

When his father died in 1966, the family firm, Milchan Bros. (there were no brothers involved in the company, although his father did have four), was worth only $60,000 and facing big debts, if not bankruptcy. Soon after the 22-year-old Arnon took over the company, he became involved with two colleagues in agricultural-fertilizer research work. The team came up with a breakthrough nutrient for iron-deficient deciduous fruit trees, and Milchan went out to sell it. "I didn't really know anything about business, so I had no inhibitions—I went straight to du Pont in Wilmington."

His contact there—what proved to be his entry ticket to the military-industrial world—was Irving Shapiro, who eventually became chairman of the giant firm. The rapport established between them was more important than the formula (although the discovery eventually led to the popular "Nu-Green" product manufactured by du Pont). Milchan's straightforward, charming manner undoubtedly won him the golden contract to represent du Pont in Israel.

Milchan, not content with his prize, had the chutzpah to go to du Pont competitors as well, and ended up representing several of them: Rhone-Poulenc, France's biggest chemical company, Ciba-Geigi of Switzerland and Hoecsd of Germany.

In running his company, Milchan decided to use technical professionals in place of salesmen. They not only sold the insecticides and fertilizers, but also advised Israeli farmers, an innovative approach in Israel that established the firm's reputation and greatly increased its earnings. Milchan opened his first foreign company in Iran, a large farm-chemical enterprise that alone brought in tens of millions of dollars annually. Another firm in Turkey, which he has since sold, did $25 million a year. His successes in the Middle East led to the founding of thirty other chemical, pharmaceutical and textile companies operating in seventeen countries. "I don't know how it all happened," says Milchan, "I didn't cheat. And I was very naive."

Milchan met with the Shah in 1972, and a certain kind of sophistication definitely followed. He became involved in the aerospace industry, the top rung of the arms trade. He represented Raytheon, North American Rockwell and Magnavox in Israel "and elsewhere."

In 1975 there was a flap in the media over a $300,000 commission paid to Milchan by a Raytheon subsidiary for a sale of Hawk missiles to Israel. The Pentagon decided not to permit Raytheon to pay the commission, because the Israel government had made it clear that it purchases directly from U.S. manufacturers without agents or middlemen. At the time, Milchan Bros. was the import agent for several aeronautics firms, including Beachcraft and the manufacturers of Bell helicopters. The Israeli Air Force bought several of the Beachcraft Queen light planes. The chief supply officer, Tat-Aluf Haim Yaron, later joined Milchan Bros., replacing another ex-general, Shlomo Lahat, who went on to become Tel Aviv's mayor. Milchan himself was never accused of any wrongdoing in the case, but he was definitely plugged in to the refinements of the military-industrial business world, and his companies were staffed with many ex-military men. Milchan himself became close friends with Moshe Dayan, Ezer Weizman and other well-known political personalities, mostly in the Labor and Liberal parties.

But at the moment of greatest expansion, Milchan started to grow bored with his businesses. He became a fixture of Tel Aviv nightlife with a reputation as a libertine. He collected art—Picasso and Magritte—and dabbled in films. His first ventures were losers (*Dizengoff '99* and a European flop appropriately entitled *Mud*), but the successful six-part miniseries *Masada* was his ticket to much grander projects. Around the same time, Milchan and his French wife, Brigitte, a model who was considered to be one of the most beautiful women in Israel, decided to move to Paris with their three children in an attempt to save their marriage. They moved to a villa outside the capital, while maintaining homes in Herzliya, near Tel Aviv, and the U.S. They were divorced in 1977, and in recent years, Milchan has been living with a woman from Sweden.

UNDER THE VENEER OF CASUAL SOPHISTICATION, Arnon Milchan is a loyal and patriotic sort, but he has engaged in some dealings for his country, and for himself, which he probably wishes he had avoided. He was already many times a millionaire and uninterested in the profit motive when he became involved in the early seventies as the key financial figure in the South African scheme that later became known as Muldergate.

Former Police, Interior, and Information Minister Dr. Connie Mulder, once the front-runner for the premiership of South Africa, was, along with Prime Minister John Vorster, the principal figure in the $160-million information slush-fund project that lasted for ten years before it ended in scandal. Their secret Information Department projects included investments in newspapers, magazines and TV stations and attempts to buy the London *Observer*, the now-defunct *Washington Star*, the influential weekly *West Africa* magazine, and other media in order to improve South Africa's image. Funds were also channeled to foes of politicians who were critical of South Africa, such as Senator Dick Clark of Iowa, chairman of the Africa subcommittee of the Senate Foreign Affairs Committee. Much of the money involved has never been accounted for.

Mulder paid official visits to Israel in 1973, 1975 and 1976, and was feted by the Labor Party government, which agreed to a consulting role in the secret project. A Hebrew University professor and a Foreign Ministry official approached Milchan together, and he agreed to become the conduit for South African funds, laundering the money through a bank in Italy. In Israel, for every such conspiracy that eventually becomes known, there are probably three or four complex and basically evil schemes that never surface.

This story exploded in 1979 because Milchan "couldn't sleep at night." He visited South Africa around that time and "saw the reality" behind the guided tour. "I didn't want to be part of covering up something so horrible—I couldn't believe a sign at the zoo that said 'Blacks, Asians and dogs not allowed.' I thought, I'm an Asian; I'm an Israeli.

"There was something totally immoral about the whole thing. There was no argument good enough to convince me that apartheid is anything but a disgrace. A Jew should not tolerate it. I refused to keep playing the game." Pretoria complained to Israel about Milchan's refusal to continue cooperating. When the story broke, Israel managed to get off the hook. In Pretoria, Mulder was expelled from the ruling National Party. (Although the scandal put an end to Vorster's career, Mulder went on to form an ultra-right-wing party.)

This experience afflicted Milchan's conscience and brought about a change of views. There were limits. So it was no coincidence that the film *Brazil* portrayed an Orwellian world ruled from an absurdly evil Ministry of Information Retrieval. The film was directed by Monty Python veteran Terry Gilliam and written by Gilliam, playwright Tom Stoppard and Charles McKeown, with Milchan's hand very much in evidence.

In 1985, when Milchan's name hit the headlines, it was not because of his film adventures or his pangs of conscience about South Africa, but because of the controversy over how Israel acquired some eight hundred switching timers without U.S. licenses. A California businessman, Richard Kelly Smyth, was indicted for sending the krytrons—which can be used for nuclear weapons—to Israel over a three-year period. *Newsweek*, which broke the story, tied Smyth's firm to a Milchan Bros. subsidiary in Tel Aviv, the Heli Trading Company.

Milchan dismisses it as "the unbelievable, stupid krytron story." The Israeli Defense Ministry ordered the sophisticated timing devices through Milchan's Heli firm. Milchan knew Smyth from North American Rockwell, where he had been an executive before starting his own company. "He was one of many clients. We ordered openly, asking if he could get $40,000 or so of krytrons. He said yes, got a license, ordered it and received the timers. His mistake was that he got a commercial license instead of applying for a State Department license."

According to Milchan, after Smyth reported a theft at his firm in 1981, the CIA, FBI and U.S. Customs were called in because of Smyth's classified position (at one time, he represented the U.S. Air Force at NATO headquarters in Brussels). The customs people came across the krytron documents and said the licensing was improper. "I knew nothing about it till three years later, when *Newsweek* called me. No complaint was ever made against me or any of my firms. The irony is that as of January 1985, krytrons, which are nothing more than accurate timers, were no longer on the list of prohibited items—anyone can import them."

Sources familiar with the affair say that the story was leaked not by U.S. Customs (whose agents have been involved in several attempts to blame Israel for improper importing of advanced technology), but by a Likud loyalist in the Foreign Ministry who wished to embarrass the then-prime minister, Shimon Peres.

A mysterious twist to the story was that Smyth and his wife vanished from their sailboat a few months after the story broke. He had been out on $100,000 bail. Some reports have claimed that the Smyths have been sighted in Israel, and that the well-connected Milchan has provided them with shelter.

In the last few years most of Milchan's time and energy has been devoted to his film productions, and he keeps only a loose hand in his other companies, delegating most of the authority. Milchan Bros. alone does $50 million a year in business, but when the firm opened new headquarters in Ramat Gan in the Greater Tel Aviv area, Milchan did not even bother to go to the ceremony. "That's what I'm very good at doing—delegating authority."

On films, he spares no expense, as evidenced by the breathtaking sets in Sergio Leone's film, or the classy special effects in *Brazil*. He loves to collaborate with authors and artists in an industry that both "fascinates and awes." He gets involved in every aspect of the productions in an easygoing way that does not seem to bother even the most temperamental movie people. But when one sees him at work with a French crew in a Paris studio, it is hard to connect him with Israel or Jewish life, despite *Masada* and the epic about American-Jewish gangsters.

Israel is said to be too parochial a place for world-class performers like violinist Yitzhak Perlman or actors like Topol or artists like Agam or big-time movie producers like Menachem Golan. And although there is much to commend in any artist who exiles himself in order to rise above nationality, the country's best writers and poets do not seem to have that same need to leave Israel in order to give full expression to their powers. Though Milchan does not look down on the possibility of doing films about his country—he says he would like to do one about the Nili Jewish underground of World War I—his children have been raised in France. His spiritual investment is there, or in the international film community. Milchan, enthralled by that exciting and sophisticated world, says he "wants to remain where the action is."

His closest friends are "shy and successful" people like himself, actor Robert DeNiro (who has starred in three of Milchan's films), and Pierre Trudeau, the former prime minister of Canada. In any case, his present world is light years away from that of fighter planes and "information" factories that plague the conscience. It means that cinema glamor, the sometimes dismal universalist urge and the guilt about the sale of swords have grabbed one of Israel's brightest sons and transformed him into an occasional visitor to the land that spawned him.

Richard T. Nowitz

XXIII

E VERYONE CALLS HIM BY HIS FIRST NAME, Teddy, like the bear he resembles, a rotund man who has been in the unique position of being mayor of reunified Jerusalem since Day One. He is unique in another way, too: no other Israeli political figure has remained as popular among both the general public and politicians across the political spectrum—and this despite a volcanic spirit and a whiplash tongue.

Of course, he also has his detractors, mainly among the extreme anti-Zionist Orthodox (and not only those who go around torching bus stops), and the extreme ultra-Zionist nationalists. He is a secular man, who does not want to see his city become a theocracy. Most Jerusalemites wish that the mayor, who approached his seventy-eighth birthday as Israel began to celebrate its fortieth, would stick around till age 120 or so.

In June 1987, when the capital of Israel celebrated its twentieth year of reunification, hundreds of newspapermen and magazine writers from around the world besieged Teddy Kollek, asking him to say a word or two for the readers of *Der Zeit* or *Figaro*, the *New Age* of Australia or *The Nation* of Nairobi. An extremely accessible man, his home phone number is in the book, though it is far easier to catch him at the office, where the workaholic mayor starts a sixteen-to-eighteen hour day at 6:30 A.M. He is very visible and very photogenic. Reporters can see and hear him all the time at the big, newsworthy events, on a tour bus with visiting VIPs, or cruising up and down the narrow streets of the capital's diverse neighborhoods to check up on the municipality's gardeners and street-cleaners.

He is known for his impatience with bullshit. At the thirteenth biennial Jerusalem International Book Fair, held in the spring of 1987, he lumbered up to the podium after being introduced as ''the guiding spirit'' of the fair. As mayor of Jerusalem, Teddy ad-libbed, he had no time to read even one book, ''so what spiritual guidance could I possibly give?'' he asked, slightly exasperated. ''We're the People of the Book, and this is the City of the Book. The city is relatively quiet and peaceful, but we have many problems before us.'' He did not go into details. The mayor received far more applause than any other speaker, including Prime Minister Yitzhak Shamir.

Nine months later, when the eastern part of the city was no longer quiet, Teddy was. After telling a television crew that coexistence was ''dead,'' and then later, after composing himself, declaring that he had said ''almost dead,'' the subdued mayor suddenly seemed to carry the weight of all his years. As the third month of the Palestinian uprising began, united Jerusalem had become a fiction. Barricades were erected in Arab neighborhoods; scores of windows in East Talpiot, Teddy's showcase of coexistence, were shattered; the Shuafat-Anata refugee camp within the city limits was under curfew; Arab schools were closed and shops in the Moslem quarter of the Old City were shuttered.

The situation in Jerusalem had ''changed in a fundamental way,'' Teddy said. ''Coexistence is not dead, but I'm sure that there will be deep scars when this is over.'' He expressed confidence that the city's adult Arab population would at some point stand up to the youths who were destroying their quality of life by blocking roads, breaking water lines and stoning cars and houses. But the mayor himself had suffered a devastating blow, and he wore his feelings on his sleeve.

I ONCE SAW TEDDY cruising around the German Colony, sitting next to his driver, at whom he barked orders: ''Over there, nincompoop, don't you know your way around Jerusalem yet?''

Teddy often lashes out at his underlings, a habit visiting Americans often find most disconcerting, but his aides have learned to live with it. Teddy's driver brought the mayor closer to a pocket park on Smuts Street, one of scores of such little patches of tree-lined sandbox playgrounds that Teddy has sprinkled around Jerusalem.

''See to it that that slide gets fixed,'' he barked to an aide in the back seat. I ran up to him and barked back. ''Have you any idea how hard it is for a child or an elderly person to cross Emek Refaim? Don't you care enough to see that a traffic light is put up there?''

Teddy sighed. ''My traffic experts all tell me that a traffic light would only complicate matters,'' he answered. ''Create more bottlenecks. Cause more accidents. It would be a waste of half a million dollars because it would tie up traffic and make things even more dangerous than they are now. But if you have some evidence that this is not so, why don't you just contact Abramovitz in the traffic division and let him in on your little secret?''

The mayor is much more likely to intervene in neighborhood traffic problems if one of his Patrons of Jerusalem is involved, like the Van Leers and their cinematheque: when the millionaires complained about how difficult it was to cross the street in front of their cultural pyramid, Teddy reacted right away, ordering a pedestrian bridge to be built.

Before the uprising, as Teddy sat in the front seat of a tour bus filled with American Jewish leaders, he pointed out the sites around his favorite new neighborhood, East Talpiot. In the back of the bus, someone was holding a whispered conversation with the Jewish Liaison to the White House as Teddy talked into the microphone. ''Will you please be quiet!'' he stormed. ''Don't talk when I'm talking.'' Nervous giggling swept through the bus. Inside David's Citadel in the Old City, a municipal employee explained how the restoration work had been carried out. Teddy grew purple in the face, sputtering to a nearby aide: ''She's idiotic, talking in the *stupidest* way, simply idiotic, *stupid*,'' while the aide tried to cool the flames with a downward waving motion of both hands.

But as Kollek once wrote in response to a huffy report in an American-Jewish newspaper about his obvious rudeness, "If everyone took each of my outbursts so seriously, I would by now have no family, no friends, and surely no staff." It is simply not part of his personality to weigh his words carefully; he is an irascible, Teddy colicky man. But so what?

AUSTRIAN-BORN TEDDY KOLLEK will go down in Jewish history as one of the great builders of Jerusalem. He has raised tremendous funds for the city, relying on his inherent charm and tenacity. Famous people have always seemed to like this prickly person, from his pioneering days on a kibbutz (Arthur Koestler dedicated his 1930s book about Palestine, *Thieves in the Night*, to Teddy and Tamar Kollek), to his tenure as Ben-Gurion's top aide, to his role as the first mayor of a reunified Jerusalem restored to the people of Israel. Only Bob Dylan did not want to meet him.

Jerusalemites are worried about who will come to the post after Teddy—no one on the horizon even approaches his caliber. There was talk that Arik Sharon, whose move to the Moslem Quarter of the Old City helped fuel the Palestinian uprising, would stand for the post, which would represent a 180-degree turn from the policies of Teddy Kollek. But everything was uncertain in the suddenness of 1988. The mayor is a moral man who has done everything possible to promote coexistence between Arabs and Jews in the capital. He remains a fervent Zionist of the old school: in his view, there is only one center for the Jews—Israel. His greatest dream is to see Jerusalem with a Jewish population greater than that of New York. As he once said about himself, "I'm very old-fashioned."

It seems that after they made Teddy Kollek, they really did break the mold. What comes next, nobody knows.

Aliza Auerbach

XXIV

THE INTENSE young Palestinian Jew who led a crusade in wartime America for the rescue of Jews from Hitler's Europe was viciously attacked by the Zionist and Jewish leadership of that age. Yet Hillel Kook, who used the pseudonym Peter Bergson during World War II, achieved great things: his efforts helped to force President Roosevelt to create the War Refugee Board, which saved up to 200,000 Jews.

But it was not enough, and Kook, still an Israeli maverick, remains haunted by his belief that perhaps a million more people could have been saved if the establishment had devoted its energies to a rescue effort instead of mounting a campaign against the "notorious" young Palestinians and their American friends who became known as "the Bergson group."

Today, Bergson/Kook is old and frail, but the mind of this man, who can be counted among the founding fathers of Israel, is as sharp as ever. His abiding concern is with the fate of his nation: Israel, he believes, is sinking in unreality, drugged on its own lies, and only a sea-change will preserve it. Israel's apparent inability to take the initiative for peace is the consequence of ignoring fundamental problems. The state of the State of Israel has brought him to the edge of despair, and his concern echoes the situation forty-five years ago, when confusion and obfuscation also reigned among the Jews.

HILLEL KOOK WAS BORN IN LITHUANIA in 1915 and lived in the Ukraine, where his father, Rabbi Dov Kook, was a chief rabbi. Hillel witnessed the bloody pogroms that followed the Russian Revolution. When he was nine, his parents brought the family to Palestine, where they lived next door to Dov's brother, the first chief rabbi of Palestine, who was already known as Rav Kook.

Hillel would soon witness more pogroms, this time by Arabs instead of Russians, during the uprising of 1929, when seventy yeshiva students were massacred in Hebron, and other Jews were killed down the street from his house in Jerusalem. After attending his uncle's yeshiva, Kook went on to study philosophy at the newly opened Hebrew University. With his best friend, David Raziel, later the commander of the Irgun underground, he joined the Haganah, the Jewish community's defense force. Following Raziel into the Irgun, he soon became a top officer. In 1937 the Irgun sent him to Poland, where he joined Ze'ev Jabotinsky and became one of his close aides. The powerful presence of the founder of Revisionist Zionism was felt by all his followers, and they emulated him in many ways—some, such as Menachem Begin, did so in dress and manners. Others, like Kook, updated Jabotinsky's basically nineteenth-century brand of liberalism while also emulating his image of dignity and pride. For three years Kook became a chief organizer in Europe of the "illegal" immigration to Palestine.

In 1940 Jabotinsky, a month before his death, summoned Kook to America, where the young firebrand would soon lead a small group of Palestinians and American converts to the cause, like famed writer Ben Hecht, in a campaign to press the Allies to create a Jewish Army. Bergson immediately made the cause an issue of concern to top government leaders. His efforts were vigorously opposed by the British, who were mainly afraid of antagonizing the Arabs, and by the establishment Zionists, led by Reform Rabbi Stephen Wise, who did not like "upstarts" or challengers to his hegemony as czar of American Jewry.

In November 1942, it was officially announced by Wise that two million Jews had been exterminated in a systematic genocide campaign, but this news, rating barely two inches in America's leading newspapers, was buried on the inside pages. It set a fire under Peter Bergson, however, and he turned his formidable energies to rousing the U.S. government to do something about the Holocaust.

He worked together with Samuel Merlin, Jabotinsky's former secretary, Jabotinsky's son Eri, Arye Ben-Eliezer (who would later bring about Menachem Begin's appointment as Irgun commander), Mike Ben-Ami, Ben Hecht and others, who frantically lobbied congressmen and government officials. They organized committees and conferences whose supporters included Eleanor Roosevelt, Herbert Hoover and William Randolph Hearst, as well as hundreds of well-known show business people, writers and lawyers. They staged a march on Washington by hundreds of Orthodox rabbis—the only such event in America during the Holocaust years—produced massive pageants about the continuing genocide, screamed their heads off in full-page ads in the *New York Times* and dozens of other newspapers, and raised money from 500,000 contributors—all in order to stir America to action.

What the Bergsonites (as they came to be called) accomplished was to put the issue of the extermination on the front pages. Bergson and his colleagues managed to wiggle out of the straitjacket of Zionist politics in order to break the silence surrounding the "Final Solution." The young Palestinians were militant and audacious in a way that was foreign, and threatening, to American Zionists. The broader Jewish leadership in America was frozen by fear of anti-Semitism in their own backyard. Instead of mounting a political campaign to press the reluctant Allies to undertake action on behalf of European Jews, the main issue became how to "liquidate" (Jewish Agency representative Nahum Goldmann's word) Peter Bergson and his colleagues.

According to a growing number of scholars (two chapters in David Wyman's highly acclaimed *The Abandonment of the Jews* lauds Bergson and his group), the Zionist establishment spent more time trying to undermine the Bergson group than opposing the efforts of the State Department, which blocked rescue efforts. Rabbi Wise and Nahum Goldmann sought to have Bergson/Kook deported. According to government documents released a few years ago, Goldmann told State Department officials that Wise thought Bergson was as great a threat to American Jews as Hitler, because his showy activism might awaken anti-Semitism in the United States.

Wise, Goldmann and other establishment leaders set up special committees whose sole function was to undermine the Bergsonites. A dirty-tricks campaign, involving the *Washington Post*, the FBI and other agencies, labeled the Bergsonites as "charlatans," "swindlers," and "clowns." Meanwhile, the Zionists impeded the establishment of a special U.S. government rescue agency only because it was the idea of the Bergson group. Nevertheless, in January 1944, President Roosevelt, responding to the storm of criticism in Congress and the press which the Bergsonites had stirred up, established the War Refugee Board, which saved tens of thousands of Jews (one of the WRB's emissaries was Raoul Wallenberg).

The maverick group also played a crucial role in speeding the timetable for Israeli independence. After the WRB was set up, Bergson and his group bought the former Iran Embassy in Washington, hoisted a blue and white flag and became known as "the Hebrew Embassy" on Massachusetts Avenue. The Bergsonites mounted a new campaign, this time for a nation-state in Palestine for the "Hebrew people." Bergson and his colleagues grappled with the Jewish identity problem: What does it mean to create a "Jewish" state? Bergson asked in a letter to Chaim Weizmann. What is an Israeli (or a "Hebrew" in the days before 1948)? What does Israeli citizenship mean in terms of the Jewish People? Bergson raised searching questions that still have not been resolved.

AFTER ELEVEN YEARS OF ORGANIZING WORK ABROAD, Kook returned home on Independence Day, 1948. Though Kook never thought of himself as a politician, at the end of 1948 Begin put him near the top of his party's list for the Constituent Assembly. Most expected that this body would be Israel's Constitutional Convention, dealing with complex issues related to the rebirth of an ancient people in its historic homeland, but Ben-Gurion transformed it into the First Knesset. (Merlin and Eri Jabotinsky also became members of the assembly-turned-legislature, and Ben-Eliezer became deputy speaker.)

In the Constituent Assembly, Kook cried out that a "putsch" by Ben-Gurion and the Labor Zionists had taken place, and he regrets to this day that he did not resign then and there, for it was evident that basic questions such as the separation of nationality and religion were not going to be dealt with.

Though Kook had learned a great deal about democracy during his years in America, he found no place for a Jeffersonian democrat in an Israel dominated by the East European mentality. He and Eri Jabotinsky split with Begin and served out their term as independents. In 1951 Kook decided to leave Israel with his American-born wife and baby daughter for a "few years" of temporary exile. He expected a new generation to emerge relatively soon that would change the new country, free it from its stifling, dangerous "ghetto atmosphere."

In America and Cuba, he made a small fortune in oil and securities. In 1968, four years after his wife died, he retired from business and brought his two daughters home, settling in the fashionable Tel Aviv suburb of Kfar Shmaryahu. He remarried, and looked for ways to get his ideas across, to get Israelis to confront the changing character of Jewish existence and to help bring about a normalization of life for the Jews who had gained political independence for the first time in 1,900 years.

He expressed his views on key questions in lectures to students and talks with political leaders and journalists. His ideas became the subject of a study by John Agasi, an Israeli philosopher, and a topic for debate among leading Israeli intellectuals across the political spectrum. His role in the Holocaust rescue effort drew increasing international attention and was treated in the BBC documentary "Auschwitz and the Allies" and in Laurence Jarvik's documentary "Who Shall Live and Who Shall Die." Kook also appeared on TV interview shows, where he had only minutes to describe difficult concepts that had taken a lifetime to formulate.

To this thoroughgoing iconoclast, the Likud and Labor parties are basically the same. Both, he charges, avoid the basic issues, such as the necessity for separation of nationality and religion, which he believes is even more important than the separation of religion and state and which is essential if a permanent solution to the conflict with the Palestinians is to be reached. If the problem is not addressed, it will lead to disaster, says Kook, the nephew of the greatest Jewish scholar of the modern era, Avraham Yitzhak Hacohen Kook, and first cousin of Zvi Yehuda Kook, founding spirit of the Messianic nationalist movement. In the First Knesset, he voted for the Law of Return. He now believes that the recurring attempts by the ultra-Orthodox politicians to amend the law in their quest to say Who Is a Jew will succeed in the coming years, but he is not one of those crying that it will lead inevitably to a schism among the Jewish people.

He believes it is only a symptom of a much deeper problem. A "post-Zionist" who deprecates the Zionist idea that there is a Jewish nation of thirteen million, he sees an Israeli nation that is already *there*, yet goes somehow unrecognized. He believes that the Zionist motto We Are One represents purposeful obscuring of the question of political loyalty—the Pollard affair is one example; the controversy over whether American Jews should speak out and even organize against Israeli government policy is another.

"The question of Who Is a Jew should be handled by a rabbinical assembly and not a parliament: the Knesset is a secular institution, which even includes non-Jews—an absurd situation. What the Knesset really should be dealing with is the question of Who Is an Israeli," Kook says.

Basically, Kook believes that if Israel does not restructure itself, it will disintegrate. He feels that Israel must change the way it looks at itself, that it is not simply a nation of Jews but a nation of 3.5 million Jews and half a million Israeli non-Jews. He has always considered it scandalous that Israeli Arabs are designated as members of the "Arab nation" on their identity cards, instead of being listed as members of the Israeli nation. (In the third month of the Palestinian uprising, Defense Minister Yitzhak Rabin said exactly the same thing, an indicaion that the themes Kook has hammered away at are finally gaining acceptance.)

His convictions emerge in a flood of ideas. In brief, he tells his fellow Israelis that they must update the way they look at themselves, change the 3,000-year-old tradition of being a "religion-nation" and build a modern democracy for the Israeli nation separate from the worldwide Jewish religion—a concept deeply disturbing to many Jews. Furthermore, he says, Israel must initiate this new approach of true integration in relations with its non-Jewish citizens. A change in perceptions is also vital to relations with Israel's neighbors, the rest of the world and fellow Jews abroad.

Kook perceives total confusion in Israel over nationality and citizenship, and religion and nationality. How does an Israeli Arab feel, he asks, when Israel is referred to as the Jewish State? Would American Jews feel comfortable if the U.S. were always called a Christian state? Jews and Israelis are not synonymous terms.

The problem of Who Is a Jew, he says, "is not with the religious people but with the secular. In the U.S., the word American is not confused with the word Protestant. In Israel, the word Jew means *both* religion and nationality.

"I feel myself to be 100 percent Jewish by my heritage and religious beliefs. I'm also 100 percent Israeli—I live here, and this nation represents the entire culture and history of 3,500 years. Nevertheless, under Israeli law, my nationality is 'Jewish,' not 'Israeli.' If you take this to its logical conclusion, it means that an American Jew is not an American, but a resident of America."

He points out that "in the absence of a Constituent Assembly, there is still no legal definition or acknowledgement of the existence of the Israeli nation." That is one reason why he is one of the main supporters of the campaign launched in 1987 to require the government of Israel to draw up a constitution.

Kook believes it is arcane to talk of Galut—to his mind, American Jews are not in Exile, despite Zionist rhetoric. His credo is that the Galut ended in 1948, at least in free countries, when the gates of Israel were opened to the Jews of the world. At that point, Judaism became an "international religion" for Jews belonging to different nations, and Israel became the nation of the Jews by virtue of the fact that the majority of Israelis are of the Jewish faith. To accept this reality would strengthen the religion and would help normalize Israel's political existence. Yet Zionists cling to the concept that Jews remain both a nationality and religion whether they are citizens of the United States or of Israel.

Kook has been saying for decades that a terrible split will occur between American and Israeli Jews because of the refusal to pay heed to these problems of identity, which are not "academic" questions but vital issues. "God forbid that we wait until the day when the American Jews have to choose sides," he told me in 1982, six years before the Palestinian uprising began to shake Israel and world Jewry. He believes that the basic change in identity he calls for, part of a general reevaluation of values, would make peace with Israel's neighbors more achievable, for the confusion of identity has long influenced Israel's position regarding the Palestinian people. "This is a perfect time for a settlement with the Palestinians—and *not* with the PLO," he says. He has long believed that Israel should initiate a peace pact with the Palestinians, but does not think that Israel as currently constituted is capable of taking the initiative.

Kook fights his anxieties about Israel's course up to now by taking a positive position regarding basic change. He dreams of a flourishing Israeli democracy with a constitutional framework, an Israel drawing inspiration from the great traditions of Judaism and the Jewish people, as well as from the American democratic tradition. Concerning the Palestinians, he says, "I believe we can achieve peace between us. I'm even utopian enough to believe that somewhere along the road, we can be allies."

Is Kook's voice just another in the Israeli wilderness? Or is that road that he wants Israel to pursue reminiscent of Isaiah's highway in the desert, leading the exiles back to Zion?

XXV

EVEN IN HIS SECOND TERM OF OFFICE, the prime minister of Israel in the year of the uprising, Yitzhak Shamir, has not been considered an appropriate subject for a biographer—in Hebrew, English or any other language. Is this a commentary on the blandness of the person, on the political bias of most journalists and writers, or on the marketplace realism of the book industry?

Many people consider Shamir the last of the founding fathers of the state. He has led a fascinating, often thrilling life: as leader of the Lehi (Stern group) underground during the independence struggle, as a prisoner of the British in Eritrea, as a top spy-master of the Mossad for over a decade, and as a tenacious politician who seems able to outfox the polished and sophisticated Shimon Peres at every turning.

Several books have been written about Peres, who reads widely (in contrast to Shamir, who does not read any books) but whose life story is a great yawn beside Shamir's. Peres is nothing more than a splinter of Ben-Gurion, while Shamir appears to be a self-created, unique entity. Part of the reason for the absence of books about the prime minister is that Shamir is still anathema to the liberal establishment, here in Israel and abroad. Another factor is Shamir himself—he is an extremely closed, mysterious figure, who does not gab at all. But his detractors say that there is no mystery, that he is the epitome of an ordinary soul, an empty vessel, intransigent and thick. All agree that he is tough.

Commentators find it easy to criticize him because of his extreme caution, his bombastic, discordant speechmaking and his apparent lack of a sense of humor. Anyone in the media who says something good about Shamir risks the opprobrium of his colleagues. It is true that his do-nothingness may have aggravated Israel's problems, that he is rarely an inspiration, that you do not know what is happening behind the flat, thin eyes and mouth. But he is a very decent man to talk to, capable of great warmth and impatient with vanity; and he definitely does have a sense of humor. One top American correspondent, who holds typically left-liberal opinions, told me he liked Shamir's approachability, even if Shamir never said much. "It's much easier talking to the right-wingers."

Like their colleagues around the world, many Israeli politicians think of themselves as the darlings of men and gods. The same American correspondent, who represents a newspaper of Olympian power, never calls Ezer Weizman, for example, even though Weizman's political position is viewed so favorably by the American media establishment. Why? "Because he's so arrogant and rude and smug and downright mean."

President Chaim Herzog has managed to alienate much of the Israeli press corps that covers the presidency, and his aristocratic airs have led to a mass defection of his staff, eighteen people in little more than a year. Shimon Peres often exudes a haughty spirit. And Haim Bar-Lev acts as if the Bar-Lev Line never fell. In contrast, Shamir is a democrat in personality—accessible, grandfatherly, decent. An American-Israeli radio reporter, catching Shamir standing on the tarmac at the airport about to embark on a trip to the U.S., went up to him and asked with a grin, "Can you take some letters for me?" (The deficiencies of the Israeli mail system are legion, and many immigrants send the bulk of their mail with travelers to the old country for much faster and surer service.) Shamir smiled, stuck out his hand and said, "Of course!" The reporter could not imagine ever kidding with Peres in the same way.

It would certainly be ridiculous to say that the way a person treats a fellow human being is more important than the momentous questions of war and peace, life and death. Because you may have been terribly exploited by a boss with a socialist philosophy does not mean you can condemn socialism. As one of Israel's leading news photographers put it, "Ben-Gurion was not nice. A bastard. But look at what he did compared to this man!" Still, I for one cannot help admitting that I like Mr. Shamir.

If a book is published about Shamir in the coming years, it will likely be either a vicious attack on the man by one of a host of intellectual enemies, or a canticle by one of the very small group of journalists who subscribe to Shamir's political vision. In either case, such a slanted book would be a shame, a missed opportunity for an objective exploration of the life and times of this enigmatic leader of an unusual nation. The appeal of biography lies, in part, in its claim to a coherent and integral view of human affairs. A good biography is based on the profoundly hopeful assumption that people really are responsible for their actions, that there is a moral continuity between the inner and outer man. Without any doubt, we ought to know more about Yitzhak Shamir.

According to one of his close aides, Shamir may be planning an autobiography—this in an age when every thirty-year-old who has found God gets a contract to write all about it. Because Shamir is such a guarded, laconic soul, we will probably get nothing more than the clothes and buttons of the man.

WHEN YITZHAK SHAMIR became Israel's seventh prime minister in October 1983, many reflected on his problematic past and shuddered. The London *Times* complained editorially that Menachem Begin was bad enough, but that this Shamir was *really* a terrorist. Many Israelis were bewildered by the sudden emergence of this small, illusive man, not only the most hunted terrorist in Palestine at one time but also a virtual outlaw in the Jewish community. They remembered Shamir as the chief of operations of the Fighters for the Freedom of Israel, or Lehi, which the British and most of the rest of the world preferred to call the "Stern Gang."

Of the three Jewish undergrounds operating during the British Mandate, Lehi was the smallest, the most fanatical, the most ruthless. The largest of the military organizations, the Haganah, was the designated defense arm of the socialist-oriented Jewish Agency headed by Ben-Gurion, the government of the prestate Jewish community. Its main political rival was the Irgun, headed by Begin. Lehi split with the Irgun when the mentor of the Jewish nationalist movement, Ze'ev Jabotinsky, and his followers in Palestine, chose to fight with the British in World War II. Lehi, led by the fanatic poet Avraham Stern (who would soon be trapped and murdered by British forces), chose to pursue its own little war against the colonialist enemy, the British.

Lehi's most effective military weapon in that war was assassination. According to some knowledgeable former Lehi members, one of Shamir's nicknames in the underground was "The Shooter." Under his leadership, Lehi gunmen shot at British officials, soldiers and policemen. To finance the underground, they robbed banks, as Stalin allegedly did in the early days of the Bolshevik movement. In one instance, Shamir, acting as judge and probably as executioner (he took his responsibilities literally) eliminated a crazed Lehi leader who was considered a threat to the entire underground.

In November 1944, Lehi carried its fight against the British to the streets of Cairo, where it assassinated Lord Moyne, scion of the Guinness clan and the highest-ranking British official in the Middle East. Moyne had blocked Jewish refugees from Hitler from receiving asylum in Palestine, and many Jews believed he deserved to be executed. "The Deed," as this most famous of Lehi's exploits came to be known, was meticulously planned by Shamir.

On the theory that the past is prologue, it was logical to assume that with Shamir's sudden rise to power forty years later, Israel had taken yet another lurch towards fanaticism. But the paradox soon became evident: Shamir's first term as prime minister was noteworthy primarily because of the defeats he inflicted on right-wing extremists in his own camp. It was he who broke the modern Jewish underground spawned by the West Bank settlers.

Shamir has a history of surprising those who take him for granted—one reason to want to know more about his career, even though he prefers us to know less. Even if he had not become Israel's prime minister twice, his story would be one of those odysseys worth telling. But there is another reason: his toughness, his Greater Israel politics and his terrorist background may provide him with the credentials to make peace one day with the Palestinians and their representatives, the PLO terrorists who, unlike the Jewish terrorists of the 1940s, attack civilians at random and deliberately kill innocent people. Although he seemed as intransigent as ever when the Palestinians in the occupied territories rose up and the Americans launched their peace initiative in the early months of 1988, no one could say for sure which course Yitzhak Shamir would finally steer.

YITZHAK YEZERNITSKY was raised in a socialist-Zionist home in Poland (his parents had participated in the abortive 1905 revolution in Russia) and as a teenager was briefly in a left-wing Zionist youth organization. After he learned of the 1929 massacres of Jews in Palestine by local Arabs, he joined Betar, the paramilitary youth group affiliated with Jabotinsky's Revisionists. A secular Jew, whose formative experience had been Polish anti-Semitism, his only political passion seemed to be the restoration of a Hebrew republic on both sides of the Jordan as an answer to the plight of the Jews.

In the spring of 1940 his name was still Yezernitsky; he would take the name Shamir two years later. (In Jewish folklore, the Shamir was a very hard precious stone, or a marvelous magic worm, that was used to cut the great blocks of granite in Solomon's Temple. The Shamir was made at twilight on the sixth day of creation, together with other extraordinary things. Shamir is also the word for dill.) Only twenty-six years old, he confronted the most fateful decision of his life. He had arrived in Palestine from his native Poland five years earlier. After a brief stay at the Hebrew University, he joined the Irgun Zvai Leumi, the more extreme of the two Jewish undergrounds. Yezernitsky quickly earned his spurs in the Irgun, taking part in several violent operations.

In 1940 the Irgun was splitting over Jabotinsky's directive to suspend military action against the British and offer to fight with them against the common Nazi enemy. The majority in the Irgun, including the military commander, David Raziel, followed Jabotinsky's order. The dissidents, led by Raziel's main rival, the firebrand Avraham Stern, disdained Jabotinsky's diplomatic approach. Stern even dispatched emissaries to Hitler's Germany and offered a deal: If the Germans released the Jews of Europe and sent them to Palestine, Stern's group would cooperate in making war on Great Britain. The plan, however, was a nonstarter and was soon abandoned.

Yezernitsky had no political agenda that anyone can remember. He vacillated for several months about whether to go with Stern. Later he recalled that even though he went with Stern he had unalterably opposed to any direct dealings with the Germans. But he supported Stern's argument that Britain remained the number-one enemy of the Jews of Palestine.

The Jewish community in Palestine regarded this policy as utter madness—Britain stood alone in fighting the worst enemy of the Jewish people in history. Stern and his followers were cast out as lepers, and the Jewish community, including old comrades from the Irgun, joined in hunting down the men of the new underground group.

After Stern was captured by the British and shot down in February 1942, the group virtually ceased to exist. Most of those who had not been killed, including Yezernitsky, were in the Mizra detention camp. Before his arrest, he was Stern's top hit man, and was now called by his underground name, "Michael." (One comrade from those days, now an Israeli journalist on the extreme right, remembers him as exhibiting great courage under fire, behaving "like a lion" during one bank robbery.)

Leadership now passed to "Michael" and Natan Yalin-Mor, an intellectual intoxicated with political ideas, who was also imprisoned at Mizra. Yalin-Mor envisioned the Hebrew underground uniting with the Arabs of Palestine in an anti-imperialist revolt that would throw out the British, establish a socialist state and maintain friendly relations with the Soviet Union. They made a strangely matched pair as they paced around the prison compound talking about what had to be done. Yalin-Mor was over six feet tall, a big bear of a man with a high-pitched voice and a round, gentle face. Muscular, narrow-eyed Yezernitsky, built like a tree stump, was not much over five feet.

What Yezernitsky and Yalin-Mor talked about in Mizra was the need to revive the underground and stoke up the war with the British. To that end, they hatched a plan: Yezernitsky and another top fighter would break out of the prison, make contact with the remaining Sternists outside, and then lay the groundwork for a larger break by the entire group held at Mizra.

Donning Polish army officers' uniforms that had been smuggled into the prison, Yezernitsky and his partner walked out of Mizra on August 31, 1942. Yezernitsky hid in the orange groves outside Tel Aviv for several days and let his beard grow. When he emerged, he had a new identity. He was now Rabbi Yitzhak Shamir, complete with beard, earlocks and black hat.

Shamir set out to rebuild the organization, but first he was forced to confront an explosive problem that had arisen within the ranks. According to all the reports Shamir was getting, Eliahu Giladi, the man who escaped with him from Mizra and was now his deputy in charge of operations, had gone off the deep end. Even in a radical group like Lehi, there were limits: Giladi was actively working on a plot to kill David Ben-Gurion and the main leadership of the Jewish Agency, whom he considered traitors. He was a brutal, frightening man who toyed with his guns and forced women into prostitution in the name of the cause.

In Mizra, Yalin-Mor had warned Shamir that one day there might have to be a "drawing of pistols" with Giladi. "I asked Michael [Shamir] to be alert to the danger, to be on guard, and be the first to draw and shoot his gun," Yalin-Mor would recount in his memoirs. "The day came and Michael remembered."

That is as close as any ex-Lehi man has come to putting it on the record that Shamir killed Giladi. But several underground veterans will say so directly, though not for attribution: Shamir gave the order and undoubtedly pulled the trigger himself.

Giladi was shot in the sands outside Tel Aviv and buried in an unmarked grave. It had to be done. "Everybody thought Giladi was clinically insane and that Shamir should kill him," one Lehi veteran told writer Sol Stern and myself, who wrote about Shamir for the *Village Voice*. "Shamir was most cautious about the decision. Giladi carried two Colt revolvers all the time and frequently threatened to kill people. The question was: him or us? It was like the American movie *High Noon*. It wasn't important who pulled the trigger. If anything, Shamir was criticized for taking so long in deciding."

On November 1, 1943, Yalin-Mor and twenty of the toughest Sternists broke out of the Latrun prison fortress, where they had been moved for tighter security. They had patiently dug a tunnel seventy-five yards long for months. Waiting at the other end of the tunnel were Shamir's men with hijacked buses to drive the escapees to hideouts all over the country.

Lehi stepped up a new terror campaign against the British, bombing police stations, shooting at individual officers and attempting two abortive assassinations of the British High Commissioner. Still condemned as an outlaw organization by the organs of the Jewish community, the group's direction was nevertheless becoming increasingly popular among many Palestinian Jews, who saw that the policy of cooperating with the British during the war had not in any way ameliorated the Jewish disaster taking place in Hitler's Europe. Indeed, it was now evident that the British had acquiesced in the murder of millions of Jews with policies that effectively locked the victims in with their executioners. Lehi's assassination of Lord Moyne in 1944 was not an unpopular deed among the Jewish people because they knew that Moyne had blood on his hands.

The assassination was designed to shock the world, and it did. Historians have suggested that Churchill was so outraged over the murder of his good friend that he turned against Zionism *tout court*. The Moyne killing is a climactic point not only in Shamir's story, but in Jewish history as well.

The British forces vented their rage against the entire Jewish community, and the Jewish Agency and its fighting arm, the Haganah, cooperated with the British to crush the underground. But soon afterward, the Zionist leadership renewed cooperation with the "outlaws" of the Irgun and Lehi, the people they publicly condemned as a "cancer" that had to be rooted out of the community.

In the struggle for Israel's independence, this became a recurring dialectic: the "moderates" would denounce the terrorists on moral and political grounds, but eventually wound up using the terrorist threat. As one ex-Lehi member, now a Labor Party stalwart, said: "We in Lehi were just one instrument in the orchestra led by Ben-Gurion—in that we were successful."

Perhaps the most revealing argument for the efficacy of terrorism (considering the source) was offered by Shamir himself in an interview in 1977 with British historian Lord Bethel. Asked whether killing Lord Moyne had helped the cause of independence, Shamir replied:

> Without doubt. It's not quite the same thing, but take the case of the Palestinians. Ten years ago nobody in the world talked about Palestinians, about a Palestinian people, about a Palestinian state. Now there's quite a consensus in the United States, in Europe, that there is a Palestinian question, a Palestinian people, a Palestinian movement for independence. And [President] Carter says that they must be given a homeland. What happened in those ten years? This is why I think killing Lord Moyne helped the Jewish cause. Governments don't give attention to any problem until such sharp methods are used. Otherwise nothing is done. There are times when you have to use such methods. But you must keep within certain limits. For instance, with us the limits were not to kill any civilians, anyone not connected with the government. In that respect we were not like the Arab terrorists today.

EVEN AFTER THE STATE was declared forty years ago, elements of Lehi continued to engage in terrorist activities. On September 18, 1948, a Lehi unit in Jerusalem assassinated another European nobleman, Count Folke Bernadotte, the United Nations mediator trying to end the first Arab-Israel war on terms that would have meant a reduction in the amount of territory allotted to the Jewish state. Ben-Gurion and the new Israeli government were stunned. Shamir went underground to avoid arrest—this time by Israeli security forces.

Who gave the order to kill Bernadotte has remained a mystery to this day. Israel Eldad, one of Shamir's fellow commanders, told me that he was "proud" of the Bernadotte killing, and that the troika—himself,

Shamir and Yalin-Mor—jointly made the decision. However, Shamir, and the late Yalin-Mor, always denied responsibility for the act.

Unable to identify the actual killers, the Ben-Gurion government released over a hundred Lehi men who had been arrested. Shamir and other Lehi leaders who emerged from the underground were ostracized for many years afterwards. "Those were unhappy years," Shamir would recall in an interview. "The adjustment was difficult." Ben-Gurion finally rescued Shamir from limbo. The old man apparently had a soft spot for Lehi: he chose one of Shamir's top gunmen, Yehoshua Cohen, to be the head of his personal security guard, and in 1955 he allowed his intelligence chief, Isser Harel, to recruit Shamir into the Mossad, Israel's secret service. When he met with Shamir, Harel asked only one question: "Will you loyally carry out all your missions even if you disagree with the policy?" Shamir's answer was affirmative. For the next ten years, Shamir was in deep cover again, becoming one of Harel's top lieutenants.

In the mid-1960s Shamir swallowed his pride and went to the former leader of the rival Irgun, Menachem Begin, and asked to join the Herut party. His first job in the party did not augur a bright future. But then, his whole career has been a study in patience. He went about his business quietly, ruffling no feathers, particularly Begin's. Begin could not tolerate anyone who showed a little bit of independence or who challenged him in any way. He had disposed of Hillel Kook in the First Knesset and of Shmuel Tamir a generation later. Shamir, in contrast, was bland and loyal and never displayed any special intelligence.

Shamir was elected to the Knesset in 1973 at the age of sixty. No one remembers him for any bold initiatives as a legislator. He was a run-of-the-mill backbencher. In 1977, when Begin unexpectedly unseated Labor for the first time, Shamir became Speaker of the Knesset, a position of little importance. In fact, this was the only time in his life that Shamir read any books—mostly biographies of British political figures, as he would tell writer David Grossman in a 1987 radio interview.

In 1980, almost through default, Shamir became Foreign Minister when Moshe Dayan resigned in protest against Begin's hard-line interpretations of the Camp David provisions for Palestinian autonomy. Shamir's tenure in that post was less than distinguished. He had no hand at all in the crucial decisions on the war in Lebanon, which he loyally supported. Nevertheless, he was strongly criticized by the Kahan Commission investigating Israeli responsibility for the Christian Phalangists' massacre of Palestinians in the Sabra and Shatila refugee camps. He was cited for failing to take any action despite receiving reports from the Minister of Communications, Mordechai Zipori, that the Phalangists were rampaging through the camps. Shamir, according to one of his aides, did not think highly of Zipori and thus did not take his report seriously. He also thought it was Arik Sharon's war and thus Sharon's problem.

In one of those unexpected twists that seem to recur in Shamir's career, it was the moral disaster of Sabra and Shatila that led to his becoming prime minister, as it caused the ouster of Sharon and eventually led to Menachem Begin's collapse. Shamir was the accidental prime minister. Like Harry Truman, he was not given much chance by the media of measuring up to the job. But although his first term was largely a holding operation, there was a conscious turning away from the adventurism and posturing of the Begin-Sharon regime. And the government led by the old terrorist chief successfully cracked down on the settlers' underground which murdered and maimed Arabs on the West Bank.

THE WORDS HIS AIDES USE MOST OFTEN to describe him are "pragmatic" and "extremely cautious." One former Lehi comrade who has stayed close to Shamir said, "He has an almost un-Jewish nerve system. He's strong and patient, solid and courageous, but with no imagination, not at all intellectual. He's very very suspicious. But he's known as a listener—he makes you feel he's open to your arguments."

Somewhere along the line, the most feared terrorist in Palestine has become a statist, a conservative with an understanding of the limits of power. He is no dove; at a Herut rally, his voice rumbling histrionically, he will reassure the masses that Judea and Samaria will remain part of Israel forever. Yet Shamir's concern with the "interests of the state" is more than a nuance. Just as Begin was able to reach an accord with Sadat, Shamir may be able to do so with the Palestinians—with Arafat, or Husseini, or whoever emerges as the Palestinians' Ben-Gurion.

No one is better placed than Shamir to point out the fundamental differences between deeds committed by the prestate undergrounds against a foreign occupier—when Jews were being marched into gas chambers— and the present situation in which Jews not only have a state but the most powerful army in the Middle East. He may have a much better chance than the sophisticated, haughty Shimon Peres of stemming the tide of atavistic religious nationalism that not only prevents talk about peace but threatens the very fabric of the nation. Like Begin, he came to the Land of Israel from Poland, which became the charnel house of the Jews. The survival of the Jewish people is in his bones, and he is no sunshine patriot. He will do what has to be done to protect Jewish life.

Perhaps because the Holocaust is not a distant memory for him, he remains an old-fashioned Zionist, believing, as he told me in an interview on the eve of Israel's thirty-ninth birthday, that the Jews of the Diaspora must be told, "Enough, it is time to go to Israel."

What worried him the most, he said, was not the conflict with the Arabs, the demographic problem or the various divisions among the Jews, but the fact "that there are too few Jews here."

Asked if he saw Zionism as essentially a rebellion against the Jewish religion or a fulfillment of it, he replied: "Zionism is a revolution, but not against religion. Zionism is a revolution against Exile, against the opportunism of Exile. Whoever is satisfied with fulfilling the religious laws but remains in Exile is an opportunist. He is also not working for Judaism, because Judaism will only survive if the Jewish people will concentrate here...Zionism is the continuation of Judaism's struggle to exist and develop. The two must go together."

It is perhaps an irony of history that Israel in the year of the Palestinian uprising is being guided by its most secretive and least creative leader since independence. With the country split in two over the cardinal issue of the territories, the elections scheduled for November 1988 will be the most important in Israel's forty years of existence. Shamir and the Likud have a strong chance of continuing in power. If Shamir continues to endeavor only to buy more time, he may preside over a schism that will once again threaten Jewish existence. Or, if he can meet the daunting challenge, he could guide a country resolved to settle the dispute with the Palestinians, the kind of country that will, indeed, be able to attract millions of other Jews to their ancestral homeland.

XXVI

IN TODAY'S ISRAEL, Henri Atlan—Sephardi, leftist, religious, doctor and eminent scientist—is a strange fish in a strange pond. But then, messengers with bad news are not really welcome anywhere. Although a significant number of people believed—at least before the Palestinian uprising—that Israel was somehow coping with the enormous problems that beset her, Dr. Atlan's prognosis is not good: he hold a basically hopeless view of the country's immediate future. As William James once wrote, "Not the Jews of the captivity, but those of the days of Solomon's glory are those from whom the pessimistic utterances in our Bible come."

Atlan, one of the world's leading scholars of the Cabala, believes that the mass return to religion in Israel, mixed with nationalist Zionism, is a poisonous brew that could lead to national self-destruction.

Henri Atlan is not a household name in Israel. Although there have been major magazine articles about him in the Hebrew press, he is much better known in France, where his books, difficult works meshing Jewish thought with modern science, are the talk of the French-Jewish intellectual world. Associates and friends say he is a genius, a possessor of *virtu*—that attribute of the Renaissance man whose brilliance is not confined to any one field. He has international reputations in biophysics and nuclear medicine, in addition to his expertise in Cabala. He is as at home with the philosophies of Nietzsche, Marx, Wittgenstein and Freud as he is with the theories of Einstein and Godel. Certainly, Atlan does not fit the stereotype of the North African Sephardi immigrant to Israel, the son of a janitor. But others find his ideas politically naive, his instincts somehow lacking. They may doubt that this particular physician, magician and soothsayer is close enough to the pulse to make a difference.

In Israel, the corner on the Orthodox leftist-iconoclast market has long been held by Professor Yeshayahu Leibowitz, whose sometimes outrageous—even obscene—comments are swallowed like Jove's nectar by the basically antireligious media. Atlan, on the other hand, comes from a different place; his is a Sephardi, Cabala-oriented world. According to Atlan, the elderly Ashkenazi Leibowitz dismisses Cabala as "idolatry."

Anyone can call himself a Cabalist. The English Gentile Aleister Crowley, a devil-worshiper known as "The Beast," was one, and in today's Israel many religious nationalists use Cabala to justify their arguments. Atlan views these people "the way a Buddhist monk must look upon the young Western hippies who dabble transiently and perfunctorily in the ancient Eastern wisdoms."

In 1985 Atlan, who holds both Israeli and French citizenship, was decorated with the Legion of Honor in recognition of his important scientific-philosophic work; one day, he may be destined to add the Nobel Prize to his collection of distinguished awards. A spiritual and literal commuter, Atlan shuttles between Paris and Jerusalem every two months as a member of French President Francois Mitterrand's national panel on medical ethics, and to lecture at the University of Paris. When he dines at the Elysee Palace, kosher food is served.

During one of his visits in March 1988, he was a featured speaker at Peace Now rallies, where he said that Israel has two alternatives: "Either get rid of the occupied territories—as Leibowitz says, 'free ourselves of the occupied territories'—or kill masses of Palestinians."

He believes that the disproportionate media coverage of the Palestinian uprising is unhealthy, "a kind of jubilation at seeing previous victims become the oppressors. It seems we've become a chosen people not by God but by journalists. But it may be the same thing, after all. We have to bear it, just as we don't like being chosen by God. We can't avoid it. The intensity of having eight hundred extra journalists over here covering the uprising has had an inhibiting effect on Jews abroad, because they don't want to howl with the wolves. But despite the often negative motivations of the media, it all helps us to become vigilant from inside."

FOR HENRI ATLAN, it has been a long journey from the small Algerian town of Blida, where he was born in 1931. A shoemaker, and later a school custodian, his father was active in the labor movement. Under the French colonial system, the Jews of Algeria, unlike those of Morocco, were French citizens. There were about a million French, including the Jews, in a sea of eight million Arabs. As the goal of every Jewish parent was to make their children French, their children did not learn Arabic. "The Arabs lived in separate quarters. We did not see them. They were just part of the landscape," Atlan recalled.

His family was thoroughly assimilated, and he did not know what Shabbat was—or Passover for that matter. He started to become aware of his Jewishness at age nine, when the Vichy regime in France enacted anti-Semitic laws. His parents were thrown out of their jobs, and Jewish pupils were expelled from schools (the Jews were forced to organize their own schools). The anti-Semitism that prevailed at that time made the Atlans and their friends and neighbors aware of who they were. "We discovered we were Jews." In Oron, where Atlan's family lived for some years, Albert Camus taught in one of these Jewish schools to show solidarity with the oppressed people.

Atlan went to France at age sixteen. He and his friends became part of an experimental school, where assimilated French and North African Jews, traumatized by the Holocaust in varying degrees, could learn about their Jewishness. In the school in Paris, which was run along the lines of a commune, ten boys and ten girls each year learned about Judaism and Jewish lore. The idea was to start a new life, a new world and a search for metaphysical truths, while at the same time becoming connected to Judaism.

Atlan became involved in the Jewish student movement. Though he and his friends stayed removed from the other groups in the movement, they did feel more in common with the Communists than with the Zionists. "The Mapainik students were, well, Mapainiks," he recalled, implying that the mainstream labor-socialist Zionists were doctrinaire, unimaginative.

Atlan continued to study Torah, Talmud and Cabala. Creating their own methods of study, he and his friends felt distant from traditionalist teachers. In 1960 he became director of the school he had attended in the postwar period and also taught there. Along the way he had become a physician, but he was only interested in basic research, especially in the relatively new field of biophysics.

He went back to the Sorbonne to study higher mathematics and physics, practicing medicine to foot the bills. In 1966 he became a professor at Rouen Medical School, but soon left when he became a fellow of the U.S. national space agency, NASA. It was a great opportunity, and he was eager to go to America, where the most advanced work in biophysics was being done.

At the NASA Research Center in northern California, Atlan conducted important research into the effects of cosmic rays and accelerated particles on human beings, using fruit flies and bacteria. The huge accelerators at the famed Berkeley Rad lab were made available for his work. Out of this research came crucial studies of the aging process; this in turn opened up the field of biological organization, in which Atlan soon became an international authority. Biological organization, in simple terms, examines the way groups of molecules are organized in order to perform some function, to do what a cell does.

When Atlan arrived in the Bay Area in 1966, there was a great deal of other experimentation going on. The scientist and Jewish scholar took LSD and journeyed to the small village of Huatla in Mexico to take the magic mushroom: while he was studying outer space, he was stuyding inner space as well. He does not regret this experience in any way.

> It was very important to me, mostly the mushroom experience. I had been studying Cabala for many years, but always in a very intellectual way. Suddenly, I saw that the authors of these books had had visions, revelations, even though the content of their books was presented in a very rational way. It was overwhelming, and I couldn't explain it. I discovered the world of mystics. I understood more the need to study the *mitzvot* [the 613 Jewish religious commandments]. When you're trying to climb a mountain, you're not even sure that there is a mountain—you don't see it, don't know. This was a look at the mountain in a helicopter. It changed my way of studying Torah. It became much more alive.

In his scientific work, Atlan left his studies of aging and went into the purely theoretical field of mathematics and information theory. At

Berkeley Atlan worked closely with Aharon Katchalsky (brother of former Israeli president Ephraim Katzier), whose life was cut short in the attack by Japanese terrorists at Lod airport in 1972. Katchalsky, one of Israel's most brilliant scientists, was doing pioneering work on irreversible thermodynamics, a different way of approaching the problem of biological organization. Katchalsky was one of the few people in the world who could understand the work Atlan was doing. Meanwhile, Atlan returned to France, where he wrote the first of two key books on organization theory and biology and taught at the University of Paris.

Katchalsky invited Atlan to become a visiting professor at the Weizmann Institute, and Atlan accepted the offer—thus began Atlan's "professional romance" with Israel. According to Professor Alex Silverberg of the Weizmann Institute, the collaboration between Katchalsky and Atlan, and Atlan's work after Katchalsky was killed, is very important, indeed. "He is one of the few in the world developing the field of biophysics." The work is a mathematical model that would allow one to understand biological interaction within a biological system, how the flow of energy is controlled.

Even before his academic romance with Israel, Atlan had become attached to the country for religious reasons. Early in the sixties he had come to Jerusalem to study with Rabbi Zvi Yehuda Kook, son of the Rav Kook and eventually mentor of Gush Emunim, which would become Atlan's nemesis. Rabbi Kook had the teaching method Atlan and his friends had been seeking for years. "It was true, the real thing, because it was based on the teachings of his father, a synthesis of [modern] philosophy and Cabala, as well as traditional studies." Zvi Yehuda Kook, the guru of messianic nationalism, was attractive to the leftist Atlan "because he thought like a Marxist."

Atlan was particularly interested in the work of the Maharal, Rabbi Loew of medieval Prague, who is best known as the creator of the Golem, but whose work was of extreme importance to Judaism because he extended and translated Cabalistic teachings into science and philosophy, having been closely involved with Copernicus and Kepler. The Rav Kook was in the same tradition, a man at home with Nietzsche and Schopenhauer, as well as with the Cabalists and rationalists of Jewish tradition.

Atlan worked on biological organization theory and thermodynamics at Weizmann for three years. Then he accepted an offer from Hadassah University Medical School to start a new department of biophysics and nuclear medicine (a diagnostic field using radioactive materials). Combining these two fields was a first in Israel, and Atlan's work included the most sophisticated areas of medical imaging, including nuclear magnetic resonance. Atlan's cell biology experiments and theoretical work won him international recognition; even before he was awarded the Legion of Honor, Atlan was in constant demand as a lecturer at universities in North America, Europe and Japan.

Though always sympathetic to the Peace Now movement, Atlan felt that the liberal-left would never learn the right language for reaching the Israeli masses—the Sephardi majority, many of whom are traditional. He believes the left must not leave religion and tradition to the right, or it will never sway the average Israeli. He himself became "chairman of the advisory board" in the short-lived *ohelim* movement of Sephardi slum residents, who organized sit-in demonstrations in Jerusalem. "They needed people without a criminal record," he recalled wryly. "In the end they were cheated by unfilled promises, as so often in the past."

Atlan's sense of mortality is very strong, as evidenced by the thick tome he published in 1986, *A Tort et Raison* (On Wrong and Right). The book is an analysis of the difference between scientific rationality and traditional rationality, in which religion—whether Jewish, Zen or Hindu—plays a big part. He also has written, in a book of essays by leading French-Jewish intellectuals, on the humanistic, universalistic Rav Kook—who, he feels, has been co-opted and perverted by the nationalistic elements exemplified by Gush Emunim.

This latter work has something in common with a 1985 book by Lova Eliav, the former Labor Party secretary-general who went several degrees to the left of the party. Eliav's book (to be published in English in the fall of 1988 under the title *New Heart, New Spirit*) is a secular-humanists' attempt to reclaim the Bible from the messianic nationalists. Atlan believes that Eliav is the only prominent member of the liberal-left camp who has the wisdom to present arguments against the continuing occupation of the territories in terms of Torah values, whereas universalism simply doesn't speak to most Israelis.

Atlan believes that Israel's central problem is the occupation of the West Bank and Gaza. It will continue until "transfer will become a real possibility." In the months before the Palestinian uprising, he was afraid even to voice such a view, because "the more we say about transfer, one way or the other, the more likely it becomes."

Despite the fact that he is an Orthodox Jew, Atlan is more disturbed than gratified by the growing number of Israelis who are becoming newly observant. "It is convenient to be religious because you don't have to think too much." It can be lethal when combined with a Zionism that is "a kind of weakness of mind."

The religious nationalists, in his view, are pursuing a false Messiah, like the seventeeth-century movement that believed Shabbetai Zvi was the awaited one. He believes that today's movement, built around the Gush

Emunim/settler philosophy with a dose of Kahane racism mixed in, will go the way of Sabbatianism. "It will blow up the mosques—and the Messiah will not come!"

The Sabbatian movement "was authentic in its Cabalistic roots," Atlan believes, but it was also subject to wild misinterpretation. "But that is what perversion is all about. You pervert the authentic, not the entirely imaginary."

Many ultra-Orthodox people oppose any Jewish state until the coming of the Messiah because the modern state can only cause violence. Atlan, who is not an obscurantist or particularly partial to the ultra-Orthodox, finds their position far more sympathetic than that of the religious nationalists. In his view, the "black hats" will not use religion to justify racism and nationalism. In the practical world, where good and evil are all mixed together, you cannot pretend to be pure, without evil or compromise, as when you are in "the upper worlds" of prayer and Shabbat observance. "Of course you should take what the Cabala calls 'sparks' of light and separate them from evil —but it is dangerous, it's what Shabbetai Zvi did." Cabala, Atlan says, is "just normal Jewish study—it was not for mystics only. Anyone who studies it knows this. The whole *siddur* [the Jewish prayer book] is based on it."

Atlan believes that Judaism, even the least Zionistic varieties, has been "poisoned by this Messianic idea." Many religious Jews now believe that "as long as they observe the *mitzvot*, they don't have to worry about leaving the territories because 'God will help us.' " He makes a chilling comparison: "When the Romans entered Jerusalem and were on their way to destroy the Second Temple, the Jews inside awaited a miracle. Even at the last minute, as the Romans were on their way up the Mount, the Jews thought that this would just make the miracle of their salvation all the greater."

Atlan is close to Rabbi Adin Steinzalz, generally considered the greatest Talmudic scholar of modern times. Although he is somewhat critical of Steinzalz's refusal to stay out of the great political debate, he has the utmost respect for the work of this rabbi. "Steinzalz is preparing the future."

Atlan, who would like to see a political Zionism based on morality and love of the land that is bereft of any false messianism, believes that some good may come out of the mass return to religion. Study does bring some constraints and has other positive values. In Israel's fortieth year, or soon after, "There might be a swing of the pendulum; and in a crude way, the return to Judaism movements may pave the ground for it."

What does the Cabala, in which numerology is an integral element, have to say about forty? "Four, and its extensions, represents a kind of totality," Atlan said. "The Passover Haggada is built around it—the four sons, the four cups of wine. Five is beyond totality. The fifth cup is for Elijah the Prophet. It doesn't exist yet, not until the days of the Messiah." Not another false one, Atlan hopes.

XXVII

NOT EVERYONE IN ISRAEL is a genius, a soldier-farmer or a Jewish savant. We have a working class—*amcha*, the salt of the earth—and an increasingly large nonworking class. Quite ordinary Jews exist right here in the Jewish state, though it may be hard to believe for some Jews abroad (a shrinking minority) who still believe that a Jew born in Israel is somehow superior.

One Jewish visitor from the United States, a well-known record tycoon, could not get over his discovery of "really stupid Jews, Jewish cops and Jewish supermarkets, and so many lame-dumb-everyday variety of Jews" in Israel—especially after all those streetwise L. A. and New York Jews, the smart lawyers and the smooth operators he knew from the entertainment industry.

Of course, there are all kinds in any nation, and Israel has its share of every type. Zionism was a striving for a normal existence in a normal state, which meant Israel would produce a normal percentage of criminals and prostitutes and ne'er-do-wells, but there often seems to be a particularly Israeli, or Jewish, twist to our usualness. For a few days in the early eighties, for instance, Israelis were spellbound by a story about the grim and ancient raven—and a poor soul whose life was transformed into a battle between nature and man.

Aryeh Nurielli's big problem will not go away: for six years now, since the ravens first started haunting him, he has been the target of a most unforgiving tribe.

I sympathize with him, possibly because the Rapoport family was closely linked to the species from at least the Middle Ages (*rapo* is from the German *rabe* for "raven"). I almost feel responsible—how many times have I wished such a curse on my enemies? But why have the ravens been tormenting this particular hapless soul, this human being who is the same age as the state, who sits all day long on the *barzilim* (the iron railings along the main streets), trying to make sense of it all?

Sara Nurielli, the mother of Aryeh, told me that the ravens who torment her son have never let up and have caused "only suffering—no money—only suffering."

It all began in Jaffa in 1982. Local residents said that it came as a sign. Of something. A two-foot-long black and gray raven was dogging the footsteps of a thirty-five-year-old man living in a dilapidated old house in the ancient port town made famous by Jonah and the Leviathan, and beautiful Andromeda and the sea monster.

At the station near the clock tower on Jaffa's main street Aryeh Nurielli told police, "This crow [sic] is driving me crazy. I'm afraid to go out of the house in the morning. I've stopped going to the square where I used to meet my friends every evening, because the raven is outside the door waiting for me and follows me." Later, a spokesman at the police headquarters, Yitzhak Cohen, told an investigative reporter that he had never heard of anything like this before. "It's strange," he said.

On one occasion, the raven appeared as soon as Nurielli managed to get out of his mother's house. Following him to a movie theater, it suddenly nose-dived toward the hapless man and, just before hitting him in the head, veered dramatically and soared into the sky.

A week after Passover 1982, everybody in Jaffa was talking about it, wondering what it portended. Newsmen were flocking to the scene (the news business was slow, then). ABC Television was there, and Nurielli was trying to squeeze out a hundred dollars for his pain. No question that he was in trouble—his thin face, framed by his straggly black hair and oily, short-haired beard, stared out through hooded eyes from the front cover of *Ha'olam Hazeh* (This World), the nation's most popular weekly, a highly successful mix of semi-porn, gossip and left-wing politics. The back cover featured a woman who had been murdered with a nail gun.

The story captured the country's imagination during the same week that a war with Syria became a possibility, and six weeks before Israel invaded

Lebanon. Nurielli's mother said at the time that her son should get paid for all the interviews and pictures. At the movie theater where Hitchcock's *The Birds* was specially screened for him by the cinema owner, photographers swarmed all over him. All Nurielli got out of it was a free dinner and horrible nightmares, possibly for the rest of his life—birds pecking at your head intent on destroying you.

When he got back to the street where he lived, Aryeh ("lion" in Hebrew) dived for the earth as the raven again swooped down on him. "We don't know what the bird wants, but we're afraid he may take an eye out," his mother said.

An American in-law told Nurielli he could make a lot of money out of his trouble, especially if he lost an eye. After all, at that very time, Moshe Dayan was defending the receipt of thousands of dollars from Israeli newspapers that wanted to interview him. The legendary hero, who had lost an eye to a bullet rather than a beak, was reportedly making $700,000 a year from these interviews and book advances. Why shouldn't the unemployed, thoroughly wretched Nurielli do well, too? Nurielli decided not to speak to the press until that big offer came along. "Aryeh's life has always been a mess," a neighbor said.

Meanwhile, the police worked on the strange case in cooperation with the Nature Reserves Authority and the SPCA. Theories abounded. The raven, perhaps trained by a man who looked just like Nurielli, may have believed that the Jaffa man was his master. Maybe the raven was seeking revenge for some wrong done him by Nurielli—perhaps he took the raven's eggs or disturbed its nest on the roof or otherwise displeased the big bird, whose species was for millennia a source of superstition and veneration.

"They remember anyone who does them wrong," Professor Aharon Shulov of Jerusalem's Biblical Zoo told me. He did not think the saga was unique. If a young raven falls from its nest and is brought to the zoo, a flock of ravens immediately descends on the zoo and tries to get him out, the professor said.

A leading Moroccan-born rabbi, of the famed Abuhatzeira clan, offered his reading of the situation, a twist on the raven's vengeful reputation. The spirit of a bad man who had wronged Nurielli and then died had entered the bird and was now asking forgiveness. Other experts suggested that the raven darting down on Nurielli was just influenced by the season—in spring, ravens perform remarkable aerobatics, tumbling, flying upside down and nose-diving.

Three weeks after the raven's first appearance, its family joined him. Traditionally, ravens presage evil, and Nurielli grew into a panic as several birds were now stalking him. He caught one and turned it over to the Tel Aviv University zoological garden. But it wasn't the main guy. His nemesis remained.

For a while, he was only going out at night. "The bird doesn't see at night," he said. Three more weeks passed, and the Lebanon war broke out; no reporter called Aryeh Nurielli for years to come.

In Jewish tradition, the raven was a clever, bitter, unclean bird, whom Noah dispatched to find out if the Flood waters had receded. The wretched bird's mission was unsuccessful, for when the raven saw the body of a dead man, he set about devouring it and never returned to Noah.

Six years after Aryeh Nurielli's few minutes of fame, as the events of the Palestinian uprising filled most of the columns of even the thickest Israeli dailies, flocks of ravens continued to torment the still-jobless man. They had never stopped. Aryeh had learned to live with it, and so had his mother. "The other day," she said, "a raven came into the kitchen and just sat there on the washing machine. Just sat there!"

Richard T. Nowitz

XXVIII

I N THE RICH green fields and under the royal blue skies of the Jewish homeland, the kibbutz has represented a life based on the physical and mental labors of a people who were once ragged and wretched behind ghetto walls. Created by secular revolutionary mystics as zealous as any black-hat or Gush Emunim believer, the kibbutz has always been a great pride for Israel. But eighty years after it all began, and forty years after the creation of the state, a terrible financial debt has shaken the rural foundations of the nation, and the whole socialist communal enterprise is in crisis.

This particular dark cloud, however, may contain a silver lining, for the often-insulated and smug collectivists, whose feelings of superiority were nurtured in relative isolation, are being forced to undergo a skin change, to reexamine and reappraise their roots and their goals. There is reason to believe that something good will come out of the adversity.

The most obvious damage has occurred on kibbutzim that have been problematic in the past, or were just getting by, but the severity of the crisis is such that it has affected even the richest and most successful kibbutzim, like dynamic Kfar Giladi, a hilly kibbutz near Metulla and the Lebanon border, one of the oldest farm and factory settlements in the country. In a highly organized place like Kfar Giladi, it may easier for the kibbutzniks to rededicate themselves to the idealistic goals their movement stands for. But in many other settlements around the country, a severe depression has set in, with no silver lining the clouds.

It is said that about 10 percent of the communally owned kibbutzim will not survive the severe economic plight affecting the nation's farms, which was caused by exorbitant interest on bank loans. For the great majority of kibbutzim, strong ideology and accumulated wealth ensure survival. But there is danger of collapse of a much higher percentage of the moshavim, where families own their individual land and property but are interdependent economically. These communal settlements are answerable to central cooperative organizations that have suffered financial bankruptcy. As Israel confronted the massive Palestinian revolt, bailiffs sent by the banks were trying to confiscate the private property of hundreds of moshav farmers in Israel proper.

All of this ruin exists in the midst of plenty. Israeli agriculture has never been stronger, annually producing $2.5 billion worth of superb fruit, vegetables, grain and other crops that could have come out of the Garden of Eden. The high quality of the produce is all the reason one needs to live in Israel, but the current indebtedness negates the plentiful rains of the last few years and even the cessation of the mid-1980s drought.

In the spring of 1987, the United Kibbutz Movement (UKM), the larger and less ideological of the two kibbutz federations, went to the government hat in hand, asking for an emergency loan of $180 million—a tide-over measure, since the total kibbutz debt probably exceeded $2 billion, according to one Agriculture Ministry source. In the rough world of Israeli politics, the humbling handout apparently hurt more than helped. Politicians linked the loan request to grants for *yeshivot* and aid to nonproductive settlements on the West Bank. Also, taxpayer resentment soared: at the time, many Labor- and Likud-oriented businesses and institutions were seeking bailout money. Now it could be said that even the proud "aristocrats" of the nation, long resented by the Likud electorate, had been forced to beg. The long crisis has had a deep emotional effect on the people of the land, setting off a profound reassessment of ideology and identity that some think is of the utmost importance to the survival of Israeli collectivism (ideology has never been important in most of the moshavim). Even their worst enemies recognize the great achievements of the communards who sought a synthesis of Zionism and radical socialism, and "built the Jewish state cow by cow, farm by farm." They persevered through the years of strenuous labor, security problems, moral dilemmas and despair; many of their settlements became prosperous model farms. The 140,000 kibbutzniks, about 4 percent of Israel's population, supply much of the food for their countrymen, as well as a disproportionate share of the industrial output. They have been the backbone of the officer corps since the creation of the Israel Defense Forces, and they have provided the world with a leaf-fringed legend of the Jewish farmer-soldier.

Some say that materialism was the snake that crawled into this utopia—at least into a number of the settlements. Kibbutz members wanted color TVs, more vacations, better communal facilities. Increasingly, they wanted their children to live at home, not in children's houses (a mainstay of kibbutz ideology), so that expensive new housing had to be built. In the moshavim, members buying through central cooperatives wanted newer cars and, instead of perfectly suitable tractors, John Deere tractors that cost twice as much. They borrowed from the banks. In the early eighties, Israelis in general, tempted by videos and Volvos, went on a wild buying spree.

It was the Age of Aridor, the former Likud Finance Minister generally credited with the near-destruction of the economy. According to Avraham Katz-Oz, a kibbutznik and Labor Knesset member who became Deputy Minister of Agriculture in the Shamir-Peres national unity government, Aridor promised the kibbutzim $250 million for development and did not pay it for many months. "Meanwhile, the kibbutzim were building, at a time when the inflation rate was 15 percent per month," Katz-Oz told me. "That meant interest of 15 to 16 percent per month." In addition, the settlements were hard hit by the decision in July 1985 by the coalition government to freeze the dollar, wages and prices.

The wild buying deeply depleted the treasuries of the less successful settlements, but it was no problem for the wealthier kibbutzim. In fact, they had great financial surpluses, which they invested in farms in Argentina and the Tel Aviv stock market to protect themselves from the runaway inflation rate, or to make more money. But they blundered all along the way. One relatively minor example was their choice of David Balas as an investment expert. Balas, who was later found guilty of financial misdeeds, lost about $60 million for the UKM.

It was hard-earned money. Not every kibbutz is a country club with tennis courts and swimming pools, as Likudniks sometimes like to portray them. Some look like dilapidated farms in the Ozarks, others like drab and dusty settlements in southwestern America.

Kfar Giladi, however, is definitely a jewel in the Zionist crown. If it is in trouble, then all of Israel is. The kibbutz's general manager, Amos Levine, thirty-seven, was born and raised on the verdant seventy-year-old kibbutz, one of the oldest in the country (the first kibbutz, Dagania, was established in 1907). He supervises a prosperous little town of 780 people who keep busy with a thousand acres of cotton, corn, peanuts, avocado, apples; a successful optics factory; an attractive guesthouse with 150 rooms (''the biggest in Israel''); and the mainstay of the kibbutz, a huge quarry and powder plant that itself owns seven cement factories around the country. It is big business at this kibbutz, $30 million a year in ordinary times. But since the crisis hit, income has fallen to $18 million annually.

''We've stopped developing,'' Levine told me over cafeteria lunch in the new, $3-million central dining room, a splendid wood-paneled building reinforced to withstand Katyusha rocket attacks. ''And that's bad—we live for development.'' The kibbutz had been hardest hit by the government's general cutback on building, including roads. The head of the efficient, computerized quarry operation, which supplies 8 percent of Israel's building materials, is Gideon Giladi, grandson of the pioneer for whom the kibbutz is named.

''The kibbutz is a very safe way of life,'' he said, ''and it took a very long time for the average kibbutznik to understand just how bad the situation is now. Everyone reads the papers, but it took about a year to bring it all home.'' One way was to stop supplying the market, where kibbutzniks bought food for cooking in their own small kitchens, sweets and toys. ''The shelves are empty now. We don't want to tempt people.''

Giladi pointed out that in the context of the general economy, his kibbutz was doing quite well. The biggest builder in the country, the Labor-affiliated Solel Boneh, was close to collapse, but its big materials supplier was still all right. Kfar Giladi was almost breaking even, though it was unable to expand or to replace old equipment—a very serious problem down the road a bit. In 1987 the kibbutz laid off sixty outside workers, cut down on vacations, transportation—even food. However, Gideon

Giladi and Amos Levine said that they were worried about the future. Will young people come back after the army and university? "But the crisis has strengthened our ideology and led to a reexamination," Giladi said. "You have to know why you live in kibbutz. Many are saying that the crisis will reinvigorate the whole kibbutz movement."

The economy as a whole must show signs of recovery before the kibbutz-moshav situation can improve, but Giladi is not sanguine. "Over $2 billion has been poured into the nonproductive settlements in the West Bank. They live on Israel; they don't feed it. That's the basic difference." The bitterness against the settlers and everything they stand for accelerated with the Palestinian uprising. On the kibbutz, it was felt that the Greater Israel people were not only a disaster economically, but that the whole country was going down the drain politically because of them.

Although Kfar Giladi's surplus had been wiped out and no new equipment was being bought, it remained a rich settlement whose problems were eminently solvable. That was not the case with another kibbutz fifteen miles to the south, Lehavot Habashan, a run-down and ramshackle member of the Mapam-affiliated Kibbutz Artzi movement. The forty-five-year-old kibbutz, with 300 members and a population of 550, was in deep financial trouble, and the farm crisis had adversely affected the general mood.

The secretaries of the kibbutz, Edit Sela and Oded Dagan, did not want to give figures, but outside estimates of the debt ranged between ten and twenty million dollars. Here too, it was the astronomical interest that pushed this kibbutz, long in the red, to the brink of collapse.

Unlike the UKM, the Artzi federation, generally much more leftist ideologically, did not go to the government to ask for help in rescheduling its debts, but tried to arrange loans directly with the banks. "We haven't gone to the government, and that makes us feel better," Dagan said. But, shaking his burly head, he conceded that his federation might be forced to do so in the near future.

In 1986 the kibbutzniks of Lehavot Habashan slashed their total expenditures by 20 percent—food, furniture, vacation time, clothing, car mileage. But it proved "too depressing," and in 1987 5 percent of the cutback was restored in the personal budgets of the kibbutzniks—money for books, chocolate, toys, clothes. "We couldn't go on like this. It was really getting sad," Sela said apologetically.

In recent years, Lehavot Habashan became "a lot less ideological," and the economic crisis seemed to be spurring that trend. More families were insisting that their children live with them instead of in the children's houses. "It helps compensate members who are very upset about the economic situation," Sela said. (In the summer of 1987, the Kibbutz Artzi federation, following the path taken by the centrist UKM many years ago, voted to do away eventually with the concept of children's houses—an epic decision in kibbutz ideological history.)

"In the last two years, our young people have been examining their lives more," she continued. "They want to know why they're living here; and they're seeking more ideology, more involvement. We're in this mess together."

AT ANOTHER ARTZI KIBBUTZ on the other side of the country, Nir Oz in the Negev, ideological reassessment was also going on. The kibbutz, whose 7,500 acres of automated farmland abut the teeming Gaza Strip, is highly productive. But its debt hit at least $13 million in 1987, and the standard of living was cut back drastically. As at richer settlements like Kfar Giladi, or poorer ones like Lehavot Habashan, the kibbutzniks of Nir Oz must make do with old equipment, without any hope of replacing combines or tractors for years to come.

There was bitterness here, too, at the way some members became "corrupted during the crazy Aridor days," according to Avi Eshel, the thirty-three-year-old head of the team that tends the fields. "We built too much and bought too much. The interest on the borrowed money killed us. But the big difference is that people work less hard. They don't want to work ten or eleven hours a day, which is what we must do."

Eshel was not talking about his own team; they had recently achieved a world record for crop yield in the potato fields. But there were others "who think less about each other and take care only of themselves. I'm very scared by all this."

The best workers on the kibbutz were equally concerned about their future, including Larry Butler, who had helped Eshel's team achieve its world record. Butler, son of a professional baseball player from Philadelphia, had been a Marine sergeant in Vietnam, a working-class Jew who had experienced a horrible tour of duty in that war. Several profiles about him had appeared in the left-wing Israeli press, detailing this man's untypically Jewish life and his hair-raising tales of the American heart of darkness in Asia. He married a Jew of Moroccan origin, brought his mother from Philadelphia to retire on the kibbutz, and worked with almost feverish determination. But after ten years he was beginning to wonder if it was all worth it, if this was where he wanted to be. He was thinking of taking his wife, children and mother to live in Jerusalem or Tel Aviv, and to feel independent once again.

THE WORK DAY GROWS longer on the farms. According to Deputy Agricultural Minister Katz-Oz, all kibbutzniks will have to work much longer days. Speaking of the UKM federation, he told me, "We are cutting our standard of living by 5 percent a year for at least the next four years. And we've vowed to increase our production by 4 to 5 percent every year."

Almost all of Israel's 290 kibbutzim will survive the crisis, Katz-Oz said, "but the moshavim are a real problem. They don't produce enough and have no way to pay back their debts." If many moshavim go out of business, however, it would not necessarily be a complete disaster. Many would become rural enclaves whose residents would simply commute an hour away to work in one of the big cities.

Katz-Oz noted that a quarter of the some three hundred moshavim produced two-thirds of the moshavim's total agricultural output. Many of the moshavim had been unproductive for fifteen years, and the current crisis was likely to bring about their dismantling.

This somber forecast certainly appeared true of at least a dozen Negev moshavim, for example, such as Brosh, Hen and Talmei Eliahu; or of some of the moshavim along the Lebanon border, such as Zarit, a depressed place where fifty families owed $3 million and were looking for outside jobs in Nahariya, an hour's drive away. There never seems to have been much communal spirit at Zarit, and a visitor can see it immediately. A tree falls across a footpath used by schoolchildren, and it is still there a month later, for one example. The head of local security wants to keep warm and leaves the patrolling to the army, fifty yards away—no second defense here.

The moshavim do not have a mutual aid structure, unlike the kibbutzim, where the wealthy settlements lend financial aid to the poorer ones. Individual ownership generally means "sink or swim." Furthermore, the central buying organizations of the moshavim have folded. A mood of defiance developed at many of the moshavim throughout Israel's thirty-ninth year, with residents chaining themselves to fences or threatening to take up arms to stop the bailiffs from repossessing their private property. Ya'acov Ivgi, the secretary of Moshav Avivim on the Lebanon border, put it this way: "If we don't get help soon, we'll simply set up camp in tents in Jerusalem and start all over again as new immigrants, because there won't be anything left here."

But a number of the moshavim are fighting hard for the survival of their communities as a whole. In the Golan Heights, east of the Sea of Galilee, Moshav Givat Yoav's sixty-two families came up with a meticulously detailed plan to pay off the huge debts incurred by about two-thirds of the community.

Yaela Ben-Yosef, a former kibbutznik, told me that Givat Yoav had enlarged its secretariat from five to nine to deal with the financial emergency—a debt of over $10 million. ''We can pay back half of it over the next ten years. But the government has to make up the rest of it.''

The moshavniks were shocked and angry over the mismanagement of the central organizations, which had encouraged more and more buying on borrowed money. Givat Yoav, founded in a pastoral valley by a group of ex-paratroopers who had fought together in the Six Day War, almost broke up over the financial mess. There were constant meetings, and emotions ran very high. ''But then we decided to rally round, to help each other and to make sure this will never happen again,'' Mrs. Ben-Yosef said.

Why should they be bailed out? ''Our farms are highly productive, and we are sticking together.'' Many of the other moshavim will close down, Ben-Yosef said, ''but not us.''

But it is the kibbutzim that really count in the Israeli economy, and if the general fiscal crisis continues in the uncertain years ahead, the very roots of a proud national institution will be threatened. For it will aggravate an even more serious problem on the kibbutz than the economy.

A member of Kibbutz Ha'ogen, Martin Lawson, put it this way: ''The kibbutz has been successful in its physical achievements. It is impossible to parallel those achievements when reviewing the situation concerning the kibbutz philosophy. It has always been far easier to solve the physical problems, but philosophical problems which involve dogmatic and doctrinaire attitudes are very difficult and some may say impossible to solve...The kibbutz ideals and aims have not been achieved. This does not mean that the kibbutz concept is a failure, but that parts of it are, and it is this that is hard for the kibbutz member, especially of the second and third generations, to accept.''

The growing political polarization in Israel is also bound to affect kibbutz life. If nothing is done towards finding a settlement to the conflict with the Palestinians, increasing numbers of the soldier-farmers who constitute the heart of the officer corps may refuse to serve in the occupied West Bank and Gaza. If that occurs, the gap between kibbutzniks and the urban masses who support the parties of the right will widen and become potentially explosive. Then, the economic crisis on the farms will seem, in retrospect, to be our salad days, when we were green in judgement.

XXIX

MARK TWAIN, chronicling the adventures of his innocents abroad in the Holy Land a century ago, gave many descriptions of desolation and shapeless ruin, of sites "cramped, squalid, uncomfortable and filthy." There is still much to complain about in the tourist's Israel of today; but to my mind, it is paradise compared to Spain, with its twenty million visitors every year, or spick-and-span Disneyland, a parody preserved in plastic. Yet in terms of tourism American Jews—not American Gentiles—abandoned Israel in the year of the uprising, a disturbing commentary on their commitment to the Jewish state.

Israel has hundreds of locations attractive to both domestic and foreign tourists. I can only touch on a few places I have visited, mostly spas and beaches. Lovers of mountains, big cities and heroic sites like Masada will have to consult other sources: I like water, and grains of sand, and history, which is everywhere you go in Israel. In 1988 Israel welcomed the eighteenth million tourist to visit since 1948—a Gentile from Scandinavia, but the Palestinian uprising and the publicity surrounding it brought the big boom of 1987 to a sudden end—tourism was off by 38 percent by the summer of 1988.

The word "spa," meaning mineral springs, originated in Belgium, but Jews had an affinity for the baths thousands of years before Belgium existed. In the spas of ancient Israel, the demons of Gehenna (hell) were said to be the source of the waters' curative powers. According to Greek, Roman and Jewish historians, the mineral baths of Israel were the second largest in the Roman world, and none of the others were comparable in quality. Today, the health-restoring mineral baths around the Sea of Galilee in the north and the Dead Sea in the south (all of the Holy Land is about the size of a typical American county, Mark Twain noted), cater to hundreds of thousands of Israelis every year. They are also attracting increasingly large numbers of American and European tourists, some of whom combine recreation with recuperation.

Many perfectly healthy people join guests who suffer from rheumatic ailments, psoriasis and other skin problems, allergies and respiratory complaints. Israel's three main spas, all located along the lowest trench in the world, the Great Rift Valley that cuts into the earth from Syria to Madagascar, share some appropriately strange phenomena—physical, religious and political. The lowest spot within the earthquake-prone depression, at 1,200 feet below the level of the Mediterranean, is the Dead Sea, where no one is supposed to drown (Vespasian tested the theory by throwing bound Jewish prisoners into the bilious waters), and where the filtered sunshine and oxygen-heavy atmosphere are unique in the world. The Jordan River—really a creek—meanders like an umbilical cord between the two "seas," which are really rather small lakes.

One of the spas where my family and I have stayed, the Ganei Hammat Hotel at Tiberias Hot Springs, was at the center of a bitter dispute in the mid-1980s: an Orthodox sect, suspecting that a new wing of the hotel was being built over an ancient Jewish graveyard, made life miserable for the hotel's owners and management.

Then there is the contention over the alligators. At the Hammat Gader spa in the Gilead hills, eight miles south of the Sea of Galilee and directly along the border with Jordan, the four kibbutzim that jointly operate the facility have built an alligator park (populated by beasts imported from Florida) alongside the hot springs and ancient Roman-built baths—bad taste, according to some of the more sophisticated local commentators, who say it detracts from the natural and archeological beauties of the site.

But children seem to love seeing the loglike reptiles parked in green pools of water, snoozing amid banana trees and Brazilian jacarandas. And Hammat Gader is very much a no-fuss, family-oriented spa, perfect for day-trippers. There are no hotel facilities at the spa because of its proximity to Jordan and the nearby Syrian border.

Outdoor bathing is possible year-round in the semitropical little valley, with its warm, mineral-rich waters, spacious picnic grounds, children's playground, restaurant and snack bar. Other attractions include a fifth-century synagogue and a Roman theater. The Roman buildings were ruined about a thousand years ago in one of the earthquakes that periodically devastate civilization along the Great Rift. In addition to a large mineral pool, there are pools for separate male and female bathing, a requisite for Orthodox Jews and for many of the Arab visitors. Hammat Gader is a funky but clean and well-kept place, where one must bring his own towel, but where entry costs only about three dollars per person.

The Tiberias Hot Springs health and recreation spas are a world away from nearby Hammat Gader. Here is a large, luxurious, fully equipped facility on a par with the best international spas. It is part of a fifty-acre complex that also includes the ancient baths of Tiberias, the Ganei Hammat Hotel and a private beach on the Sea of Galilee. Tiberias, site of the tombs of Maimonides and Rabbi Akiva, has attracted health-seekers probably since the time of the "Galilean Man," who lived some 100,000 years ago in the caves along the northwest tip of the lake. Legends associate King Solomon with the hot springs; he was said to have ordered the demons of hell to provide hot mineral water for his bathing pleasure. The author of the apocryphal Book of Enoch also considered their origin to be in the fires of hell, which were eventually ordained as a cure for the sick. The sages of the Talmud praised the healing powers of the hot springs and the grounds around them. Two thousand years later scientists have found that this ground emanates radium.

Not surprisingly, the hot springs have inspired a great deal of superstition, sometimes with sound medical basis. In one of the old bath-houses built by the Turks two centuries ago, still in partial use, there is an ancient marble effigy of a lion crouched over a large pool. Many local people believe that if a barren woman bathes in the pool and then mounts the back of this lion, she will become fertile. In fact, the waters have been shown to cure certain gynecological disorders.

In the huge modern complex across the street from the damp old baths, Israeli and European physio- and hydro-therapists, masseurs and medical staff supervise a variety of treatments for visitors who suffer from rheumatic and locomotoric problems, fractures, respiratory and gynecological ailments.

ABOUT 150 MILES DUE SOUTH, not far from where the Jordan River trickles into the Dead Sea, the area is as barren as the Galilee is verdant. The only luxury hotel in the area, the Moriah, is located a few miles from the supposed site of Sodom. The Moriah is a swanky recreation and health facility, set in a lunarlike landscape about two hours' drive from Jerusalem. The environs include many places of Biblical and historical interest, including the Qumran caves, source of the Dead Sea Scrolls, and the massive fortress and palace ruins of Masada. In contrast to the bald, harsh environment of the Dead Sea where the Essene sect lived in awesome austerity, Tiberias looks like a languid and luxurious fleshpot.

The Dead Sea's western shore is dotted with mineral springs, where the Romans also built bathing facilities. The creamy aquamarine waters of the sea, ten times saltier than the Mediterranean, leave a glossy, unpleasant slick on the skin. It is a little like taking a hot bath in a mixture of baby oil, mineral water, vinegar and salt.

Visitors to the area say they get "high" on the clean, dry air, which has one of the highest oxygen concentrations in the world. Added to this is a heavy concentration of the natural tranquilizer bromide in the atmosphere. The air is almost pollen-free, and there is virtually no pollution. Not many places like this are left on the earth. Even the sunlight is different: with more atmosphere than anywhere else on earth, the Dead Sea air filters out some of the effect of the sun's ultraviolet radiation, minimizing the danger of sunburn on even the hottest days.

The mud, too, is special, formed of organic, plant and algae residue and enriched by minerals from the hot springs and the Dead Sea. The black, toffee-textured mud is mined by the kibbutzniks of the nearby oasis of Ein Gedi, who also package and market "Dead Sea Mud" for export. The mud's therapeutic qualities reputedly heal many arthritic ailments.

Besides the Moriah, there are several two- to four-star resorts around Sodom, all of which provide treatment for psoriasis, the skin affliction that affects about 3 percent of humanity. The quakes and fire and brimstone that occurred along this deepest slash in the earth have made the Dead Sea, like the Sea of Galilee, an inspirational place to get healthy, or simply to relax.

SODOM IS HALFWAY between Jerusalem and Eilat, the unaesthetic but vibrant resort port on the Red Sea. With the state, Eilat was founded in 1948; consequently, the fortieth anniversary celebrations were especially important to this town, which was in the midst of a tourist and development boom until the Palestinian uprising reduced tourism to a trickle. In 1987 an all-time record number of 1.5 million tourists, mostly Europeans, flocked to the beaches of Israel, and Eilat was one of their favorite places.

Eilat is expensive, and record numbers of Israelis are opting for a week in Greece because it is so much cheaper than their own country. The lure of foreign travel has always been very strong for Israelis: 700,000 went abroad in 1987 (20 percent of the Jewish population), and they were not looking for a particularly "Jewish beach" out there in the great world. Eilat, in any case, would not qualify.

But Eilat does draw a large body of secular Israelis (they still outnumber the foreigners) and they can find a thoroughly international atmosphere there. Many of the European women visitors go topless on the stony, narrow Eilat beaches, which would present a problem for observant Jews. But Eilat is more or less considered "liberal territory," while religious beaches, with segregated bathing, exist elsewhere along Israel's Mediterranean coastline. Galei-Zans, near Netanya, caters especially to Orthodox tourists, and Haifa has two "religious" beaches. In an age of renewed religious belief, a growing number of Christian tourists also tend to go to the beaches favored by observant Jews, avoiding topless Eilat.

But a number of religious people do come to Eilat, and most of the major hotels serve kosher fare; however, the beaches are considered out of bounds. "We'll just be staying around the pool," Meir Avidan of Jerusalem told a fellow traveler on the forty-minute flight from Jerusalem's Atarot airport to Eilat. He and his wife, both sabras going to Eilat for the first time, were headed for the five-star King Solomon's Palace Hotel. Friends had told them that Eilat was worth it if you avoided the beaches. "We'll see for ourselves if it's too uninhibited."

The King Solomon, which rises above a manmade lagoon a hundred yards from Eilat's main beach, is a first-rate hotel, thanks to the interest and care of its owner, British travel magnate David Lewis. Since the early 1980s, Lewis has bought up a quarter of Eilat's approximately four thousand hotel rooms and has poured money into improving the infrastructure around his hotels, as well as into the upgrading of services.

Lewis, head of Britain's "task force for investing in Israel," is an intense, dedicated man who is not interested in putting his money in Israel to be charitable—he wants to show that investment here is good business, that high standards will create profits. In developing the North Beach area, he won several battles in the long war against Israel's notorious red tape. The bureaucracy can be very discouraging to investors, "but it is not a killer." Lewis frequently visits his growing Eilat empire, flying his own jet down from London.

"Israel has to pay its own way, and that means stand on its own feet, not relying on internal tourism but attracting foreigners, foreign currency," said Lewis, a great booster of Eilat's many attractions, including "the coral, the tropical fish." And he has added to the plus side of the ledger; he is not one of those responsible for the savaging of the land, the cruel, crude boxy construction that mars Eilat's natural beauty. He and his employees show good taste. The pool area of his main hotel, for example, is landscaped with large, burnt-sienna colored rocks from the coast.

Lewis brings in large groups of British and German tourists on package tours, which present great savings to visitors, but there are no equivalent package deals for American tourists. "There's no market yet for Americans—they don't want to take the long flight and stay only in Eilat," according to Dr. A. Braun of the Tourism Ministry. He told me that only 9 percent of the tourists to Eilat are Americans.

Dr. Braun ascribed Eilat's boom to the peace with Egypt, the abatement of the Qaddafi terror threat after the U.S. bombed Tripoli, and proximity to Europe—Eilat is the nearest sun-and-sea resort where sunshine is guaranteed year-round. Like many other knowledgeable Israelis, he gave a lot of the credit for Eilat's growth spurt to David Lewis—"He really has done it."

In an Israel that is becoming increasingly sensitive to religious questions, Eilat has become a sort of symbol for secular rights. Several major hostelries, like the Club Mediterranean on Coral Beach, halfway between Eilat and Taba, are nonkosher. As in the Labor-oriented city of Haifa, buses run on Shabbat.

There are really two Eilats: the resort of the middle-class or well-heeled tourists, and the bohemian, youth-oriented town, where backpacking students sleep on the beach, finding menial jobs at the many cafes and restaurants or at tourist attractions like the glass-bottomed boats or the "Texas Ranch," a poor man's Frontierland.

These youths love to wind-surf or snorkle or scuba-dive in the Red Sea, with its spectacular tropical fish and magnificent ridged coral, which pulsates like live brain matter. There are also many campers, and a significant number of tourists who stay in two- or three-star establishments.

Eilat is a loose and easy place for beachcombers; but many Israelis, and foreign tourists as well, prefer the big beaches along the Mediterranean coast to the isolated little city at Israel's southern extreme.

IF PRICE AND COMFORT were the determining factors, Israel would simply not be competitive with the other Mediterranean countries. But Israel has its special history and a particular kind of beauty that will always attract large numbers of visitors, no matter the cost. Eilat's Red Sea beaches are not as sandy as the Mediterranean shores, though the coral beauties of the Red Sea make up for it.

I rented a Ford van for a week to take my wife, our four little children, two relatives, food supplies and a barbecue to the beach at Tantura, north of Caesarea—opposite Zichron Ya'acov—on the Mediterranean coast. Rent-a-cars are very expensive in Israel. With gas, the van cost $550, about the same price as the weekly rate for a luxury car. But it was well worth it: there was plenty of room for eight people, crates of food, luggage and a barbecue.

For ninety dollars a day we rented two "igloos"—homely, concrete mushrooms without stems—at Moshav Dor, which shares the Dor beach with Kibbutz Nahsholim's more elegant guesthouses. The Dor coast ("Tantura," the Arabic name, is more widely used) is one of the most breathtaking beaches in Israel, a quiet place with a breakwater that creates a shallow natural lagoon where children can frolic without worrying their parents too much.

Every time there is a storm at Tantura, ancient shipwrecks emerge out of the shallow waters. One hundred sixty-seven of them, some dating to the pre-Biblical era, were discovered between 1982 and 1987. The area has been an extremely rich source of archeological finds; and a lovely museum at the kibbutz, restored from a glass-factory built by Baron de Rothschild in 1893, exhibits treasures taken from the sea and from nearby Tel Dor. The international excavation project at the tel is the largest of its kind in Israel today.

History is all around a visitor to this paradise beach, which lies opposite a row of islands used by migrating birds in autumn and spring. Biblical Dor, the capital of the Carmel coast, suffered defeat at the hands of Joshua, but the Canaanite city was not conquered until the time of David. Dor was as famous as Tyre, up the coast. During the Hellenic period it became an important fortress, and topless Aphrodite was worshiped. (Today, Tantura is not at all like Eilat—no topless bathers were to be seen along the coast when we visited in early summer.) Napoleon slept here: the French jettisoned their cannon at Tantura after their bloody defeat at Acre. Now, those weapons are on display along with rotted relics of ancient marine disasters, Egyptian, Minoan, Roman and Israelite artifacts.

Tantura has become an increasingly popular resort for Israelis in recent years, and foreigners are just discovering it. Reservations at Moshav Dor or at Kibbutz Nahsholim often must be made months in advance. Kibbutz Nahsholim ("wild surf") provides comfortable cabins and single-story units for prices considerably higher than at Moshav Dor. Some tourists might prefer to stay in nearby Zichron Ya'acov, the rustic cliff town built around Baron de Rothschild's wine fields, but accommodation there is overpriced: one pays for the spectacular view overlooking the coast around Tantura. Here one hears no echoes from Gaza.

The closest five-star hotel to Tantura is the Dan Caesarea, about twelve miles down the coast toward Tel Aviv. The beach is beautiful, and Caesarea is also rich in reminders of the past. Other beaches on the Mediterranean coast worth a visit include Nahariya, Achziv, Haifa, Machmoret, Netanya, Herzliya, Tel Aviv, Palmahim and Ashkelon.

Of course, there is much to complain about, as any tourist who has visited Israel can attest. Toilets are difficult to find and, if discovered, likely to be horrifyingly dirty. The streets are not clean. Many of the people who work in the tourist industry come straight out of a Russian hotel, where the service is not exactly extended with a smile. Grumpy, angry, inefficient personnel characterize even some of the most luxurious spots. Everybody is a bureaucrat and a Hebrew king or queen, and the customer is always wrong. But despite it all, the land of Israel represents a kind of heavenly harmony; and there is nothing quite like a day at the wide white beach of Herzliya, or in the Devil's waters along the Sea of Galilee.

XXX

THE HOARY AXIOM that originated in the Near East—"the enemy of my enemy is my friend"—has served as a foundation stone for Israeli foreign policy since the 1950s, when the "Periphery Doctrine" was conceived. In the case of Israel and Iran, the policy may be an example of a handicap based on old myths rather than a sound approach based on current realities. And even after the truce to the Iran-Iraq war was declared, there was no evidence that government policymakers would know which gears to shift.

The Periphery Doctrine, formulated under David Ben-Gurion, put special emphasis on Israel's ties with non-Arab countries on the periphery of the region: Iran, Turkey, Cyprus and Ethiopia. The Foreign Ministry wished to show that the region did not belong exclusively to the Arabic or Islamic world. Economic and military ties were especially strong with the Shah's Iran—the Persians were enemies of Israel's enemies.

In the years since Ayatollah Khomeini's revolution, Israel's Foreign Ministry (really a Foggy Bottom in miniature, even when ruled by a flawed genius like Abba Eban) continued to cultivate certain Iranian leaders and armed Iran in its long war with Iraq. David Kimche, the former director-general of the ministry and a central character in the Irangate affair, was instrumental in pursuing the policy of the Periphery Doctrine. In the early 1980s, Kimche, an icy, tightlipped former spymaster, helped forge the disastrous Israeli alliance with the Christian Phalangists of Lebanon, also in the spirit of the Periphery Doctrine. Kimche went on to snow Ronald Reagan's men into the arms adventure with the terrorist state of Iran. Kimche was later pushed out of his job at the ministry for internal political reasons, but the policy he helped set remained very much in place, despite the convulsions of Irangate.

After the furor over the Iran arms scandal, Prime Minister Shamir consistently denied reports that Israel was continuing to supply arms to Iran, either directly or through independent Israeli arms merchants. He said that both Iran and Iraq were threatening to Israel, and the ideal situation was for them to continue to fight each other—a plague on both their houses. It really was difficult to know which side was more evil. But it was certain that both were deadly enemies of Israel. Many Israelis were concerned that the end of the eight-year war meant that victorious Iraq might march toward ''the Zionist Satan,'' as Baghdad calls Israel. Iraq now has the biggest army in the Middle East, experienced by years of combat, certainly capable of gassing Jews as they have gassed to death thousands of Kurdish civilians (in March 1988, 5,000 Iraqi Kurds were exterminated, causing the whole world to concentrate further on Israel's inhumane attempts to suppress the Palestinian rebellion).

Defense Minister Yitzhak Rabin apparently held a conflicting view to Shamir's; in any case he did not pick his words as carefully. According to a report in *Ha'aretz,* Rabin told a group of Israeli correspondents in November 1987 that ''Iran is Israel's best friend,'' and that there was no reason to change Israel's policy toward Teheran. The Khomeini regime would not continue after the ayatollah's death, he predicted. ''We should not forget,'' Rabin added, ''that for many years we had friendly relations with Iran, and that during the difficult period of the oil crisis of 1973, the Iranians helped us.''

But in July 1988, when the long war appeared to be ending, Rabin said that "one of Israel's fears is that the Arab world and its leaders will mistakenly believe that the lack of an international response to the use of rockets and gas [by Iran and Iraq] affords them a legitimization of sorts to employ them. They know full well that in regard to Israel this is an entirely different matter. If, heaven forbid, they dare to employ these means, the response will be one hundred times stronger."

Throughout the 1980s, most of Israel's policymakers continued to believe that Iran's fundamentalist fever was just a passing phenomenon, that the hysterical chants about conquering Jerusalem for Mohammed were simply showbiz. But as author Anthony Sampson wrote in December 1987, "The more facts that emerge about the scope of the illicit arms trade with Iran, the more they demonstrate that there is no consistent or rational Western policy."

Several Israeli Mideast scholars and political experts were aghast over what they considered to be the government's continuing failure to come to terms with the new realities in the region. The search for "moderate" Iranian leaders was, in the view of some experts, a foolish fancy. Even after it became evident that Khomeini's agents helped fuel the Palestinian uprising by enlisting Jihad fundamentalists, particularly in the Gaza Strip, Israeli leaders still seemed to lean towards Iran. Of all the government leaders, only Ezer Weizman, a minister without portfolio or clout, called for a change in Israel's policy in the Gulf War.

"The Periphery Doctrine hasn't been valid for ten years," according to Joseph Alpher, the deputy director of the Jaffe Center for Strategic Studies at Tel Aviv University. "Yet it was the reason for Israel's arming of Iran." Some of the Israeli experts, including Amazia Baram of Haifa University, a specialist on Iraq, had said for years that Israel should have ceased all arms deals with Iran and should at least acquiesce in the U.S. arming of Iraq. Baram posited that Baghdad's "pragmatic" leadership might be ready to modify substantially its former belligerency against Israel.

Alpher and Baram both said that Israel's Iran policy was misjudged. But only Baram was saying that Israel should have tilted all the way over to the Iraqi side. The Iraqi army is over three times as large as it was in 1973, the last time that Baghdad sent forces to fight Israel, and no one can be sure that Iraq will be too war-weary to send its army to fight Israel once again.

One of the government's strongest proponents for tilting toward Iran in the war was Uri Lubrani, a former ambassador to Teheran in the Shah's last years, and in the 1980s coordinator of Israeli policy towards Lebanon. Lubrani was on record as saying that Iran was using the Shi'ite militias in southern Lebanon to extend its influence. "They regard the Shi'ites in Lebanon as a major manifestation of the successful exportation of the ayatollah's revolution," he said in a 1985 interview. "After all, it's the only place where they have made headway. For example, that was certainly not the case among the Shi'ites of Iraq."

Professor Alpher, for one, did not understand the logic of Israel arming Iran, which then armed the Hizbollah Shi'ite terrorists in south Lebanon in its armed struggle against Israeli soldiers. "What could be more ridiculous?" he asked. Several months before the Palestinian uprising, he saw no immediate risk to Israel from Iran, except for the Lebanese situation. But he perceived a long-term risk if Iran won the war. "Israel has an interest in seeing that Iran does not emerge triumphant." But one never really knows in the Middle East. Some say that the Hizbollah ("party of God") has a secret alliance with Israel against the Palestinians, who have been trying to regain the "state-within-a-state" that they controlled before Israel invaded Lebanon in 1982. In the wake of the Iran-Iraq truce, the Hizbollah were reportedly in shock, unable to believe that holy Iran had admitted defeat. Perhaps now they will ally themselves with Israel—anything goes! And it is just as logical to argue that Israel and the Palestinians will one day be allies, against whoever is the enemy—most probably the fundamentalists. At a three-day international conference in January 1988 on the "Iranian Revolution and the Moslem World," Martin Kramer, of Tel Aviv University's Dayan Center, said that the Hizbollah's immediate aim was not to transform Lebanon into a fundamentalist Islamic state. The more immediate business was to help Iran "liberate" Palestine." They want one big Islamic state covering the whole Middle East, a map drawn with "the blood of the martyrs who wage the jihad." The Dayan Center's Eli Rekhes, tracing the Iranian influence on the uprising in Gaza, said that Islamic sentiment and Iranian revolutionary fanaticism "offer Palestinians an authentic Islamic explanation and a perceived solution to both the personal stress of the individual and the collective situation of Palestinian society." It is, in short, irresistible—apparently, even to Israel's Persian Periphery advocates. At a Knesset committee meeting called to air the reasons why Israeli intelligence failed to predict an Iran-Iraq ceasefire, parliamentarian Yossi Sarid put it this way: "Any additional surprise is likely to be one surprise too many."

XXXI

T HE *NEW YORKER* ONCE assigned journalist Jacobo Timerman, the
short-time immigrant to Israel from Argentina (he lasted about
two years), to write at length about a Zionist Congress. But
Timerman, who composed his reflections about the Lebanon war for that
august magazine after a twenty-four-hour visit to the Lebanese snakepit,
apparently was either bored to death by the Zionist Congress or just could
not get a handle on this dinosaur of the Jewish world.

A few serious journalists have written extensively about Israel's quasigovernmental dinosaur, the Jewish Agency, and the World Zionist Organization (WZO), its parent albatross that weighs down the neck of the
Jewish people. I refer readers who wish to know more about the ins and
outs of these expensive bureaucratic monstrosities to Israeli reporter
Charles Hoffman's work. One can learn what a morbid, diseased world
this Ottoman structure represents; but few people are willing to plod their
way through it, including most of the Diaspora Jews who contribute about
half a billion dollars annually through the WZO and Jewish Agency.

When the Thirty-first Zionist Congress convened in Jerusalem in early
December 1987, Israeli editorial writers asked the right question: Who
needs these distributors of the badly needed largess? For while the Zionist

idea still may be alive to some people, the Agency and the WZO can only be described as anachronisms at best. In essence, the related bodies serve as little more than the "private patronage emporium" of the major Israeli political parties, as one critic put it.

The main criterion for a post abroad or a high position in the Zionist bureaucracy is how much the candidate has done to come to the aid of the party. There is no such thing as free democratic election to the Zionist Congress. Young activists, members of groups such as "Telem"—the Movement for Zionist Fulfillment—held an "alternative congress" on the subjects of immigration and absorption while the official congress droned on at the National Convention Center, Binyanei Ha'ooma. While Telem was asking whether Theodor Herzl, the founder of political Zionism and president of the first Zionist Congress, would approve of the Thirty-first Congress, the crusty old horses and political hacks of the Jewish world made deals in the long hallways of Binyanei Ha'ooma, which was turned into a kind of museum, where the Ethiopians were given a corner to sell ceramic statues.

Telem issued a broadside stating:

> The spiritual vacuum in contemporary Zionism is so stark as to be undeniable. And what of the vast sums expended by the Zionist movement in the past year—how many more school-books could have been bought for the pupils of Ashkelon, in place of one campaign ad...in place of the satellite hook-up with President Chaim Herzog at last year's Zionist Assembly in Philadelphia...How is it that so many Zionists have sold their souls for a seat in the World Zionist Congress?

Well, that may be a bit hyperbolic. It is difficult to imagine Mephistopheles winning souls so cheaply, but any observer who is not totally obtuse would agree that the patient is about to expire. The choice of the very capable Simcha Dinitz to lead the Zionist organizations into the nineties will not help revitalize the dinosaur. Israelis and potential Israelis in the so-called Diaspora will demand, one day in the not-too-distant future, that the Jewish Agency and the WZO go out of business, and that the donations from abroad be better spent. It was all neatly described by an American Jewish leader, Rabbi Wolfe Kelman, head of the Rabbinical Assembly of the American Conservative movement: "The major philanthropic activities and disbursement for Israel are controlled by Zionist political parties and their Diaspora counterparts who, in most instances, are reminiscent of the English rotten borough system of the early nineteenth century."

A FEW MONTHS BEFORE the congress, I attended a session of a five-day meeting of the Zionist General Council, which was held in Jerusalem to lay the groundwork for the big event. This convention was supposed to deal once again with the nagging problem of the relationship between the WZO and the Diaspora fund-raisers, a potentially explosive issue. But no matter what is discussed at such meetings, most Israelis do not care about the remote world of Zionist politics. The council's convocation generated only a smattering of minor articles in the back pages of the local press.

If you asked a thousand average Israelis what the "Caesarea process" means—the decision reached regarding division of power between Diaspora and Israeli Jews in the Zionist movement—not one would know. It all has to do with petty politics, lots of money and generally unattractive people. The outgoing Zionist Executive Chairman, Arye Dulzin, a toothless lion since his concession to critics not to run for re-election in 1988, told the opening session of the gathering that the coming Thirty-first Zionist Congress must do everything to unite the Jewish Agency with the Zionist Organization and establish a single "democratic Zionist movement" which would "represent the entire Jewish people," an absurd notion tied to a decayed Zionist belief that even the Jews of America or England owe their first allegiance to Israel and not to their host countries.

Dulzin criticized the fund-raisers, the people who were responsible for getting rid of him, and said that "all the recent debates revolve around problems of governance and the distribution of power... The process of Zionization and drawing together has come to a standstill." He was a pitiful figure, a defrocked Jewish leader whose appearance generally created low moans from Israeli, as well as Diaspora, audiences.

On the second day of the convocation, longtime American Zionist leader Charlotte Jacobsen put the blame for the impasse on the Israeli Zionist leaders. "All we've talked about for two years is our organization. We're not putting our own house in order. You can't have it both ways. You can't dictate to Diaspora leaders without involving them," said the fiery, tough Zionist politician. Her comments elicited cheers from the Diaspora representatives and scowls from the Israeli professional Zionists.

A large percentage of the money donated to the Zionist organizations—some say more than 30 percent—is spent on administration; that is, the organization itself consumes huge sums. A graphic illustration of how the Zionist organizational structure feeds on itself while preening in the mirror arose at the meeting with a report by the Histadrut labor federation comptroller criticizing an outlandishly expensive WZO film.

The film, a 160-minute history of Zionist Congresses from Herzl to Dulzin, was made four years earlier at a cost of $280,000 and had yet to leave the dusty shelves of the Zionist storeroom. Dulzin, who approved the project, is much in evidence in the film, which is constructed completely from archival material. Why did it cost so much to make a film out of old clips? Dulzin's defenders said that the high cost was because one hundred copies were made, and that translating the film into several languages was also expensive.

Who would sit through such a film was another problem. One of the few people to have seen the film, a disgruntled Jewish Agency official, put it this way: "Boring!"

"Dulzin makes a lot of mistakes," a top aide told me. "What can I tell you? They've taken his power away, and he doesn't look well because of it. The breed thrives on power—look what it did for Golda in her old age—and when you remove the power, you've pulled the plug."

While various speakers paid lip service to "the need to strengthen the Zionist movement," it was easy to see how the organized Zionists had little to do with real Jewish problems. The honored guest speaker at the second session was Simon Shnirman, a two-time prisoner of Zion who arrived with his wife, child and mother from the Soviet Union the previous day. But the Shnirmans had already run into problems in the homeland they had struggled so long to come to: the absorption center in Tel Aviv where they had expected to stay told them, "Sorry, no room."

Shnirman's wife, Lisa (who took the name Leah upon arrival in Israel), said it straight out to Absorption Minister Ya'acov Tsur, who was introduced to the Shnirmans in a corridor while the speeches droned on. She told him, laughing, "One day in Israel and we're already refuseniks again!"

The delegates that morning were supposed to be talking about Soviet Jewry, but the two-year battle over internal control of the organization dominated discussion. Real problems, about absorption or the immigrant housing shortage, for example, were ignored. Labor Zionist Chairman Yechiel Leket, an Israeli, did make a relevant suggestion at the opening session: that the WZO/Jewish Agency eliminate duplication and waste, and hand over immigration absorption to the government. But basic questions—such as should the Jewish Agency exist at all?—did not arise. Nor were they likely ever to be discussed. Until they collapse, the Zionist pork barrels will probably produce more films about why world Jewry should continue giving money to support the vanishing dinosaurs. And the Jews who come to Israel—usually despite the Zionists—will have to fight a constant battle to solve their housing, labor and other problems.

XXXII

SCIENTIFIC ACTIVITY IN ISRAEL is as progressive as anywhere else, and the competition for a place in the highest ranks of Israel's scientific institutes is at least as fierce as in any country where there is a disproportionate number of highly educated people. But if the competition is tough for Israeli-born scientists or American immigrants, it is even tougher for those from the USSR, who do not know "the rules of the game" in a Western society. Nevertheless, a significant number of Soviet immigrants at Israeli universities and at the Weizmann Institute have overcome their handicaps in the confrontation with Israeli society and risen to the top echelon of the nation's scientific establishment.

The Weizmann Institute is named after a pre-Soviet-regime Russian Jew and scientist, Chaim Weizmann, who was elected Israel's first president forty years ago. Today, most of the scientists at "Israel's MIT" are native-born, but Russian Jewry still represents the largest potential pool of immigrant scientists. At a time when the Israeli scientific world has been especially hard hit by economic cutbacks, it is worthwhile to look at the experience of two of the Weizmann Institute's stellar performers: biophysicist Edward Trifonov and structural chemist Valeri Krongauz.

Many problems confront the new immigrant from the Soviet Union, including a Rip Van Winkle effect. Resuming advanced work after several years of being denied employment in the sciences in the USSR, he must also learn the ins and outs of a totally different system of research and professional status.

According to Harry J. Lipkin of the Department of Nuclear Physics at the Weizmann Institute, "The average Soviet immigrant does not have the background to understand, for example, what tenure means and how to get it, how to get grants and budgets for equipment he needs, or even how to order equipment." Lipkin, a veteran of the Manhattan Project, is also the chairman of the Scientists' Committee of the Israel Public Council for Soviet Jewry. He has a huge physicist's head on his shoulders, writes essays on scores of different topics, and works assiduously on behalf of the immigrants, helping them to adjust to a different world. "There's also a general problem in Israel about what to do with middle-rank scientists, who aren't superstars. No institution or university is going to give preference to Soviet immigrants over local talent."

Professor Trifonov, of the Institute's Department of Polymer Research, was one of those who faced an uncertain future when he reached the Vienna transit camp in 1976 and opted for Israel instead of the U.S., where work in his profession would have been easier to find. Born in Leningrad in 1937 and brought up in Siberia, Trifonov studied physics, physiology, mathematics and biochemistry at the Moscow Institute of Physics and Technology and did postgraduate work at the Kurchatov Institute of Atomic Energy, specializing in physical studies of DNA.

His studies of genetics did not lead to any expansion of his Jewish consciousness. His father, whose surname was Machulan, had been a communist youth instructor until he was swallowed up in Stalin's gulag in 1938. His mother later married a Stalin victim who had survived the camps, a non-Jew who adopted Edward and gave him his Russian name. When Edward Trifonov turned sixteen and was issued an internal passport, he was listed as "Russian" instead of "Jewish" under the designation for nationality.

By the early 1970s, however, as the Jewish emigration movement grew into a mass phenomenon, Trifonov became involved with the activists, taking part in the scientific seminars held in refuseniks' apartments. He applied for an exit visa in 1975, and after a year of struggle got permission. There was no logic as to why he, an outstanding associate professor of molecular biophysics who had worked in atomic energy, received a permit, while others, including a Chinese classics professor and a soccer player, were refused on the basis of "possession of state secrets."

"I wasn't particularly Jewish or Zionist," Trifonov recalled. "I just couldn't tolerate the system." He had had telephone contact with friends who had emigrated and found temporary work at the Weizmann Institute, but no one could promise that he would find employment in Israel.

"In Vienna, I wasn't sure where I'd go. My interest in Israel was growing, but I still wasn't sure. I asked myself—What am I? Jewish or Russian? I'd say Russian in most everything—culture, language. But in the Soviet Union I was always reminded that I was Jewish. Whether I liked it or not, I was Jewish. My wife and I decided to try Israel instead of America—at least I would feel a sense of belonging." Trifonov's wife, Lena, is a biochemist.

Israel was rough going at first, as it is for most new immigrants. It was difficult to get suitable jobs. Finally, a temporary place was found for him at Weizmann, on the recommendation of Professor Heinie Eisenberg of the Polymer Department, who knew of Trifonov's work. The Jewish Agency provided funding for the usual three years. After this period, the tenure question comes up, and the new immigrant is left to the mercies of a competitive system wrapped in a pseudosocialist framework.

"People didn't understand me at first—I came out of a different tradition. Here, you have to fight to get grants. You don't have that kind of competition in Russia."

Trifonov was interested in purely fundamental research, for which there is no lack of funds in the USSR. In Israel, a proper budget is available only for those involved in experimental and applied research. Although he needed a staff of five or ten, he had to make do with one assistant. "But I'm not complaining—this is a reality here," he said. "I didn't know that theory was not respected. Fortunately, I succeeded, and people recognized what we are doing."

The big payoff for Trifonov's work—the study of the mechanisms and language of DNA, the hereditary genetic material—could come in twenty or thirty years. The function of DNA is to code for proteins, and one of the main challenges of molecular biology in this century was to unravel this code. Trifonov has postulated a second code in the DNA, which he has called the "folding code," whereby the DNA provides instructions for its own smooth folding in the chromosone, the minute bodies found in the nucleus of living cells. In his first five years at the Weizmann Institute, Trifonov "broke" the code for folding, shedding more light on DNA's structure.

He managed to do this breakthrough research while adjusting to a new country and a new way of life. "When I first came here, I felt a vacuum. People were not open to me. I was sort of a strange body. Slowly, I got to know my colleagues, made friends, and came to feel very comfortable, at home."

While he counts his blessings, Trifonov expressed concern over Israel's process of absorption of new immigrants. "We witness many tragedies. People who are forced to leave." About 180,000 Soviet Jews came to Israel in the 1970s; many of them were highly educated people who could not find work in their fields. "Israel got a great present of educated people eager to work. But the country just wasn't prepared." He did not think the situation had changed. Even if the Soviets decide to open the floodgates once again, he doubted that there would be proper employment opportunities.

"I know that the brain drain in Israel today is tremendous. In a sense, the authorities are not to blame. But a special government effort should be made to face this problem. . . If Israel can't offer jobs to make the immigrants happy, it shouldn't call for aliya."

ANOTHER PROMINENT WEIZMANN INSTITUTE SCIENTIST, Professor Valeri Krongauz, also came from the USSR in 1976. He echoed Trifonov's concerns about the lack of job opportunities for scientists. "There's not even enough jobs for local graduates. It's even worse for Russian Jews," said Krongauz, whose work on quasicrystals has gained international attention. He too called for a national effort to prepare for any great influx of immigrants. "I myself had a very rough time at the beginning. I didn't expect to have so much trouble finding work."

Krongauz, who was born in Gomel in 1930, received his Ph.D. in 1957 from the Karpov Physical-Chemistry Institute in Moscow and his Sc.D. (the highest scientific degree awarded in the USSR) in 1966 from the same institute. He was comfortably off in the Soviet Union, a well-known scientist in charge of a big staff. "But I wanted to go to Israel, because I always felt very Jewish—many others came here without any Jewish background. People always dream. These may be idealized. But you can't betray your dreams."

Krongauz, who would become the first Russian immigrant to receive tenure at the Weizmann Institute, was not an activist in the USSR. He got out quietly, without having to hurdle the usual barriers. In Israel, he struggled to find work. "I was given a stipend for two years. I didn't understand that it was only temporary; I didn't know what tenure was. When I finally did realize it, I saw that my chances were very slim."

Professor Ernst Fischer of the Structural Chemistry Department pushed hard for Krongauz to be accepted. Another positive factor working in Krongauz's favor was his ability to publish papers abroad. "But it is tough going, especially for Russians who don't know the rules of the game. No one knew me at first. My papers had all been published in Russian. Russians are isolated. When an American professor comes here, everyone knows his work. My English was awful, and I agonized over my first paper." American immigrants, and of course Israelis, knew how to work the system, how to obtain comfortable housing, for example, while the newly arrived Russian had to face an onslaught of problems. When Krongauz, then forty-seven, came to Rehovot from an absorption center, he was given a room in a student dormitory. Colleagues from America or other countries got apartments. "I started from the bottom here," he said.

Krongauz became a full professor in 1987. His work, an extension of his pioneering research on quasicrystals, has been featured on the cover of *Nature,* the prestigious international weekly journal of science. The practical applications of Krongauz's work derive from his in-depth studies of the chemical and physical properties of quasicrystals, an important factor in laser technology.

Krongauz won his acceptance the hard way. He now believes that Israel must do more preparatory work if it is to attract Russian-Jewish scientists. "Of course there is a wide range in the capabilities of the Russian immigrant scientists; there's no argument about that. But people should recognize the difficulties the Soviet immigrants face. They should respect and accept them as they do the American scientists. Soviet Jews are very hard workers, very industrious. We must help them get good jobs."

Dr. Joseph Irlin, a noted Moscow oncologist and a refusenik for eight years until he was allowed out in November 1986, knew a job was waiting for him in Israel at the Weizmann Institute, but he did not realize how fast he would have to run in the three years leading up to the tenure question. On the day in 1980 when he applied to emigrate, he lost his job at the Moscow Oncology Center. He tried to keep up with scientific developments by working in various libraries, but he was barred from using the library at the Academy of Sciences. Nor could he receive scientific journals, available only to those with special clearance.

When I met him, a few weeks after his arrival at the Institute, he was just settling in, studying Hebrew, trying to improve his English and working six hours a day in a lab, feeling his way. "Soviet scientists with the highest degrees are as good as American or Israeli scientists," he said. "But newcomers like myself need help for the first steps. I've received support here from many scientists, like Harry Lipkin. Conditions are new for me. Newcomers need time, very much time."

Professor Lipkin gets depressed when he hears of Jewish scientists from the Soviet Union and Eastern Europe "who are now full professors at some of the best universities in the West, after they had spent several years in Israel, wanted to stay, and were unable to get tenure at any Israeli institution. I am even more depressed when I know their field and know that their professional qualifications are much higher than a number of Israelis in the field who subsequently received tenure." These stories reach the USSR and undoubtedly hamper efforts to influence refusenik scientists to come to Israel.

All of the veterans, new immigrants and their friends said that the continued goodwill of their colleagues was not enough. The adjustment period should be extended from three to five years, for example, and Israeli officials should do their utmost to make life easier for scientists who can contribute greatly to the nation's intellectual advancement. But no one I talked to was sanguine about the chances for any significant change, and most felt that any inflow of scientists from the Soviet Union or anywhere else will be dwarfed by a growing brain drain as Israel begins its second forty years.

XXXIII

W HEN BRITISH STATESMAN R. H. S. Crossman visited the pitiful 98,000 Holocaust survivors held in Displaced Persons camps after the war, he found that morale was always highest in centers where the seeds of a kibbutz had been organized. "In an environment of utter hopelessness, the Zionist faith expressed itself in self-organization and self-discipline. Their own civilization and communal life as Jews had been destroyed. Their homes, their synagogues, their libraries, everything had perished. But here in the camps a new community was growing up in anticipation of the new life in Palestine."

What happened to that spirit? In this new, postdesert generation, can the "Zionist faith" be a total substitute for the Jewish faith? What is the legacy of the Holocaust forty years after Israel burst into existence?

Many Holocaust survivors are still alive, and they can be encountered everywhere in Israel. One of the witnesses to the most horrible crimes in human history is Chaika Grossman, a leader of the leftist Mapam party, and a legendary heroine of the ghetto resistance in Poland. She was brought up in Hashomer Hazair, the Zionist youth organization which is the backbone of the leftist Kibbutz Artzi federation and the Mapam party. At the age of nineteen, she joined the Jewish underground, becoming a courier between the ghettoes and a liaison between Jewish fighters and the Polish resistance. The pretty blond girl who assumed the name Helina Woronowitch was able to pass as a Gentile. She managed to enter and escape from the Warsaw ghetto several times and braved great dangers to take part in the revolt of the Bialystock Ghetto. She was caught on several occasions but managed to extricate herself. After the ghettoes were pummeled into dust and the remaining Jews shipped to the death factories, Grossman joined the partisans in the forests, fighting until 1944, when the Soviet army arrived. She spent the next period trying to rescue Jewish youths to bring them to Eretz Israel; after the war, she again encountered that same fierce Zionist spirit which had so impressed R. H. S. Crossman.

In 1948 Grossman sailed on the appropriately named *Providence*, which carried two thousand survivors to their ancestral homeland. Soon afterwards, she joined Kibbutz Evron. She became a member of the Knesset in the mid-1960s, and through the years she has consistently led the left-wing socialists opposing alignment with the centrist Labor Party. Today, she looks back at the "spirit of '48" and laments its passing. "We live in another era, now. Back then, it was the first days before the revolution. Now it's one or two generations later. Those who came out of the camps, who had formed kibbutzim while still there, lived on hope—the hope of getting to Israel. That helped keep them alive. Now we have a state. There was spirit and faith then—that it was possible to build Zion."

The Holocaust survivors arrived in a country engaged in a war for survival. Many fell in battle. The years immediately following were filled with difficulties: temporary housing, little food or consumer goods, a war situation. "But there was belief—not only in a state, but in a special, beautiful state. We were a people seeking to be more just, a people pursuing justice. There wasn't any racist spirit, because these people knew what results from chauvinism and racism."

Grossman does not believe that the Zionist dream is broken. The communist dream, however, has been shattered, says the Mapam leader, whose party was closely identified with the Soviets in Israel's first years of independence. Grossman visited the Soviet Union in 1987 and was reunited with resistance friends who chose communism over Zionism, to their profound regret.

The watershed event in Israel's forty years was the Six Day War, and Grossman says bitterly that Israel's leaders became "megalomaniacs," passing on their affliction to the people. "Everyone acquired a nationalistic ego. Those who didn't, like us, were called 'traitors.' Sometimes, I'm surprised we are still a democratic state. But I don't know what will happen when we have to decide between being a democracy, or a state dominating one-and-a-half million Arabs."

But she remains optimistic about the peace process, which has a certain momentum of its own. "There's always a dynamic. The nation doesn't stand still." The peace process itself will "lower the tension we live under" and make Israelis more open to the prospects of a settlement to the long conflict.

But "there are many here whose politics represent a return to the *shtetl*. I don't speak only about the religious. But Gush Emunim wants to return us to the ghetto." She despises their form of patriotism. "The search for peace partners is what is really patriotic—in the world as a whole and in the Middle East in particular."

EVERYTHING CHAIKA GROSSMAN sees comes through the prism of her experience as a witness to the extermination of millions of Polish Jews. She is not alone. The percentage of survivors and their children in the Israeli population is quite high. Aharon Appelfeld, a survivor who is perhaps Israel's finest novelist, said this in a 1987 interview with the *Jerusalem Post*'s Edward Grossman:

> I haven't any doubt that the fear arising from that experience is passed on from generation to generation. The problem is whether, besides the fear, a certain significance is also transmitted. For instance, does a youngster here today understand that it's important for the Jews to have their own state? For someone like me, it's self-evident. The fact that there's a Jewish state makes me happy—I'm not speaking about its character, that's another question, but the very fact that it exists. And this is true, I think, of most people with my life story who live here.

Chaika Grossman believes that "Appelfeld is absolutely right." She says it is crucial to know the facts of the Holocaust, to understand what it was like before the Jews had a state. People simply do not understand the significance of the Final Solution. "Why did the Nazis keep killing the Jews, including the young and strong, when they needed manpower? They were even killing Jews hours or minutes before the Russian troops arrived. The reason was because it was part and parcel of the ideology to destroy this people. The message that Hitler gave even in the bunker was 'finish killing the Jews.' That has never happened to any other people, where the ideology and action were focused and directed and carried out against one people."

Was she moved by Menachem Begin's emotional speech in April 1981 to the first World Gathering of Jewish Holocaust Survivors? Begin, his voice trembling, addressed the audience gathered at night in the plaza adjoining the Temple's Western Wall. "*Mir zaynen do,*" he declared in Yiddish. "We are here. Where is the Emperor? Where is his might? Where is Rome? Jerusalem lives forever! We are here."

Over the years, many Israeli commentators criticized the way Begin, Golda Meir and other leaders used, or misused, the Holocaust to drive home a point. Always one of Begin's harshest critics, Chaika Grossman despised the way he constantly used the Holocaust as an analogy. "Begin once gave a speech comparing the Maronite Christians of Lebanon to the Jews in the Warsaw Ghetto, and said that because of the Holocaust we should fight alongside the Christians. It was nonsense to compare the two situations." On another occasion, when Begin, under pressure from rabbis, wanted to combine Israel's annual marking of Holocaust Day with the Tisha B'Av day of mourning for the destruction of the First and Second Temples, Grossman wrote a public letter saying that it was an idiotic idea; and Begin eventually dropped his plans. (This issue is bound to rise again in Israel, because leading rabbis and Orthodox scholars do not want to see Holocaust Day appropriated in a secular manner.) Golda Meir also misused the Holocaust analogy, "but it wasn't as bad because her Hebrew was not rich, like Begin's."

Grossman is bothered when people throw around words about six million "heroes," because most of the Jews were just ordinary people. The danger is to dilute the truth. "When I speak to schoolchildren, I tell them the facts: what Jews could and could not do, that the European Jews were people just like everybody else—a mother who wants to guard her frightened child, a father who doesn't join the partisans because he would have to leave his wife and children. There were terrible dilemmas."

Chaika herself came across her mother on a transport in Bialystock. They looked at each other, and her mother asked the young underground fighter, "Where are you going?" They were the last words between them.

"What people ever stood before such dilemmas?"

When asked if she thought the Jews were capable of ever committing genocide, she said: "I can't respond to that question. I've seen bright, good people turned into animals." Even the SS, she says, were once ordinary people.

One scene that will stick in her mind to her last day occurred in early 1943, when she stood among a throng of Poles outside the Warsaw Ghetto wall. They were cheering, laughing and applauding as they watched a Jew who had hanged himself from the balcony of a house next to the wall. Chaika could not understand how the Poles, themselves a conquered people, could "hold a party" as they watched the man dangling from the rope. Although she also saw a few women in tears, "you only could hear the haters, the ones who were cheering." She does not say so explicitly, but Chaika Grossman does seem to fear that the religious extremism in Israel today could cause terrible bloodshed as the uprising developed.

Several months before the *intifada* began, she told the Knesset, "There cannot be an enlightened occupation! Let all who hold Zionism dear cast off any illusion that an occupation that lords it over a million and a half Arabs can be humane." The gap between a Mapam atheist and the nationalist-religious right is vast, and Grossman does not appear to have much hope that it can be narrowed by people like Lova Eliav, a man of the left who tries to use the religious tradition to reach the average Israeli. Grossman has not believed in God since she was ten years old, but she says, "I love the Torah, and I studied the Talmud...I'm a rationalist." She recognizes the fact that "now that we have a state, there's no common language." She remains a classic Zionist in her belief that the majority of world Jewry should live in Israel. But before that is possible "we need to forge a common language, and not concentrate on territory." Chaika Grossman believes, with almost religious fervor, that a flood of moral evil has inundated the Land of Israel, and that the nation may not endure long enough to celebrate an eightieth birthday unless the land is justly repartitioned between Israelis and Arabs.

XXXIV

THE MIZRACHI BOYS headed for the playground right after breakfast, right after their father had yelled at them about something
while he choked on an olive pit. Avi, risking a box on the ear,
said, "You must be sick of olives by now," since his father sold millions
of pickles and olives a year in the Mahane Yehuda marketplace and was
forty years old and always yelling.

The gang wasn't there yet, just Avner, small sickly Avner with his little
yarmulke. He was sitting on the bars around the decayed kiddie carousel.
Avi went over to him and messed around. He held Avner upside-down
across the bars until he got tired of the hollering. The three brothers kicked
the soccer ball around a little in the middle of the basketball court. Actually, it was both a basketball court and a soccer field, and that was the
source of the confrontation.

An Ashkenazi woman came over with her little kid, who was holding
a basketball. She asked politely if the Mizrachi boys could let them play
basketball on part of the court. An argument ensued. Avi, big and strong
for his thirteen years, called her "the daughter of a whore." He told her
to buzz off, that he and his brothers had signed up for the court the day
before. She got shaking angry, the blood draining from her face. She used
the Hebrew words for "primitives" and "hooligans" in a way that has
become a code, since they are usually applied to the tough kids of North
African or Asian origin. Mutual hatred hung in the air.

The woman was soon joined by a man, whose Hebrew betrayed an
American origin, three more kids and another basketball. He also claimed
the right to some of the territory. After another exchange of sharp words,
the Mizrachis went back to their soccer game, while the others played
basketball. They frequently got in each other's way. "Just wait till the
rest of the team gets here," Avi shouted at the man. "We play here every
Saturday morning from ten to two. This is our place. Nobody else's."

Reddening, the man called them "idiots," saying he could see their end,
that they would end up in prison. He also called them "primitives." Avi
and his brothers cursed him back. "How old are you?" the man demanded. Avi curled his lip and answered mockingly, "Twenty." He made
fun of the man's accent. The man spat out "lowlife," and Avi called him
"a dirty Arab, just a dirty Arab." The man, boiling at this point, blustered:
"You're an Arab!"

He and his kids and the woman and her boy started up a game. Avi
and his brothers sauntered over to the same side of the court and set up

their goals with rocks and started kicking the ball around, with Avner in there too.

The man stopped dribbling and yelled at the brothers that if their ball hit him or any of the little kids, he would kill the scum. Avi, almost his height, went right up to him. "You threatening us? Is that what you're doing? You threatening us? Because we didn't threaten you. This is our court between ten and two every Saturday. That woman is always bothering us. She don't know what she's talking about. You don't either. The whole neighborhood's behind us. Just wait till the rest of the team gets here, till the head of the team gets here."

Suddenly, the man's face contorted and throbbed in hatred. He screamed in a chilling, maniacal voice at them. It shook the whole playground. Then, just as suddenly, calm returned. The man and the little kids he was playing with moved to the other half of the court and started their game again. The Mizrachis stayed pretty much out of their way. But after a while, Avi moved one of the goals closer to where the enemy was playing. The man sidled up to Avner and tried to win him over, telling the little religious boy that what the three brothers were doing was against the religion. But Avner, who obviously had been tortured many times by Avi Mizrachi, sided with his tormentors and played soccer with them in defiance of the man, and perhaps of God. In ancient Israel, which was also constricted and small and full of discord, men moved their neighbors' boundary stones in the night.

A big, handsome teenager named Dror came onto the playing field at about eleven o'clock, and Avi told him how the man was hassling them. Dror went up to him and told him politely that it was the Mizrachis' territory from eleven till two every Saturday. The man spun on Avi and said, "I thought you said it was yours from ten?" Avi said, "We meant eleven." The man had cooled down by now and seemed to feel some respect for the light-skinned Dror and was listening to him. Finally, he said, "I believe you." That seemed to be that. But the man and his kids kept playing basketball, while the three brothers, for some reason, stopped playing soccer.

They hung around the little carousel and teased Avner for the next hour, till the rest of the gang showed up. By that time the man and his kids had finished their game and walked away; the woman, who lived across the street from the playground, left with her kid too. Avi turned to Dror and declared, "It's our playground, and we'll do what we want. They can go to hell."

XXXV

"THOU SHALT NOT CURSE the deaf, nor put a stumbling block before the blind," says Leviticus 19:14, a precept that takes into account human callousness and cruelty. In a protest "tent-in" outside the prime minister's residence, which began in the summer of 1987 and was continuing months later into Israel's troubled fortieth year, a handful of discontented disabled veterans were claiming that the Defense Ministry's Rehabilitation Department was guilty of putting a stumbling block in front of their lives.

The media were sympathetic; so much so that in at least two cases they sought no reaction from the government's side. Nor did the newspaper reporters speak to veterans who were satisfied with the benefits accorded Israelis wounded while in service. That the group of protestors never exceeded ten veterans, plus friends and relatives, out of the nation's 50,000 disabled veterans should have put the whole story into some kind of perspective, but the tendency is to believe that the government cannot do anything right. Furthermore, defenders of the veterans administration say that Israel's treatment of her war-wounded and other disabled army personnel is second to none in the world. About 5,000 of the 50,000 veterans have disabilities ranging from 50 percent to 100 percent. Only one of the protestors, Avner Nagar, was among the 100 percent disabled. Paralyzed from the waist down, he is confined to a wheelchair; he is also deaf in one ear and suffers periodic back pains. A spokesman for the group, Joel Miller, who became 30 percent disabled when his shinbone was shattered in a military training exercise, told me that Avner was in desperate need of a "Quickie-2" American wheelchair, which costs $1,300 in Israel and $400 in the U.S. "He can't afford to buy it," Miller said, "and he was also turned down for a loan." Avner himself told me, "I'm a man who suffers all the time." He said other veterans were "too afraid" to join the protest, and he threatened to commit suicide if the group's demands for more aid were not met.

The broad, rough-hewn face of another protestor—call him Yosef—showed that he had been through plastic surgery. He said that though the financial aid was adequate for him, he wanted a little more respect. "It's a problem in Israel. Clerks act as if the money is theirs. They're doing you a favor. If they don't like you, they're mean." Miller interjected in English, nodding towards Yosef, "He's not pretty to look at, so he gets a rougher time. The social workers are all burnt out. They have no patience. We ask for compassion. Life is so difficult, so overwhelming, that it can destroy you.

"The Disabled Soldiers Union is embarrassed by our demands, by the information we give out. There's so much money around. Many American Jews give money so we veterans can travel outside Israel, stay in five-star hotels to relieve the constant distress. The government and the union pick veterans to go abroad to raise money, but none of us has ever been chosen—there are many who have never gone abroad. But we know of one vet who has gone to America four times in five years."

The protestors had gone to court to obtain the annual report of the Israel Defense Forces Fund for Disabled Soldiers. "In one year, $266,551,534 was dispersed," a protestor named Yehuda said. "Is it just for the administrators? True, I have a new car [worth $40,000], but it's steel. I need money for food." Yehuda, 40 percent disabled due to a leg wound, said bitterly that his wife had "said good-bye" after his injury. He was getting only 710 shekels a month (about $450) support from the government. Yosef got 1,100 shekels per month, Avner about 1,500.

Another protestor, whose severe injuries were the result of a jeep accident, was trying to get the veterans administration to increase the percentage of his disability. "He was brain dead for several hours," Miller asserted. "He was on the way to the freezer when he came out of the coma. He's had two heart attacks in the last six months. His back goes out, or his legs, whenever he has a brain spasm. And he can't have sex—that alone should be 100 percent disabled."

Some of the protestors had been thrown out of the veterans union, and the officials in charge of the ministerial department that deals with the disabled veterans refused to have anything to do with the small group. Nor did Prime Minister Shamir pay any attention to the demonstrators in their tent around the corner from his residence. The protestors continually threatened to take wild action. Another spokesman for the ten, Amar Ben-Krayot, said during the first week of the protest, "If they don't come through, there'll be war in the streets. Our disabilities have placed limitations on us. But we're all trained soldiers, and we haven't forgotten how to fight."

LAWYER AHARON FARKASH is a wheelchair-bound veteran who has fought for years to get Jerusalem municipal officials to take into account the needs of handicapped people when approving plans for new buildings. If it were not for him, and people like him, people in wheelchairs would not be able to get through the doors of many hotels, public toilets or elevators.

A veteran of the Yom Kippur War of 1973, Farkash survived "without a scratch" while his friends died all around him. But Israel's highways take a much bigger toll than all of the wars combined. While still in service in 1975, he lost use of his legs in an accident on the Tel Aviv-Jerusalem highway.

Farkash had a one-word reaction to the complaints of the disabled protestors, *bubbameisas*, a Yiddish expression meaning "tall tales," or bullshit. "Everyone who is 100 percent disabled got a 'Quickie-2' wheelchair," he said. "I got mine two months ago, after they measured me for it a couple months before that. I didn't pay anything for it. The ministry ordered according to the need, and it was a very big shipment."

Farkash got his law degree in 1980, five years after the accident that left him a paraplegic. Since he began his practice, he has represented handicapped groups who seek access to buildings such as clinics, hotels and commercial centers, campaigning for ramps, broader doorways, elevators where there are only escalators. The Knesset passed a law on such access, the kind of law that exists in the United States. "But here, it's different," Farkash said. "I can't say why—perhaps it's lack of thoughtfulness. People will say, 'I didn't think of that.' " Jerusalem's garish Great Synagogue, for example, was built in the early eighties without a thought for handicapped Orthodox congregants. When Farkash went to check the $10-million building, he found that there were two steps to get into the bathroom. On Shabbat, no elevators operated, only an escalator, which wheelchair people could not use. "What was their problem?" the Orthodox Farkash asked. "Couldn't they afford it?"

He had no complaints about the government's treatment of disabled vets. "How much you get depends on whether you work or not, the size of your family, and the nature of your disability." He gets about 1,200 shekels a month (about $800), because he works as a lawyer and takes home a salary check every month. "The handicapped have much higher expenses than normal people; often, they need a full-time helper, for instance."

Anyone with a 100 percent disability gets a free new American car or a Volvo. "I get a new car every five years. I can't sell it. It's called a 'medical vehicle.' Someone with a 50 percent disability gets money to buy a car without paying the usual 200 percent tax. He can buy a new car every three years and sell it. I also got a big house in Ramot (a middle-class Jerusalem suburb) from Defense Ministry loans. Under the law, I'm entitled to a 120- to 130-square meter apartment as a gift. Or, you get the cash equivalent to buy a bigger place like I did—about $120,000. There's no country in the world, in my opinion, that treats you as well."

He "thanks God" that his injury came while he was still in uniform and not a few days after his service contract expired. "This way, you have a father—the Defense Ministry. They also paid for my education, including law school, plus other expenses. They take care of you, give loans and grants to open a business. Most of the taxi cabs in Israel are owned by the handicapped. The ministry tries to help you return to normal life.''

Farkash takes part in sports for the handicapped, goes abroad, and has nothing but praise for the way the Defense Ministry treats the vets. His complaints are reserved for the managers of public buildings who do not consider the needs of people confined to wheelchairs—for example, only one of Jerusalem's score of movie theaters is free of architectural barriers. Even at the Western Wall, Judaism's holiest site, there is an absence of toilets for paraplegics. ''I love this city, but that situation is a disgrace.''

ARYEH FINK, the Defense Ministry's director of the Rehabilitation Department, told me that the ten protestors did not have ''the best records'' in the service. He said they were trying to exert pressure by unlawful means, and he accused one of them of physically assaulting a social worker and threatening to murder her. He said that Israel's care for its injured veterans was at least on a par with that of the U.S., Sweden and France. ''The ministry spends about $340 million annually on the veterans and on the families of deceased soldiers under a law enacted in 1949.''

One example of where the ministry's money goes is Beit Halohem (''House of the Fighter''), a sport and rehabilitation center with wide expanses of lawn, swimming pools, work-out rooms and lounges. The Tel Aviv center, the brainchild of Yoske Lutenberg, himself a disabled veteran of the 1948 war, needs about a million dollars a year to operate. There is a similar center in Haifa, and an $8 million facility is on the drawing board for Jerusalem. At Beit Halohem, disabled vets can go for a couple hours of special exercise or physiotherapy, while their wives, children or girlfriends swim, take art classes or watch movies. The center is always crowded with people who come from all over Israel. Lutenberg, while proud of his accomplishments, feels that there should be more facilities like Beit Halohem for the disabled vets. Israel's lack of ramps, wide entrances and special toilets is due to the fact that the laws on the subject ''have no teeth...this is surprising in a country which has been at war for most of its four decades.'' But people like Lutenberg and Aharon Farkash are working in a positive way to correct the situation.

According to Gil Yaniv, Jerusalem's assistant city engineer, ''There are more than 400,000 disabled persons in Israel as a result of wars and automobile accidents. We have got to be more sensitive to their needs.'' Yaniv and other planning officials have pledged to step up enforcement of regulations designed to give easy access to buildings. He attributed the new policy to Farkash, who had taken the initiative to fight for the rights of the handicapped.

Despite the tiny minority's gripes, some of which are undoubtedly legitimate, Israel's overall attitude to its veterans with torn bodies is that they deserve only the best. The weak are not being singled out to be robbed or crushed. It just is not so.

Richard T. Nowitz

XXXVI

THE MARKETPLACE is a rolling frenzy, a dusty place where shoppers seek bargains while the bird of night perches ominously, hooting and shrieking. Israel's marketplaces in the main cities are crowded, dirty and teemingly alive. During election campaigns, right-wing politicians know they have to stop there. But the philosophers and scholars ignore the shouk. It is an oversight; anthropologists should run a market stall for a year. Historians of the city should pay attention to what happens there. Even Fernand Braudel, who portrayed "ordinary life" in the Mediterranean world of Philip II, only touched on the slice of reality supplied by the marketplace.

In Western countries the central markets are vanishing, or they have been turned into shopping malls: Les Halles has become a shiny glass emporium of Parisian boutiques, and the Farmer's Market in Los Angeles is nothing more than an expensive tourist trap. Lagging behind the U.S.

and Western Europe, Israel is not yet a total supermarket society. Bargain-hunting Israelis continue to flock to the town centers—the Mahaneh Yehuda shouk in Jerusalem, the Carmel Market in Tel Aviv—to buy produce and clothing that is 25 to 40 percent cheaper than in the supermarkets or neighborhood mom-and-pop stores.

Most of Jerusalem's bus lines stop at the shouk (the Arabic word for marketplace), dislodging streams of veteran shoppers. Tough old women of Kurdi, Moroccan or Yemenite origin, wearing scarves over their hair, mingle with the black-hat Orthodox denizens of Geula and Mea She'arim, the densely populated neighborhoods that adjoin Mahaneh Yehuda (literally, "Camp of Judea").

The Number 18 bus travels one of the main lines passing through Jerusalem, moving from the slums of Katamon to the slightly higher grade of housing projects in San Simon, through the now expensive Greek and German Colonies, past the King David Hotel to the city's main thoroughfare, Jaffa Road. It goes on to the bus station in Romema and then to Kiryat Yovel, but many of the passengers have already gotten off at Jaffa Road's midpoint, where the shouk is located.

The shoppers, mostly women, bring plastic baskets, colorful nets or shopping carts; a good number of them are buying food for families of ten or twelve. The constant hum of the crowd is accompanied by the Oriental-Greek-Sephardic Israeli music blaring from little kiosks with names like "King of the Cassetas." The smoky smells of charcoaled meat and freshly baked bread mingle with the acrid odor of garbage and polluted puddles of water. The best "steakiah" and falafel stands are located here, like Sima's, which does a roaring business selling a heavily spiced mixed grill of hearts, livers and steak with onions. The heart of the shouk is lined with tightly packed stalls on both sides of a narrow walkway. Other stalls and shops are located along the little capillaries that branch from the main artery.

The vendors' cries punctuate the constant din; they try to outshout each other as they hawk their merchandise. The shoppers are bumper cars, rarely saying "excuse me" as they meander along, lugging trays with thirty eggs, and bulging baskets and carts. As on the bus, one sees a wide variety of head coverings: gangster caps, yarmulkes, broad-rimmed black fedoras, scarves. The funky, lively atmosphere is akin to that described in accounts of New York's East Side at the turn of the century.

One vendor's sonorous voice momentarily reigns supreme: *"Shekel echad, shekel echad, tiras, tiras"* ("one shekel, one shekel, corn, corn").

Israel's produce is bountiful and beautiful. In midwinter you can get carrots, artichokes, eggplant, celery, various kinds of lettuce and cabbage, cauliflower, red and green peppers, melons, tomatoes, cucumbers, kiwis, potatoes, onions, parsnips, oranges, tangerines, lemons, five kinds of apples, juicy red pomegranates, beets, turnips, radishes, squash, zucchini, chard, two varities of avocado, two kinds of persimmons, bananas, fresh dill and parsley and other spices. Other stands sell nuts, cookies, candies and dried fruit by the bulk, wide varieties of pickles and olives and cheeses and pasta and coffee. There are numerous butcher shops as well, often displaying fish still flopping in their death throes.

The vendors themselves engage in constant "fraternal" banter, frequently using the Arabic phrase for "your mother's cunt" (curse words are lacking in Hebrew), or calling each other "Arab," which is by far the dirtiest word they can think of. Most of the physical work, the loading and unloading of innumerable wooden crates, is done by Arab teenagers, most of whom are simply treated like dirt.

The vendors in the shouk are all right-wing politically. They used to vote for Menachem Begin, but the Likud party of today is much too tame for them. They prefer Tehiya or Meir Kahane. "It's better if the Arabs get out," one vendor posits, even though he depends on Arab labor. "That's why I'm for Kahane."

The vendors, with few exceptions, are the mere scum of the earth, rivaled only by Jerusalem's taxi drivers for their coarseness, dishonesty and discourtesy. They provide fertile ground for the racism that has escalated with the Palestinian uprising. They are braggarts who wear thousand-dollar big-linked gold chains around their necks. They are bullies with pot bellies hanging over their belts.

There must be an exception, of course, and if he is ever discovered, he will become famous. A small stand along the main artery, known among the vendors as "the Kurdi shouk" because most of the stall owners are from Kurdistan, costs about $50,000 and brings its owner about $200 profit on a good day. (This information is hard to come by—the vendors will "put on" an inquirer, saying that they make a profit of at least $700 a day, and that their stands are worth $150,000, and that "Arabs own the stands.") Stalls along the capillaries and in a smaller shouk nearby cost from $25,000 to $50,000. These stalls are owned by Jews of Moroccan, Iraqi, Persian or Yemenite origin. An Ashkenazi shouk dealer in produce is as rare as a black swan.

In the back of the shouk is a small square lined with former restaurants, which a decade ago served Iraqi and Kurdi food. Now, the tables, inside and outside, are crowded with gamblers playing cards or sheshbesh all day long. For the vendors and their workers, the day begins at 4:00 or 5:00 A.M. and ends at 7:30 P.M. in the winter—and as late as 9:00 in the summer. The shouting and hustle and bustle gets more frantic in the half-hour before closing, and the prices often come down suddenly, especially on Friday afternoons, just before Shabbat.

In contrast to the vendors, the shoppers are a more representative mix of Israelis, but there is a disproportionate number of religious people because of the shouk's location. Every New Year, towards Yom Kippur, the market air fills with chicken feathers and dust as the ultra-Orthodox search for a chicken who will take their sins away in the *kapparot* ceremony (in which a live chicken is swung around the head and then slaughtered).

Like the majority of their countrymen, most vendors defraud the taxman; there is often no other choice if you want to survive in Israel. The shouk vendors, like the local neighborhood greengrocers, do not like competition from the Arab women and children who come in from the West Bank villages carrying enormous loads of greens or citrus fruit or sabras (the sweet cactus fruit) on their heads. These Arabs are really a movable minishouk, lining a street near a neighborhood clinic, or just off the district's main shopping thoroughfare. Even in the midst of the Palestinian uprising, many of them braved their way into Israel proper.

One winter day I stopped at a local greengrocer's to buy fresh dill. He was busy talking to two men in a car with radio-telephone antennae. A few minutes later, just outside my house, these same men confiscated the fruit and raffia baskets of an elderly Arab woman and put them in the trunk of their car. The two men—detectives responding to official complaints by the various fruit and vegetable dealers of surrounding neighborhoods—explained to her in Arabic that it was illegal for her to sell produce without a license. Bystanders said it was the right thing to do, because the produce was probably polluted. (It is true that lettuce and cabbage from certain parts of the territories are sometimes contaminated and can cause dysentery or even cholera.) The greengrocer joined the crowd, adding that the Arab women do not pay taxes and do not have overhead; he deemed this unfair competition. This particular greengrocer was notorious for having jacked up many of his prices to at least 50 percent higher than better-quality produce at the shouk, where profits were not exactly wanting. But no one was going to impound his produce. Many of the bystanders had bought from this Arab woman for years, but no one said anything in her defense—she knew the risk, and it was just too bad.

The shouk, wherever it is, is a basically cruel place. All the people in the Land of Israel, Jews and Arabs, know that very well.

XXXVII

HE ISRAELI JUNKIE-CRIMINAL was chained to his bed in the orthopedic ward of the increasingly seedy Hadassah Hospital, overlooking Ein Kerem valley in Jerusalem. He had broken his back in an
attempt to escape from prison and was not about to take flight again;
he was shackled to the bed, nevertheless. In addition, a police guard was
stationed outside the criminal's door. A male nurse from England, a
clandestine Christian missionary who was really not too good at keeping
his apostleship secret, simply could not restrain himself—this was a
remarkable opportunity, a truly captive audience among the recuperating
crippled Jews.

The blond angel plied the criminal with pamplets about The Light, about
how Jesus Christ the Jew would "come again" as soon as all the Israelis,
including Barabbas the Junkie, would convert to the True Faith.

The English angel became a favorite of many of the patients because
of his fresh good looks and attentive manner, which stood out all the more
against the gray life of the run-down, depressing hospital. The hospital,
once the pride of half a million American-Jewish Hadassah ladies and
all Israel, had seriously deteriorated in the early 1980s; towards the end
of the decade it had become a kind of stepchild, offering a stark contrast
to the bright new Hadassah Hospital built on Mount Scopus on the other
side of the city.

The redeemer in a white hospital gown was one of many foreign or Arab
nurses at Hadassah-Ein Kerem, at work in a nation where nurses' salaries
are on a par with those of teenage sales clerks. Nurses from wealthier countries do not come to Israel to make money. They have become increasingly important in many Israeli hospitals where the shortage of nurses is
severe, and the overworked Israeli nurses frequently scream at the doctors.
The Englishman worked hard and well, a relief for patients from the
sometimes bitter, rude or exasperated Israeli nurses.

Because they got so little attention from the indigenous staff, the patients
appreciated the Englishman all the more. At Hadassah, as at many other
Israeli hospitals, a patient rings the nurses' bell and no one answers—
especially galling in the orthopedic ward, where almost every patient needs
physical help. One woman patient broke into tears after spending thirty
minutes on the bed pan, with no one coming to help her off and take away
her bowel movement.

Obviously, missionaries could have great success tilling this fertile soil.
Why not convert to the religion of love and niceness? The angel from
England could say, after Eliot, "I'll convert you! Into a stew. A nice little,
white little, missionary stew!"

The male nurse with the faraway look in his eyes was very sorry for the shackled criminal with a broken back, and he told him stories about the Lord—mixing the two Christian Lords, "father and son," to the confusion of the Jewish criminal. He also related the saga of a priest who had made a condemned man on Death Row very happy, indeed. The accommodating Israeli policeman watching over the criminal knew some English and acted as the translator for the nurse, who succeeded in making the junkie-criminal feel a lot better about going back to prison and doing his time.

When the criminal arrived back at Ramle prison, the guards confiscated the missionary pamphlets and queried him about them. Missionaries have never been too popular in Israel, but there was particular sensitivity at this time because of the many press reports about the embittered Israeli leftist who had converted to the Anglican church, Mr. Mordechai Vanunu. Having revealed Israel's nuclear secrets to the world, Vanunu was being recommended for the Nobel Peace Prize by no less than Graham Greene. Vanunu's Australian Anglican priest was giving press conferences in Jerusalem chiding the Jews for denying Christ...er, Vanunu. Vanunu would be found guilty of treason and espionage in March, 1988, and sentenced to eighteen years in prison.

Feeding the antimissionary fever was the story of the Mormon center in Jerusalem, which had also been in the news since 1985. This particular church—whose extremely vehement enemies within the Christian world make Israeli foes look like pussycats—had succeeded in establishing a huge university on the Mount of Olives, thanks to the worldly, humanistic Israelis who pooh-poohed the Mormons' history of aggressive missionizing. The ultra-Orthodox were up in arms about it, and for a while it seemed the campaign would not stop until the Mormons' big center was dismantled. Antimissionary individuals, and organizations like the ultra-Orthodox Yad L'Achim ("Helping Hand to the Brothers"), published statements by Bruce McConkie, the chief Mormon theologian. "The Jews were cursed and smitten and cursed anew because they rejected the gospel, cast out their Messiah and crucified their King...the Jewish denial and rejection of the Holy One...made them a hiss and a byword in all nations...so shall it be until they repent and come unto Him whom their fathers slew..."

The furor died down after the Mormons pledged in writing that they would not engage in missionizing in Israel. But nerves were left raw.

Most observant Jews despise missionaries of all persuasions because they regard them as soul-snatchers. They see Christian missionaries as members of the biggest, most successful cult in history, who are still out to destroy Judaism. In the Talmud, the loss of even one soul is regarded as the loss of the whole world, just as the saving of one soul represents the saving of the whole world. Given the fragility of Jewish existence in an era when 40 percent of the Jews were exterminated, one soul is all the more important. Therefore, it would not matter if the number of Israelis who convert were four thousand a year or just Mordechai Vanunu and four others.

So when the junkie-criminal back from the hospital ratted on the missionary nurse, it was no surprise that a complaint went out to the national police. A knock on the door followed. The Englishman was told by the police that it is not legal to missionize in Israel, that it is simply not allowed; they ordered him to leave the country. The nurse was very upset. He loved Israel and wanted to live in the country for the rest of his life; he knew he had not controlled his mouth. But when you are happy and have all the answers, it is hard to restrain yourself, to keep from blurting it all out. He took a lawyer.

Proselytizing per se is not illegal in Israel, but a 1977 law states that whoever gives or promises money to someone to change his religion is liable to imprisonment or a large fine. Broader legislation was introduced in the Knesset in 1987. There was no evidence that the nurse offered any material inducements to the criminal, but he was told that he would still have to leave. At the last minute, as he was departing for London from the airport, an Israeli woman friend arrived with the lawyer and told him that they had won a reprieve—if he did not proselytize again, he could stay. Officials at the airport put a little cross in his passport, a kind of scarlet letter, and he promised not to missionize again. He lied, of course. An Ethiopian Jew who works at Hadassah, and other Israelis, soon heard the same whispers of salvation. But the nurse was allowed to stay on, because he was needed.

The Ethiopian Jew at Hadassah had lived as a child among Christian missionaries, who had been very good to him, providing food and medical care. But these missionaries were regarded by many Ethiopian Jews as their worst enemies. The victims—Jews who converted—were never accepted by the Christian Amhara people and were regarded as pariahs by the Ethiopian Jews as well. Some of the nineteenth-century missionaries to the Falashas, as the Ethiopian Jews were called, were themselves apostate Jews. One of them, Henry Stern, traveled among the villages saying, "I'm a Jew, just like you." He and his colleagues succeeded in converting thousands of Falashas, leaving them in limbo.

Today's "Jews for Jesus," or "Messianic Jews" as they like to call themselves, preach the same sermon as Henry Stern to Jews all over the world. They are Jews, they say, who happen to believe in the divinity of Jesus. But no Orthodox Jew can or will ever accept this; in fact, many nonobservant Jews, like myself, regard "Messianic Jews" as traitors to their people and their traditions.

Perhaps there is something hysterical and ghetto-like in the "overreaction" of many Israelis to the missionaries. Secular humanist religionists dismiss the whole concern about missionaries, defend the Mormons and their sprawling new center on the Mount of Olives, and heap scorn on believing Jews for their "ghetto mentality." In fact, a poll in early 1988 showed that a startling 78 percent of Israelis (or, about the whole of the secular population) would accept Jesus-Jews as Israelis, if these Jews wished to settle here. Some more balanced observers, who cannot be pigeonholed as fuzzy-brained liberals, have also said that it is absurd to be afraid of the missionaries, that the Jews lived among the Gentiles for thousands of years. What is so horrible, they ask, if a few Christians are allowed to live here and preach their religion?

Moshe Dann, an American-born former history professor who became an activist fighting various cults and missionary groups in Israel, is aware of the problems that arise in a democratic society that seeks to restrict missionary activity. The missionary question raises many important issues, especially the question of how the state defines a Jewish apostate who seeks to emigrate to Israel. But Dann, who is Orthodox, believes that "efforts to convert Jews amount to ethnocide, ethnic destruction...We cannot but be outraged that, after all that has been done to the Jews in the name of Christianity, including its involvement in the Holocaust, Christian missionaries are not ashamed by their attempts to convert us."

Naturally, when vandals or arsonists strike at a Christian bookstore or church, the general Israeli society condemns such action. Moderate voices try to explain the differences between Christian friends, Christian residents or citizens of Israel, who refrain from missionizing, and the fundamentalists who believe they must convert the Jews or delay the Second Coming. All too often, there are stories about how ultra-Orthodox fanatics attack mixed couples. In November 1987, for example, a new immigrant from the USSR and his non-Jewish wife were beaten up by Hasidic zealots in the Jerusalem neighborhood of Neve Ya'acov.

Moshe Dann believes that the Kahane followers or fringe ultra-Orthodox elements who engage in violent activities aimed at the missionaries will only succeed in winning support for the proselytizers. He discerns three main groups engaging in missionary work in Israel: the traditional missionaries, such as Baptists and Anglicans; "Messianic Jews," such as Jews for Jesus; and pro-Israel Christians, including the Voice of Hope radio station and the International Christian Embassy in Jerusalem. An estimated one to three thousand of these missionaries distribute literature in Hebrew, English, Arabic and Amharic, the language spoken by the majority of Ethiopian Jews.

What seems certain in the coming years is that a large number of missionaries, including many apostate Jews, will be coming to Israel as the third millennium approaches, for many Christians believe that their Messiah will return in the year 2000. Moshe Dann believes that the Jews for Jesus will try through the court system to become recognized as another stream of Judaism, like the Orthodox, Conservative, Reform or Reconstructionists. Two cases involving "Messianic Jews" were brought to Israel's High Court of Justice in 1987: a couple from Zimbabwe, the Beresfords, claimed that despite their belief in Jesus they should have all the rights provided for Jews returning to their ancestral homeland under the Law of Return; and an Israeli citizen, Aryeh Sarko-Ram, also a "Messianic Jew," was demanding to be returned to his army reserves unit, which threw him out for proselytizing. Both the Beresfords and Sarko-Ram denied that they were baptized or had otherwise become Christians.

The cases presented a major dilemma for Israel's rabbis, scholars and legal experts. According to Yosef Ben-Menashe, the lawyer representing both the Beresfords and Sarko-Ram, "the larger issue is the issue of freedom of conscience." And on the other side, Moshe Dann said that "the missionary challenge forces us to say what Israel is all about; it forces us to examine the nature and identity of the Jewish state."

Julius Berman, chairman of the Task Force on Missionaries and Cults of the Jewish Community Relations Council of New York, believes that the Beresford case "raises questions as to whether or not the community is prepared for the challenge. Obviously most Israelis do not understand who these people are or what their goal is." The Christian fundamentalist goal, he says, is to bring about "salvation," which requires "converting twelve thousand Jews from each of the twelve tribes"—a daunting challenge, since Jews of the modern era have no idea which tribe they are from. "The hope of the fundamentalists is that through their usage of Jewish religious symbols and Jewish cultural traditions, through their adoption of Jewish causes (such as Soviet Jewry), and through their support for the State of Israel, their religious values will gain acceptance in the hearts and minds of many Jewish people. If doing so requires that they deceive the unknowing Jewish target by claiming to be Jewish, so be it . . . The Zionist sentiments of the Beresfords and other Hebrew Christians are nothing more than a result of their belief that Israel plays a central role in the Messianic vision."

A NEW NEIGHBOR OF MINE, an American who lived many years in Sweden and emigrated to Israel with his wife and six children, tried to show me The Light one Saturday night. This former musician had seen the Truth, been in close touch with God, and could lead me there. The bad people were the rabbis of the last two thousand years, who only kept people away from touching and feeling the Spirit, he explained.

I felt genuinely repulsed, just like an Ethiopian Jew who must perform ablutions after coming into contact with an idolator. I told him exactly that, but he kept on trying. I also felt that he and his reborn Christian wife had come to Israel under false pretenses. They had stayed for over a year at an absorption center, on money provided by heavily taxed Israelis, yet later could afford to pay up to $700 a month rent. He had told people he came to Israel because of his "Jewish roots." Our previous neighbors, fundamentalist Christian-Zionists, never tried to win our souls. They kept their religion to themselves, and our kids and theirs became very close friends in the three years they lived in Israel.

Perhaps it is harder for apostate Jews to refrain from missionizing. When my sad-faced new neighbor approached me a second time, I told him that I thought that the otherwise-daring Nietzsche had been too afraid to place the blame for Christianity squarely on Jesus. Nietzsche made Paul the villain. It was a little like blaming Stalin and not Lenin as well for the excesses of communism. My own feeling was that Jesus was another Shabbetai Zvi, a false Messiah, and Paul was his Nathan of Gaza. In this ecumenical age, a Jew is not supposed to voice such beliefs. But, I told my interlocutor, I really believe that the true identity of Jesus, as good a rabbi as he may have been, was closer to that of the anti-Christ, and the Holocaust was the fruition of his self-delusion. I told him that I believe the Jewish Messiah will come one day, and that he will disabuse the world of its belief that God had a son who should be worshiped as another god.

For some time after that, the missionary family not only left me alone but steered clear of me as if I were a vampire, werewolf or the Devil himself. But after a few weeks, the former Jew approached my wife and tried to get her to accept missionary literature, and he left a letter for me, saying that "the Jewish Bible says the Messiah would come two times," with quotes from Isaiah, Psalms and Daniel. "The Bible said the Jewish people would reject the Messiah the first time he came (Isaiah 53:1-3)," was one of his references. But this passage is not about an individual, as the Christians would have it, but about exiled Israel and the Babylonians. Yet this ignorant man had the gall to dismiss the Jewish interpretation of the Jewish scriptures.

Most Israelis have never been approached by missionaries. The real problem, in the view of many secular Israelis, is that some of their children are being grabbed by Jewish cults in the ultra-Orthodox world. They are looking for deprogrammers to rescue their children from schools of Talmudic study. Other Israelis are falling prey to well-known authoritarian cults like EST or Scientology. But if Moshe Dann and Julius Berman are correct—and the evidence does seem to confirm their point of view— Christian missionizing in Israel's fifth decade is likely to become a major problem, one that challenges the entire legal and rabbinical system.

XXXVIII

TROTSKY'S GRANDSON, David Axelrod, is one of them. So is Uri Zohar, a former bohemian and entertainer who was once Israel's leading film director. He is a rabbi now. One of the pioneers was Adin Steinzalz, the son of socialist parents who has become perhaps the greatest Talmudic scholar since Rashi died eight hundred years ago. Thousands of Israelis, and numerous Jews of the Diaspora, are busy being "reborn." All of them are part of the Teshuva Movement—the return to Orthodox Judaism.

They are called *ba'alei teshuva* or *hozrim b'teshuva* (penitents or repentants, or "those who return"), and most of them join the so-called black-hat centers of learning. These *yeshivot* preach a "Torah lifestyle." The students include former Israel Air Force pilots, artists from kibbutzim, and doctors and scholars from Oxford or the Ivy League colleges or Johannesburg Medical School. They are told that only the fools among the Jews believed that the Enlightenment of the eighteenth and nineteenth century had shed light on the darkness of the ghetto.

"It has taken us nearly two hundred years to finally realize that the true Enlightenment can be found in the light of the Torah, in its moral values and intellectual rigor and honesty, in a way of life which illuminates the emptiness and essential immorality of secular society," according to Pinchas Kasnett, author of a tract published by Ohr Somayach, a Torah college headquartered in Jerusalem. Ohr Somayach ("Light of Happiness") has been instrumental in advancing the Return Movement. The fifty rabbis there have found fertile ground in the repugnance felt by sensitive or spiritual people towards a pornographic, materialistic Western world.

The Ohr Somayach people try to stay out of politics, but many of them can be identified as being close to Agudat Yisrael, a non-Zionist party of the ultra-Orthodox (they despise this newspaper term, probably rightly). The Return Movement also includes people who define themselves as "modern Orthodox"—that is, those who keep the *mitzvot* (the 613 commandments), but do not live ghettoized lives and are often quite liberal in their politics. And at the other end of the spectrum are the penitents who join Gush Emunim, the vanguard of the settlers' movement whose sartorial identity is the knitted yarmulke instead of the black hat. Other penitents come from the criminal element, and the dregs of society. The Shuvu Banim ("Returning Sons") Yeshiva, located in the Moslem Quarter of Jerusalem's Old City, caters to Sephardi former criminals who have become wildly religious—and who are a thorn in the side of those who seek coexistence with the Arabs. The Yeshiva of the Diaspora, which dominates Jerusalem's Mount Zion, has long been known as a refuge for Ashkenazi refugees of the American drug culture.

Other newly religious people go even further to the right than Gush Emunim or the God-intoxicated *Lumpen* of Shuvu Banim. For instance, many immigrants from the USSR have taken their rebellion against a totalitarian system to another extreme. David Axelrod, Trotsky's grandson, lives with his family in the heart of Arab Hebron and feels close politically to Meir Kahane's fascistic movement. He told me this much on the telephone when I sought an interview with him, but the new immigrant did not want to talk to any writers or journalists.

Axelrod, a computer engineer, and his wife, Annette, celebrated the birth of their son in mid-1987: the great-grandson of the founder of the Red Army. Of course, this was an ironic twist of history, one which the settler movement could capitalize on. Trotsky, as well as many other revolutionary socialists of Jewish origin, took the assimilationist view, holding that there was no future for the Jews as a separate community, and that Zionism was nothing more than a fabricated nationalism.

Now, his great-grandson has been circumcised—a ceremony that marks the reconfirmation of the covenant between the Jews and Elohim—and is going to grow up in the heavily fortified small Jewish settlement located in the center of the West Bank city, a stone's throw (no pun intended) from the tomb of Abraham and Sarah.

David Axelrod struck me as a strange, cranky man who nevertheless had the healthy reaction of guarding his privacy. Former filmmaker Uri Zohar was also most reluctant to be interviewed. One friend of his said that the intense, high-powered Zohar had sought publicity and renown in his former life as an entertainer and director, and now he was understandably going to the other extreme. Zohar's closest friend and costar in the old days, the popular Israeli singer/actor Arik Einstein, wrote a song about his friend shortly after Zohar's "Return":

> He did teshuva
> He's learning Torah now
> And with him are the wife
> And children
> And a year has passed
> Nothing has changed
> It's the same melody and words
> But the heart, it wants much more
> It tells a different story
> And repeats and says
> That I have lost a friend.

In another twist of fate, Arik Einstein's lost friend became his in-law: the singer's daughter joined the Teshuva Movement and married Zohar's son in a wedding attended by three thousand guests.

"There isn't a house in Israel today that doesn't know someone who has returned to Torah. Pilots, artists, engineers...it's like the final stages of birth: nothing can stop it," Rabbi Zohar said in a rare interview in 1987. "I meet with the people, not the Israeli WASPs, the establishment. The Sephardim know what's happening in this country. They see what is happening to the children on the streets, what is being poured into their souls by movies and television....One who is not constantly thinking in Torah terms runs the risk of being dragged back down into the morass of routine, habit and disconnected detail...the Torah itself is described as a structure with its feet on the ground and its head in the heavens. That is freedom.

"It is freedom based on knowledge which allows one to gaze over the whole length and breadth of the Creation and to be able to partake of every facet of life in just the right amounts, and above all, to know why you're doing it."

THE SPARK THAT MAY HAVE SET OFF the Israeli mass movement (there have always been individuals or small groups who became newly religious) was the Yom Kippur War of 1973. Ohr Somayach began shortly before the war, in response to the desire of three young men who wanted to know more about Judaism and their Jewish roots.

In the late seventies, three main groups could be found among the penitents of Jerusalem, according to Janet Aviad, a Hebrew University sociologist whose book on the subject is now somewhat outdated. One group came out of the American-Jewish upper- and middle-classes, veterans of the "youth culture" of that era. A subgroup was comprised of young American Jews from Orthodox or traditional homes. In contrast to the first group, "seekers and experimenters," these Jews sought a strengthening of religious beliefs that they already held. The second large group were Israelis of Western background, who came from homes where some of the religious traditions were honored. The third large group were also Israelis, but mostly North African or Asian Jews from disadvantaged neighborhoods and development towns.

Within a decade of its founding, Ohr Somayach, which catered mostly to the first and second large groups of penitents, had mushroomed into a sprawling college campus in Jerusalem, with branches in Tel Aviv, Zichron Ya'acov (one of the earliest secular Zionist settlements in the Land of Israel), Rehovot and Monsey, New York. Yeshiva "task forces" were dispatched to Europe, North America and South Africa, holding three-day seminars for the Jews of San Francisco or Cape Town. Only the much larger Habad movement—followers of the Lubavitcher rebbe who lives in Brooklyn—could show such rapid growth. There was an obvious need, and the Habad Hasidim and new institutions like Ohr Somayach filled it.

An Ohr Somayach rabbi, Simcha Wasserman, put it this way: "Teshuva is in the air now, inflammable; one has only to strike a light and it flames up." One of those who caught the spirit was a young South African doctor, Akiva Tatz, who loved rock 'n' roll, and thought that "Dylan had said it all." He first became interested in the Jewish religion when he heard a talk in Johannesburg on medicine and Torah. His interest developed while he served in the South African Army, and blossomed during a visit to Israel. He was attracted by "the values of the Torah community...modesty and self-control."

Like others who discover religion, he saw or felt light everywhere: from the "glowing Shabbos table" to "flashes of clarity" to the "radiance" on the faces of those who study Torah. The religion's grandeur became obvious to him: "There is no limit to its depths." A single word can become the whole world: "One can become enraptured with the clarifying of structure alone."

Tatz, whose youthful face is framed by a black beard and the black old-fashioned brimmed hat favored by many of the ultra-Orthodox, was impressed by the discipline and learning he encountered among sharp-minded rabbis, including a former professor of analytical philosophy at Johns Hopkins. Tatz says that "secular education pales in comparison." His medical studies were much easier.

He learned from the learned—rabbis who knew the entire Talmud by heart—about such mysteries as the origin of the universe. And thus, he was assured of happiness amid the rapidly changing vicissitudes of life. For Tatz believes that the reward for a "Torah lifestyle" is "eternity, a payoff beyond description or imagination." Such convictions would be entirely comprehensible to Iranian Shi'ite fundamentalists, or to some African animists, or American evangelical Christians, or Vietnamese Buddhist monks.

One of Tatz's friends at Ohr Somayach was a crack pilot in an elite squadron of the Israel Air Force before he became newly religious. Many secular Israeli parents, who have "lost" their children to the world of the yeshiva, feel that the Teshuva Movement is little better than a cult. Their sons sometimes become totally alienated from them, and will not even drink a glass of water in the nonkosher houses they grew up in. Other parents encourage their offspring's romance with the Torah. In one case at Ohr Somayach, an American father flew to Israel with the intent of forcibly taking his son home. Instead, he joined up, too.

When a pilot "defects" it disturbs more people than just the immediate family. A report in early 1987 asserted that seventeen pilots had left the service to take up the Torah Life—a great blow to the Air Force. Israeli pilots are considered the cream of the military, and great amounts of money are spent on their training. But flying in a rarified atmosphere or dodging missiles in combat can make any man wonder what it is all about. That is precisely what happened to Allon. While flying the highly amplified Israeli version of the U.S.-made Skyhawk, he "began to wonder about spirituality."

He attended a *shiur,* or lesson, at the yeshiva, asked questions, and sought guidance from a rabbi. He decided that his "swinging" life was empty. So he asked for a six-month leave to study at Ohr Somayach. And that was that.

"You disappear down the rabbit hole and no one hears of you again," a still-wordly penitent (he continues to write for racy American magazines) told me when I said I was going to visit Ohr Somayach. Another writer friend, who keeps a traditional home, also warned: "Don't get caught." That is basically how the Teshuva Movement is perceived by outsiders, even by some religious people.

When the pilot informed his superiors that he wanted a leave of absence, the commanding general of his base questioned him closely, perhaps saying to himself, "Well, there goes a million dollars worth of training." Allon answered, "I've discovered that to ensure the survival of my people, I need to know more than how to fly a Skyhawk."

Another former pilot at Ohr Somayach had been Israel's representative and a guest of the American government when the Israel Air Force received its first F-15s. In the seventh year of his service, this dedicated and skilled pilot began to feel that "something wasn't quite right. When you're climbing to the top, you can always fool yourself into believing that the solution is somewhere up there. A little more money, a little more prestige, a better-looking girlfriend..."

Judaism had never entered his mind. "My parents came from Yemen as children. I had no contact with Judaism, none whatsoever. I was ignorant, and full of hate for religious Jews." He went to the East to study Zen, and eventually came back to his Jewish roots. "There is a saying in the yeshiva that 'understanding the question clearly is half the answer.' My year abroad of searching and questioning had prepared me for my experience at Ohr Somayach."

Akiva Tatz, in his book *Anatomy of a Search: Personal Drama in the Teshuva Revolution,* dismissed the charge that his yeshiva and others like it engage in brainwashing. "It's the opposite, everything is ruthlessly questioned and critically examined."

There is a women's section at Ohr Somayach, and the men are divided into various language groups—including a new section for Jews who managed to get out of Iran. Thousands of newly religious people have passed through Ohr Somayach's portals in little over a decade. Unlike *hesder yeshivot,* which combine Talmudic study with army service, the people at Ohr Somayach do not serve in the army, a source of deep resentment among secular Israelis and religious-nationalists.

According to Rabbi Avraham Edelstein, an Ohr Somayach administrator, there are few Russian immigrants at the yeshiva because they have already become religious in the USSR and can bypass the institutions that cater to the newly religious and go directly into the regular yeshivot. There are no Ethiopians at Ohr Somayach "because none have asked to come here." Most of the Ethiopians who pursue rabbinical studies are at Jerusalem's Machon Meir, a yeshiva whose students serve in the armed forces.

A general detachment from the physical marks the Torah community: men avoid even looking at women, and premarital sex is forbidden. Married women are expected to bear many children, since "be fruitful and multiply" is one of the Bible's commandments. In the age of AIDS and the revolt against promiscuity, the Orthodox Jewish views are likely to gain many more adherents. A woman is regarded as "a reflection of something very high, a being tuned to the forces of creation," according to Tatz.

His book makes no mention of the high rate of sexual neuroses that plague the ultra-Orthodox community. Tatz recalls a visit to the yeshiva by a beautiful girl whom he and two other yeshiva friends had known in South Africa. "Immodestly dressed," she could not believe how her old friends backed away from her. They gave her a long-sleeved shirt to wear. She was bewildered, ignorant of the penitent's "ever-present terror" that some woman from his previous life, unaware of the religious prohibition on male-female contact, might sully him with a handshake. The revolt against an obviously overpermissive society goes to the opposite pole.

At certain hours, the huge *beit midrash,* or synagogue/study hall, of the college is filled with davening men in black suits. They hold on to lecterns loaded with large books—the "black crow people" as poet Yehuda Amichai termed them. On the bulletin board is a rigorous daily prayer schedule, a list of sick people who should be visited, notices of special lessons. When Tatz meditates, his sparkling black eyes closed, he sees visions and feels "that this place is, in a deep way, the fulcrum of the world."

There are many rival institutions, reflecting different streams of Orthodoxy, which also claim to be the repository of truth. All of them are bound to attract many new adherents, as wild, dark times rumble toward us.

Caption (vertical, right side): *Richard T. Nowitz.*

XXXIX

"...a middle-class girl may have the illusion that a prince will come and marry her. This is possible, and a few such cases have occurred. That the Messiah will come and found a golden age is much less likely."

Freud, *The Future of an Illusion*

A S ISRAEL ENTERED its fifth decade, theater-goers were flocking to a smash hit called *Pangs of the Messiah (Hevlei Mashiach),* a portrayal of a gloomy future conflict within the Messianic Greater Israel settlers' movement and between the Messianists and the majority of Israelis. Why was this basically pedestrian play filling up large auditoriums night after night ever since it opened in June 1987, six months before the Palestinian uprising provided the nation with another kind of drama? The playwright, Motti Lerner, is a political foe of Gush Emunim, but he did not demonize the settlers in his play. "I aimed to write about real people in a real situation," he told an interviewer. The settlers' leaders concur that Lerner avoided stereotypes. But despite the throngs of Israelis paying $20 a ticket to see the play, there was something definitely missing—perhaps the quality of believing in belief.

Heinrich Heine, that noble poet and apostate Jew who certainly regretted his apostasy, wrote that "the prophet who wishes to write a new apocalypse will have to invent entirely new beasts." This play was not a new beast. But the reaction to the play, and the play itself, do seem to shed light on Israel's immediate future. For what is happening now definitely has deep significance—in *these* surroundings.

The surroundings give it its importance. *Pangs of the Messiah* is set in a Jewish settlement in Samaria some time in the near future, as a peace accord with Jordan is in the air. The playwright, alas, did not foresee King Hussein's decision to renounce Jordan's claims to the West Bank. Lerner concentrates the action on the family of a Gush Emunim leader, a glib but basically humane character called Shmuel Berger. His family and relatives are split over what means to use against a government that they perceive as stabbing the settlers' movement in the back.

When the Jewish terrorist underground of Gush Emunim activists was revealed in the mid-1980s, the whole Greater Israel movement split over the issue of whether or not the twenty-seven young men—the cream of the movement—should be condemned for their random killings of Arab college students, the booby-trapping of West Bank mayors who were PLO supporters, and the delusionary dream of blowing up the Moslem shrines on the Temple Mount.

In the play, Gush Emunim leader Berger tells the local Israel Army commander, who is about to abandon the area's main base under the conditions of an accord with Jordan, that he is prepared to go to any lengths to defend his family and his settlement, which are being sold down the river by the Israel-Jordan agreement. "How can we have arrived at such a situation, with a question mark over our existence?" he asks. His long-bearded young son-in-law, a former member of the Gush underground who has served his time, takes part in the blowing up of the two Moslem shrines on the Temple Mount in order to derail the agreement with Jordan.

Shmuel Berger's reaction is shock and disgust: "How dare you do such a terrible thing? Are you a human being at all? Have you a brain? A heart? There can be no forgiveness. Not from me. Oh Master of the Universe, I swear that I will have nothing to do with [my son-in-law]." He is incredulous that the radicals could be so sick, so deluded as to "force a war on the entire world."

His son-in-law, Benny, answers him with chilling clarity:

> You know that this war is a just war. Shmuel, there is no difference between this war and our other wars. You yourself said that our victories were a sign of Redemption. You know that it is permissible to rebel against the kingdom in order to perform a higher commandment—that the purification of the Temple Mount is exactly that sort of commandment... We settled here to cause an awakening below, which would prod along a wakening above, which would bring Redemption. It's not because the government wanted it, but because the Almighty wanted it. You called on us to do His will and not to stop until Redemption was achieved.

Berger calls this "blasphemy": "The Lord's will is concealed from us. Who can peek behind the curtain? Who?"

Pangs of the Messiah became an Event, attended by Israelis from right and from left, secular and religious; and the reason is that everyone knew—even before the Palestinian uprising—that Israel was at the crossroads.

When the Kingdom of Judah fell, the Jews who hoped to regain independence prayed for the coming of their Messiah, a man born from the root of Jesse—King David's family. The messianic hopes of two thousand years ago were basically political, but included the wish for peace under a realm of righteousness. The Apocalypses written by strange Jewish cultists during that era were mainly concerned with the End of the World. Because they were permeated with *Angst*—a deep despair of the "real" world—these writings (with the exception of the Book of Daniel) were excluded from Scripture. The great rabbis also rejected the apocalyptic movement, recognizing the danger of guessing when the Messiah and a better world would come.

But anyone who has witnessed the two most momentous events in Jewish history in the last two millennia—the extermination of European Jews and the bursting forth of Israel—can be forgiven for venturing the guess that the Messianic Era may be upon us. And that, of course, would make Israel's next forty years even more interesting than its first.

BUT MORE BLOODSHED and anguish appear to lie ahead. We are at war, and it is a terrible tragedy because the fight is between right and right. But the Palestinians who want it all, just like the Israeli Jews who want it all, must come to realize that they will self-destruct if they cannot reach a compromise. Nobody is going to get everything they want. Eventually, lines will be drawn. Many Jewish towns and settlements in Judea and Samaria will have to be dismantled—or the Jews there will have to be ready to live in a Jordanian-Palestinian state; many Palestinians will be moved from their towns and villages to what I believe will be an eventually independent entity in the eastern half of the West Bank, demilitarized and joined to a Jordan where the Palestinians are the majority—and those who stay behind will have to accept becoming Israelis.

Israeli Arabs—600,000 of them—have been polarized by the uprising, and even "moderates" among them, like Mahmoud Darwish, the well-known poet who lives in Paris, have been spewing out hatred for Israeli Jews, saying that there is no place for an independent Israel in the PLO's paradise. But they are the ones who are in danger—for any irrendentism will be crushed. Israeli Jews, on the other hand, will have to change completely the status of the Arab minority, who are second-class citizens in everything but name. Israeli settlers will have to stop threatening to destroy the Jewish people if they do not get their way. Ron Nachman, the ambitious Herut mayor of Ariel, the "capital of Samaria" with 8,000 Jewish residents, told me, "If for reasons of state Israel wants to commit suicide [and withdraw from part of the territories], we won't be part of it. Only if the left and the Arabs are in control will Judea and Samaria be divided. In my opinion, it will bring big civil war."

But it is the settler movement itself that is becoming suicidal, as evidenced by the incident at Beita village in April 1988, in which a Jewish girl and two Arabs were killed. In the midst of the uprising and heightened tensions, settlers from Elon Moreh decided to take a hike through an area near Beita village, south of Nablus. The teenagers were escorted by two men who had been in trouble with the Israeli army on several occasions. Romam Aldubi, a twenty-six-year-old eccentric, had repeatedly caused disturbances in Nablus and neighboring areas and had been barred from Nablus by the army command. The other guide, Menachem Ilan, had been convicted of helping to cover-up for a settler who killed an eleven-year-old girl in Nablus. These two guarded sixteen teenagers on the hike and did not bother to notify the army, as is customary, of their hiking plans. Details of the incident were unclear at first, but the army version laid a great deal of blame on Aldubi, who, after killing one Arab stone-thrower, was beaten viciously by the local Arabs and left in a comatose state. He was looking for trouble, and he found it.

In a situation verging on war, how could the parents of the teenagers allow them to go hiking in the face of the enemy? It showed a profound disregard for life, something these religious people are supposed to value above all else. Yet nationalist politicians like Arik Sharon and even moderates like Zevulun Hammer of the National Religious Party put all the blame on the Arabs and on the Israeli army command, calling for the dismantling of the large village, despite the fact that several of the women of Beita gave refuge to the teenagers who were being stoned.

I personally feel closest to Israelis who despise both the left and the right, who understand that we cannot allow ourselves to be dragged into a civil war, who believe that the Palestinians have a right to a nation (though no more right than the Kurds or the Estonians or the Armenians, for that matter), and that we must reach a settlement. I do not believe we need an international conference, or even direct talks with our enemies. It can be done unilaterally, within a five-year time frame. Henry Kissinger said in February 1988 that international guarantees are not worth a damn and that the whole issue of a peace treaty is overblown. Mutual recognition did not stop Iran and Iraq from their long and horrible war, nor did it solve the India-Pakistan conflict. Israel should work out a position with the Americans and then unilaterally announce that it is prepared to withdraw from parts of the territories.

To my mind, the line can be drawn roughly from the west side of Jenin at the top-center of the West Bank map, down through Nablus, Ramallah, part of East Jerusalem (the Old City and most of the new neighborhoods would remain in Israel's hands) down past Bethlehem, curving west to divide Hebron (between Israel and Palestine) and then veering sharply east and north to the upper fifth of the Dead Sea. If Jordan with its mainly Palestinian population is included in the new state, that would provide the Palestinians with territory twice as large as Israel. Tiny Gaza would remain in Israel's hands, with its half million Palestinians given the option of compensation and removal fifteen miles away to Palestine, or Israeli citizenship.

Nobody would be happy, but that is to be expected. Israel must preserve itself, and do justice at the same time. The only other option is the wasteland, a habitation of wild dogs. It is not supposed to end that way. Isaiah said that the ravenous beasts are to be banished, "And sorrow and sighing shall flee away." We shall see.

XL

I N MAY 1988, I rode in the back of a small open Jeep as Roni, the captain of our "Company A," roared down a sandy side street in pestilential Jebaliya, pursuing a mob of stone-throwers. He tore through a twenty-yard-long putrid-smelling puddle in this rat-infested Gaza refugee camp where the *intifada* began.

Jebaliya is a teeming hellhole, generally regarded as the most violent and nightmarish place in the territories. Spent silver-gas candles, black-gas grenades, Palestinian and Islamic flags, black mourning banners (for Abu Jihad) and assorted junk tied with string to a rock had been lobbed up to the electric and telephone wires and dangled above the streets—the voodoo look is cultivated, and adds to the ominous atmosphere. The Jeep parted the waters of the big puddle, splashing both sides of the shanty-town street; and it all came back down on us. Pure liquefied shit—open sewage—and we were covered in it. It seemed to be a perfect commentary. It was also the only time I had ever seen our captain, a grim young ex-paratrooper, crack a smile.

Certainly, there had not been much to laugh about since the first day Company A moved into the fortified post (I called it "Fort Apache") in the center of this densely populated square mile—60,000 people, about six to a room. That first day, two Palestinians were killed as we were attacked by frenzied mobs whipped up by Moslem fundamentalists and PLO nationalists. The "natives" test each new reserves unit immediately upon its arrival, and our somewhat panicky reactions were duly noted. They could see that part of our company—the potbellied men pushing forty or even fifty—were not like the paratrooper reservists we were replacing. Stones and rocks rained down on us, and sometimes it was truly terrifying.

"*Ya Maniac!*" the Arabs yelled at the soldiers looking out from Fort Apache. "If you're a man come out here without your gun," one said in fluent Hebrew—40 percent of Gaza's men commute to work in Israel. Taunting is constant, though no Israeli seems to take it personally, and words are not what bring the soldiers out—the officers respond only to the erection of burning barricades across the roads, or large groups of youths stoning Israeli vehicles. The defiant youths encourage the chase, the cat-and-mouse game. They have laid traps all around—on one occasion, a bomb had been planted in waiting for the arrival of our patrol.

Our adobe-like fort, really just a police post, was manned by four soldiers and a few policemen on the December day in 1987 when the *intifada* began, right here, after four local people were killed in an auto accident at the Jebaliya intersection (near the entrance to the village and camp area and three miles from Gaza city). The rumor swept the camp that the Israelis had murdered the four. That falsehood, along with the successful attack on an army post in the north a week earlier by a single Palestinian glider pilot, is what triggered the uprising.

The scores of men in the reserves company I served with and the hundreds of men in our battalion and the dozens of paratrooper, border police and other regular-army units who also patrol Jebaliya, are portrayed by the media—within Israel and throughout the world—as part of the Goliath Machine versus little David with his puny stones. (Even our great king becomes a Palestinian in the continuing and relentless cooptation of Jewish history.) In addition to being seen as David against Goliath, the Palestinians are called protesters, and compared to the followers of Martin Luther King and Gandhi, or the peaceful Russian peasants who marched on the Czar's Winter Palace. We Israelis are cast as the Nazis, shooting out the eyes of nine-month-old babies.

The truth is that with a number of exceptions Israeli soldiers are typically restrained and decent men under frequent attack by people who openly yell not "We Shall Overcome" but "Death to the Jews" and who punctuate their chants by throwing Molotov cocktails and pipe bombs and lethal building blocks from the roofs. (Our battalion had twenty-five injuries, with four men hospitalized, but such information is rarely mentioned in the media reports.)

IN GAZA I SAW WITH MY OWN EYES (and through powerful binoculars) how grown men send children to the "front," pulling the strings from behind, quite willing to sacrifice others, knowing that the nine-month-old baby who is wounded by a rubber bullet will make headlines around the world, and that no one will question the responsibility of the infant's mother, or of the Palestinians who actually invite such incidents. No one will mention the hysterical religious fanatics in the refugee-camp schools who preach holy war and suicide—martyrdom.

The founder of the Arab Legion, Sir John Glubb, noted in his book *A Soldier of the Arabs*, about events in the 1950s, that "when the schoolmasters received the word from the extremist politicians, they turned all the children into the streets. On some occasions, the teachers had written on pieces of paper the slogans which the children were to call out. A mass of children, shouting and singing, waving flags and throwing stones, blocked the traffic. It was difficult for the [Jordanian] police to disperse the crowds of big girls or even little boys and girls... When sufficient confusion had been created, the roughs took over the riot." The method, over thirty years later, remains the same.

The mother of one of the two nine-month-old babies who lost eyes in two separate incidents in Jebaliya in late May and early June 1988 proudly announced to the press that her daughter would become "the Moshe Dayan of the Palestinian revolution." One Jebaliya father told us frankly that he was prepared to sacrifice a couple of his nine children because there "is no other hope," and the PLO will compensate all martyrs.

As for our own soldiers, many of them felt that their hands were tied. They were warned that they would face imprisonment if they used live ammunition against stone-throwers in any but a life-or-death situation. Even the use of rubber bullets and tear gas was strictly controlled, though there were cases when a newcomer to a patrol never heard that day's orders, or someone loosely interpreted the "immediate danger to life" rule. Accidents or misjudgments happened—as when tear gas was fired into a closed housing compound. One of our men, an ex-convict from Russia (*not* a prisoner of Zion type), fashioned a Molotov cocktail of his own and might have thrown it if an officer hadn't heard about it and taken it away from him. But I doubt whether any other army or police force in the world would act with more restraint than the Israelis have: the approximately two hundred Arab fatalities in six months of a widespread violent uprising is a remarkably low figure.

In Jebaliya, this stronghold of the Khomeini like Moslem fundamentalist revolution, I did witness some instances of Israeli brutality during the month of Ramadan (when the Moslems fast during daylight hours). But the worst beatings I saw were by Palestinian militants of their own people—for example, the face of an old man (a "collaborator" because he tried to stop his children from stoning soldiers) had been pummeled into bloody hamburger by the young men who were staging the daily disturbances. With the aid of one of his sons, he crawled to us for help. "The Jews are better than our own people," he cried bitterly to his son. "You throw stones at them, but it wasn't the Jews who did this to me."

I also saw several of our own soldiers stop hot-headed fellow Israelis from hitting bound and blindfolded prisoners. The kibbutzniks were the best about this—they simply would not allow it. The worst incident I witnessed was when a strapping corporal with a sadistic grin threw a blindfolded, bound prisoner into the grill of a truck parked just outside the "Ansar 2" prison compound in Gaza. But even that was not so bad— during the Vietnam War I myself experienced a worse beating by San Francisco police for simply being in the vicinity of a peaceful demonstration (by people who were demanding an end to war, and who were not throwing bombs or big rocks).

AND SO HERE I FIND MYSELF—a past supporter of Journalists for Amnesty International, an anti-Vietnam War activist of the 1960s, and a present supporter in Israel of a political solution based on territorial compromise—condoning a certain amount of beating.

During one week in the middle of my thirty-day service in Jebaliya, our security forces backed by the army rounded up three different terrorist cells in and around nearby Gaza town. These twenty terrorists had automatic rifles, grenades and explosives. Although on one occasion they had carried out a mission against an Israeli patrol, all their other actions had been directed against Israeli civilians, bombing a city bus in Rishon Letzion, for example. Now one of these groups was about to launch a suicide human-bomb attack on the throngs of people at the Tel Aviv Central Bus Station. Hundreds of lives might have been lost if the Israeli security forces had not managed to press the detainees to reveal the terrorist plot.

I found that many of the left-wing or left-center reservists in my unit, who believe as I do that we must arrive at a territorial compromise with the Palestinians, had no "psychological problems" arresting suspects or pursuing people whose aim is to kill or maim as many Israelis as possible. Yet one reads constantly in the Israeli media, with its left-liberal slant, that many Israeli psychologists are alarmed about the growing risks to the country's mental health, that the army is not as it used to be, that its actions are "inhuman." In contrast, one simply never sees praise for the army, for the average soldier or reservist who is doing what has to be done. It is all terribly distorted by people—whether journalists or psychologists—who do not mind stretching the truth in order to get their political views across.

Indeed, all of us in Company A—left, right and center—were astonished at the difference between what we saw first-hand, and what the media were telling us about it. I was the only writer-journalist among the men, who as in any reserve company came from all walks of life. But we all felt that the media distortions were immense, and as sinister as the worst instances of very real Israeli abuses (such as the now-famous incident of four soldiers beating two detainees, filmed by Israeli CBS cameramen).

On our last day of service, the colonel in charge of our battalion and three others in Gaza ranted against the Israeli media. He told us how they cut and distorted, and he cited examples of Israeli journalists who tapped into the army internal radio network for their scoops, or who impersonated army officers in order to obtain information from secretaries at military headquarters in Gaza. Many of the reservists—leftist and rightist alike— nodded in agreement with the commander.

THE PROBLEM ARISES from the fact that the media are part of an Israeli Labor-oriented establishment that shares the view of other establishments in the West and in the East Bloc and in the Third World which want Israel to withdraw in favor of an autonomous Palestinian entity if not a state. (I am one of the minority within this majority of journalists, favoring the Allon plan, which involves returning no more than 60 percent of the West Bank to the Arabs.)

These journalists are political animals who put their stamp on every sentence they submit about the territories. They are the ones who shoot the footage for American TV, work as stringers for all the major newspapers in the world, and often provide most of the story an American or a Norwegian reads under the byline of a well-known reporter. One strident Peace Now type, a snake to work under, is in charge of a news service bureau, manages the news of a major Israeli daily, is the representative of a large Canadian newspaper and an English Sunday newspaper, and is a favorite commentator for the BBC, CBC and ABC (such is life in Israel—everyone needs at least two incomes). No one says anything about possible conflict of interest, or monopoly. Nor is he shy about getting his opinions across.

Twenty-one Israelis have refused to serve in the army reserves in the territories—one of them is assistant managing editor of a major daily newspaper (he selects the stories that go on page one, oversees the headline writers, fashions the story in a way he sees fit). Yet the newspaper never even reported that he spent thirty days in prison rather than serve in Gaza (although the paper did run a long, very favorable magazine piece about the group of twenty-one, mentioning some of their leaders, but not the aforementioned journalist or another journalist-"refusenik," as they call themselves).

A reporter who covers the West Bank for Israel Television—a very decent man who like all of his predecessors eventually arrived at the position that Israel must withdraw immediately from the territories—greeted the news that I was going to serve in Jebaliya with the comment: "So you're going to beat Arabs?" He happens to be one of the more balanced journalists, and there are several like him who have done an important job in covering the *intifada*, revealing Israeli abuses along with Palestinian. But the impression they convey of a once noble Israeli army turned into brutalizers of children and freedom fighters is simply false.

As for foreign journalists, of the eight hundred covering the Palestinian uprising, practically all of them also believe that the Palestinians deserve support as underdogs searching for national identity and deprived of many basic human rights. (In 1942 the *Washington Post* totally ignored the systematic extermination of millions of Jews. In November of that year, Rabbi Stephen Wise's press conference confirming State Department findings of two million systematically murdered rated a few inches on the inside pages of both the *New York Times* and the *Post*. But the *Post* in six months had already run 300,000 words about the *intifada*.)

Thus, the foreign reporters and the Israeli media form a community of interest, and they are constantly rubbing each other's backs, financially as well as politically. Some of them, like David Grossman, are eloquent, and the *New Yorker* will rush to publish their work. Grossman's book was sympathetic to and understanding of the Palestinians. Such a book from the other side, looking kindly upon Israelis, is unlikely to be produced by any Palestinian writer/reporter.

ONE OF THE MANY "BLEEDING HEART" REPORTERS in Israel is a very solid young American who unfortunately knows or cares little about the background to the Jewish-Arab conflict. He believes that the root of the whole problem is Israel's presence in the territories, and that if the troops would only refrain from responding to every tire-burning and barricade, and withdraw to the periphery, the casualty rate, at least, would go down to a more acceptable level. In Jebaliya, I found that there was constant debate among the soldiers and the officers about this point. But the view that prevailed, and to which I now subscribe, is that there can be no "withdrawal" in the face of violence—every incident must be responded to or there will be ten more such incidents within minutes.

Furthermore, there are large numbers of Palestinians who might pay lip service to the uprising, but who want to live under Israeli sovereignty, and who know that a Lebanon-style bloodbath will be the first fruit of a Palestinian state. I watched small Jebaliya children stoning cars with local Gaza license plates and demanding "protection money" from the drivers, who eventually chased them away and cleared the road of the peanut-version of revolutionists we all frequently faced.

These territories were the price paid by the Arabs for constant war against Israel. They cannot be allowed to get the land back by burning tires or burning down forests in Israel proper or becoming the darlings of the world media. Israel will not be so easily defeated.

Indeed, why should our enemies be rewarded? Should the territories be conceded because of the ongoing violence? Or because of an increasing willingness among Palestinians to die for their cause? The *New York Times* may think that the name "Abu Jihad" means "Father of the Struggle," but everyone in the Middle East knows that *jihad* means "holy war," not "struggle," and that a "holy war" is what most Arabs believe they are engaged in.

I KNEW THAT THIS SPELL OF RESERVE DUTY would be especially important, coming as the Palestinian uprising headed toward its half-year point
and during the Moslem holy month of Ramadan. A good friend of mine
said when he heard I was going to the Gaza Strip, "Of course, be careful;
but try also to take a really close look at what is happening there. Open
your eyes. Open your third eye."

Eyes, or the lack of them, are automatically associated with Gaza. The
Philistines took Samson there, putting out his eyes and binding him with
fetters of brass and placing him in the prison house to work. Blind John
Milton, in "Samson Agonistes," wrote about the Israelite Judge being
"Eyeless in Gaza, at the mill with slaves." The rabbis said that the eyes
are the agents of sin; Samson's eyes had lusted for Philistine women. Samson took vengeance for his eyes, slaying thousands when he brought the
house down on the Philistine lords and himself. The Palestinians are now
vowing to take vengeance for their own lost eyes. Many commentators
have said that modern Israel suffers from a "Samson complex" rather
than a "Masada complex," that it will end up destroying itself along with
its Arab enemies.

My own feeling is that places like Jebaliya are festering wounds that
must be eliminated. For years, the PLO resisted any change in the status
of the refugee-camp inmates—when a new neighborhood of well-built
homes was erected alongside Shati refugee camp in Gaza (a place second
only to Jebaliya in horribleness), the refugees refused to budge. Their
miserable camps are a hothouse of insurrection, and the PLO wants them
there until Jerusalem and Jaffa are liberated. If I had my way, the camp,
which British Assistant Foreign Minister David Mellor called an affront
to humanity when he visited Jebaliya in January 1988, would be bulldoz-
ed, and its residents sent to nearby Gaza town or a few miles away to
the West Bank. Samson tore out the Gate of Gaza and carried it on his
shoulders forty miles to Hebron—why not now? Because it would be called
"transfer," or "a second Lidice."

There are so many myths about Gaza—in a 1971 PLO booklet, Gaza's
140 square miles with a population (at that time) of 450,000 was termed
one of the most overcrowded places on earth. What about Los Angeles
or Mexico City or Tokyo? They, and a thousand other cities, all have a
much higher population density. Yet just about every journalist repeats
this ridiculous claim. What *is* true is that the Jebaliya and Shati camps
are criminally overcrowded—though, again, I have visited refugee camps
in Sudan, such as Wad Kali, which are *twice* as densely populated as
Jebaliya, and have seen worse living conditions in dozens of countries.

In any case, Jebaliya has become, for the Palestinians, the symbol, the
very essence, of the *intifada*. That is why it is likely to become the site

of some horrible climax to the passion play that will burn on. Meanwhile, some of the myths about the uprising's moral and political costs to Israel are also dissipating.

The Israeli Army chief of staff, Dan Shomron, announced in early 1988 that every able-bodied Israeli male between the ages of twenty-two and fifty would be spending sixty-two days in the army reserves during the year, instead of the usual thirty-five to forty days, and that this was the price for holding on to the territories. My own feeling at the time was that this would swell the numbers of Israelis who will vote for Labor, the party willing to trade land for peace, and I was heartened. What I found in Gaza was that none of the soldiers, even after thirty days of being "up against the shit of Jebaliya," had changed their political views, but that all were prepared to do what must be done to break the *intifada*.

The spirit among members of this battalion, whose average age is about thirty-five, had not been higher in years. Our three young lieutenants, who ranged from an extremely cautious man to a slightly reckless daredevil, were all superb: honest, straight, courageous, tough but compassionate, businesslike. When I thought of the newspaper articles I had read about the "psychological traumas" affecting just about every soldier in the army and the "dangerous consequences of the renewed violence" to Israeli society, it seemed to me that compared with those psychologists and journalists, the much-abused and supposedly unhinged Israeli soldiers, splashing through excrement, were the real models of sanity. The Israeli Army has not been Nazified, as some "peace activists" would have it. Despite some instances of brutality, and even manslaughter, the Israeli Army remains one of the most decent in the world. But that is not the main issue—Israel is at the crossroads. We face either a permanent state of war, or peace—may it come speedily in our time.